PRIMARY PROFESSIONAL STUDIES

PRIMARY PROFESSIONAL STUDIES

Edited by ALICE HANSEN

Los Angeles | London | New Delhi
Singapore | Washington DC

Learning Matters
An imprint of SAGE Publications Ltd
1 Oliver's Yard
55 City Road
London EC1Y 1SP

SAGE Publications Inc.
2455 Teller Road
Thousand Oaks, California 91320

SAGE Publications India Pvt Ltd
B 1/I 1 Mohan Cooperative Industrial Area
Mathura Road
New Delhi 110 044

SAGE Asia-Pacific Pte Ltd
3 Church Street
#10–04 Samsung Hub
Singapore 049483

 LEEDS TRINITY UNIVERSITY *Acc*

Editor: Amy Thornton
Production controller: Chris Marke
Project management: Deer Park Productions
Marketing manager: Catherine Slinn
Cover design: Wendy Scott
Typeset by: C&M Digitals (P) Ltd, Chennai, India
Printed in Great Britain by Henry Ling Limited at The
Dorset Press, Dorchester, DT1 1HD

© 2015 Chapter 1, Alice Hansen; Chapter 2, Adrian
Copping; Chapter 3, Sally Neaum and Rebecca
Walters; Chapter 4, Denis Hayes; Chapter 5,
Jonathan Glazzard; Chapter 6, Mary Briggs;
Chapter 7, David Morris; Chapter 8, Tony Ewens;
Chapter 9, Denis Hayes; Chapter 10, Pat
McPherson; Chapter 11, Tony Ewens; Chapter 12,
Sandra Eady and Cathryn Hardy; Chapter 13, Mary
Briggs; Chapter 14, Mary Briggs; Chapter 15, Kate
Adams; Chapter 16, Jonathan Leeming

First published in 2011 by Learning Matters Ltd.
Reprinted in 2011. Second edition published in 2012.
Third edition published in 2015.

Library of Congress Control Number: 2015940819

British Library Cataloguing in Publication Data

A catalogue record for this book is available from
the British Library

ISBN 978-1-4739-1607-4
ISBN 978-1-4739-1608-1 (pbk)

At SAGE we take sustainability seriously. Most of our products are printed in the UK using FSC papers and boards.
When we print overseas we ensure sustainable papers are used as measured by the Egmont grading system.
We undertake an annual audit to monitor our sustainability.

Contents

About the contributors

Kate Adams is Reader in Education at Bishop Grosseteste University College Lincoln, where she also leads the Doctor of Education (EdD) programme and lectures in Education Studies. She is an experienced primary teacher and teacher trainer. Kate's research interests lie in childhood, particularly in understanding the world from children's perspectives. Her recent books include *Behaviour for Learning in the Primary School* (2009) and *Unseen Worlds: Looking through the lens of childhood* (2010).

Mary Briggs is an Associate Professor in the Institute of Education at the University of Warwick. She teaches on a wide range of different education courses and has published widely in the educational field. Her specific research interests are in mathematics education, leadership, assessment and mentoring and coaching. She has worked in a wide range of settings including children's homes, special, primary school and universities.

Adrian Copping is Senior Lecturer in English and Literacy at the University of Cumbria. Adrian teaches English Education on undergraduate and postgraduate courses. He also teaches on a Master's level PGCE course and leads the university's Lancaster-based PGCE cohort. He began his teaching career in Lancashire primary schools where he was a class teacher and subject coordinator before becoming a teacher educator. He is also Chair of Governors of a local primary school and is research-active, currently looking at peer and co-teaching.

Sandra Eady is a Senior Teaching Fellow at the Stirling Institute of Education, University of Stirling where she is Coordinator of the BA Primary Professional Education Programme. Sandra has extensive experience as a teacher educator on both undergraduate and postgraduate professional education programmes in England and Scotland. Prior to this she has worked in a number of different primary schools. She gained her PhD in primary science from the Institute of Education at the University of Warwick. Her research interests include the professional education including Master's level programmes and primary science. Sandra regularly disseminates her work at conferences and through journal publications.

Tony Ewens worked as a teacher and head teacher in primary and middle schools in Devon, then as the county's advisory teacher for religious and moral education, before moving into initial teacher education as a lecturer at St Martin's College (now the University of Cumbria). Specialising in philosophy of education as well as RE, he became Head of Education and Associate Dean at St Martin's College. Upon the formation of the University of Cumbria Tony was appointed Head of Education Studies. He retired in 2008 and is now a freelance consultant, significantly involved in the training of school governing bodies. He is also a member of the Blackburn Diocesan Schools' Committee.

Jonathan Glazzard is Senior Lecturer in Primary Education at the University of Huddersfield. He leads the Primary Education provision as well as teaching on the Master's courses. Prior to his work at the university Jonathan worked as a primary school teacher with responsibility for the coordination of special educational needs. His research interests lie in the area of inclusive education and Jonathan has a number of publications within this field.

Alice Hansen is an education consultant and the director of Children Count Ltd. Prior to this, she worked in initial teacher education for 12 years as a senior lecturer in primary mathematics and later as a PGCE programme leader. Her work focuses mainly on curriculum development in England and abroad. She also publishes mobile applications for trainee teachers, teachers and parents. Her research interests include technology-enhanced learning and teaching in mathematics.

Cathryn Hardy is an education improvement adviser in Shropshire, with specific responsibility for mathematics in primary schools. As part of this role, she is seconded to Edge Hill University and teaches on mathematics education undergraduate and postgraduate courses including the Specialist Primary Mathematics Practice programme (formally MaST). She is involved in leading a wide range of CPD for teachers at every stage of their career, and classroom-focused, school-based development is a particular specialism.

After spending 17 years in the classroom, including two deputy headships and head teacher, **Denis Hayes** worked for the University of Plymouth for 20 years and became professor of primary education in the Faculty of Education. His research interests include tracking the experiences of trainee teachers on school placement and the development of classroom teaching skills. Denis is now an education writer and speaker and has published extensively.

Jonathan Leeming has more than 16 years of classroom teaching experience, both in the UK and abroad and has taught across all primary phases. He currently works as a senior leader and Year 2 class teacher at Moorside Primary School in Lancaster where he leads mathematics. He is a mathematics specialist teacher (MaST) and is now working on the final part of his MA in primary mathematics pedagogy. Jonathan is accredited by the National Centre for Excellence in the Teaching of Mathematics (NCETM) as a professional development leader.

Patricia Macpherson has extensive experience of safeguarding and child protection in pre-school settings, schools and higher education institutions. Her work in this area is rooted in her interest in children and young people's personal, social and emotional development and the contribution of schools and educational settings to this. Patricia has been a designated teacher for child protection in schools and principal safeguarding officer in two higher education institutions. She has written and delivered child protection courses and she participated in the NSPCC project that resulted in the publication of 'Training to Protect: A child protection resource for teacher training' (NSPCC 2003).

David Morris has over 20 years' experience in the education sector. He is currently a Senior Lecturer at the Cass School of Education, University of East London, where he is involved in initial teacher training. David has worked in both the Primary and Secondary sectors and has taught computing to children in every year group from Nursery through to Year 11. David is a published author and has delivered research papers at both national and international conferences. David's research interests are student voice, leadership and technology.

Sally Neaum is Lecturer in Education with a strong interest in the pedagogy of early literacy. Prior to this she worked as a nursery and primary school teacher, as an adviser in Early Years and inclusion, and in initial teacher education. Sally has published extensively in Early Years and primary education.

Rebecca Walters has a background in primary teaching, working across Key Stages 1 and 2 but with a particular focus in the early years. Rebecca currently lectures in the Education section at Teesside University with an interest in pedagogical approaches to learning and development in the early years.

Introduction

Right now primary education finds itself in a changing landscape brought about through new curriculum reform. This book, which forms part of the *Transforming QTS* series, supports you as a trainee teacher to address the challenges and exploit the opportunities throughout your training, and into your first years of teaching.

Transforming QTS: The complex role of the trainee teacher

Curriculum reform cannot happen overnight. It is a process that takes a long time and is dependent on the extent to which the profession embraces the imposed changes. As you train to become a teacher you will be exposed to a number of schools, educational settings, tutors, teachers and other students, and all will have different responses. You will observe numerous ways of approaching children, teaching and education. At times you may find this very challenging, but you will always learn more about how you feel about education from the context you find yourself in.

As this edition goes to press a new government is in power but there is an intention to continue the previous coalition government's aspiration (Noble-Rogers, 2015) for schools to have a high level of autonomy, to innovate, have high expectations of children, and deepen academic knowledge through learning from each other (Gove, 2010). Indeed, the Expert Panel for the National Curriculum Review stated, 'Schools should be given more freedom over the curriculum. The National Curriculum should set out only the essential knowledge (facts, concepts, principles and fundamental operations) that all children should acquire, and leave schools to design a wider curriculum that best meets the needs of their pupils and to decide how to teach this most effectively' (DfE, 2011, p.6). Furthermore, the Review was emphatic that it is important to distinguish between the National Curriculum and the wider school curriculum as experienced by all the pupils in school, explaining that 'the National Curriculum should not absorb the overwhelming majority of teaching time in schools' (p.6).

In order to be a successful trainee teacher in this climate, you will need to acknowledge and embrace your own highly complex role. Your teacher training is not about ticking off a list of competencies or demonstrating you can deliver a prescribed curriculum. Instead, you will be required to **take risks, ask questions**, and make **informed decisions** based on **collaboration** with others in a timely and professional way. Your training will ask you to reflect on your **values**: how do they impact on the way you think of yourself as a teacher and the way you develop relationships with the children you teach and your colleagues? Understanding **child development** and that all children develop in different ways and at different rates because of **prior learning, learning styles** and **individual needs** are explored throughout the book also. It is not enough to focus only on children's learning. Your *own* learning and proactively approaching your own **personal professional development** through **reflective practice** and **research-informed teaching** is a core aspect of the extent to which you will succeed on your course and as a teacher.

These emboldened terms are some of the themes you will find within the book as you read it. Of course, these are not new. These aspects have evolved out of existing good practice. Indeed, in one of his earliest speeches as the Secretary of State for Education, Michael Gove stated, 'I want to celebrate the gains which have been made – and one of the most important is the development and deepening of culture in which we recognise that it is professionals, not bureaucratic strategies and initiatives, which drive school improvement' (Gove, 2010). By fulfilling the aspects identified above, you will achieve success in the high status profession you have chosen to enter.

Using this book

Structure of the book

Throughout this book the authors have drawn upon their extensive experience of teaching and mentoring trainee teachers. This book aims to reflect and address aspects that concern you as a trainee teacher at any stage of your course. It is presented in four sections.

Section 1: The curriculum
This section explores the development of the primary national curriculum used in schools, and shows how schools and trainee teachers can design learning opportunities using a range of approaches. The philosophies and approaches that are used in the Early Years Foundation Stage are discussed in Chapter 3, explaining how children in the early years are supported in their development and learning.

Section 2: The developing child
Over the last 50 years, the centrality of children in the primary phase has been acknowledged and embraced. Therefore this section considers aspects related to child-centred teaching and learning, issues of inclusion, and transition and progression. In this edition a new chapter considering children's voice has been included, to emphasise how the focus on children as learners is evolving in the primary school.

Section 3: The developing teacher
The Teachers' Standards require you to demonstrate appropriate professional attributes. These reflect teaching as a profession and this section challenges you to consider what it is to be a professional, including among other things how to safeguard children and your role as a trainee teacher and teacher in the wider school community. It will also encourage you to think

about how you form your own teacher identity. Personal professional development is a key component of your initial teacher training. It began the moment you prepared for an interview on your course, and will continue throughout your career. This aspect of developing as a teacher is discussed in this section also.

Section 4: Teaching skills

The 'nuts and bolts' of teaching are also important, and these are reflected in the Teachers' Standards. This section will support your assessment of children, planning for teaching, management of behaviour for learning, and managing the classroom environment.

Features

This book contains a number of features to support your learning.

At the start of each chapter you will find a list of **Learning Outcomes**. These provide the intended focus of each chapter. You can skim these to see the structure and content of each chapter.

Each chapter will help you to demonstrate some of the Teachers' **Standards**, and a list of the relevant standards appears at the beginning of each chapter. You may wish to search for individual standards that you have identified as areas for development, or make a note of your reading and associated activities in your teacher training notes.

Each chapter contains a number of **Activities** that help you to become actively engaged in the content of the chapter. Sometimes the activity will ask you to reflect on your reading or placement experiences, or there may be a task that you will need to undertake. You may find it helpful to undertake the activities with a friend, or discuss the outcomes with your tutors or school mentors.

Case Studies are provided to illustrate how the ideas presented in each chapter can be achieved in a real context.

Research underpins quality teaching. Each chapter contains **Research Focus** features that highlight key literature in the area being discussed. The features provide an overview of the research.

Each chapter concludes with **Further Reading** and a **Learning Outcomes Review**, which asks you to reflect upon the key components of the chapter.

Note

This introduction has explained that education is currently placed within a changing landscape and Chapter 1 particularly explores this further. We are clear about the direction of travel that many areas of primary education are taking, and those areas are addressed in this book – making it the most up-to-date and helpful book available to trainee teachers today. However, as this edition went to print, the Department for Education was continuing to make fast and widespread changes to education, particularly in relation to assessment. Therefore, please be aware that while every effort was made to reflect the current state of education at the time of writing, there may have been subsequent changes that are not reflected in this edition. Remember that it is a key part of your professional development as a teacher to make sure that you keep up to date with legislation and change at government level, so monitoring the key education websites and specialist press should be a regular part of your practice.

References

DfE (2011) *The Framework for the National Curriculum. A Report by the Expert Panel for the National Curriculum Review*. London: DfE.

Gove, M. (2010) Speech to the National College Annual Conference, Birmingham, 16 June. Available from www.education.gov.uk/news/speeches/nationalcollegeannualconference accessed 2/10/12.

Noble-Rogers, J. (2015) Universities Council for the Education of Teachers (UCET) Update. National Primary Teacher Education Council (NaPTEC) Conference, London, 17 April.

SECTION 1
THE CURRICULUM

1. Transforming teaching and learning
Alice Hansen

Learning Outcomes

By the end of this chapter, you will have:

- reviewed the development of teaching and learning in English primary schools since the 1940s;
- reflected on how this development impacts on our current teaching and learning practices in primary schools;
- considered your own professional knowledge and competence, by reflecting on how you are contributing to the 'transformation' of teaching and learning.

TEACHERS' STANDARDS
A teacher must:

3. Demonstrate good subject and curriculum knowledge
- demonstrate a critical understanding of developments in the subject and curriculum areas, and promote the value of scholarship.

4. Plan and teach well structured lessons
- contribute to the design and provision of an engaging curriculum within the relevant subject area(s).

6. Make accurate and productive use of assessment
- know and understand how to assess the relevant subject and curriculum areas, including statutory assessment requirements.

8. Fulfil wider professional responsibilities
- take responsibility for improving teaching through appropriate professional development, responding to advice and feedback from colleagues.

Introduction

Teaching is entering a new evolutionary phase, where the government is committed to a vision of a 'transformed school curriculum' (DfE, 2010a), where 'ministers are committed to giving schools more freedom from unnecessary prescription and bureaucracy' and where teachers are encouraged to 'consider new approaches' (DfE, 2010b).

In order for you to make sense of these statements, this chapter is laid out in three parts.

1. *Where have we been?* provides a historical journey through the development of the national curriculum and other pertinent education milestones since the 1940s.

2. *Where are we now?* outlines the current statutory and non-statutory guidance you must be familiar with.

3. *Where are we going?* asks you to consider curriculum reform and what transforming teaching and learning for the future looks like.

Understanding the historical and current contexts is essential for you to critically and professionally move forward in your teacher training.

Where have we been?

This section reports a very small part of the history of education in England. It is mainly concerned with government-related documentation from the 1940s to 2010 and is intended to provide for you a skeletal outline of the intention of the government of the day. Although you should be aware that political parties and changes of government impacted significantly at various times during this period, detail about the government in power at the time is not given here. For more information about this, see the Further Reading section.

In the 1920s and 1930s, Sir Henry Hadow wrote six reports about education, which are widely recognised as informing the development of the English education system as we recognise it today (Plowden, 1967; Gillard, 2006). One of these reports, *The Primary School* (Board of Education, 1931), stated that 'the traditional practice of dividing the matter of primary instruction into separate subjects, taught in distinct lessons, should be reconsidered [as long as] provision [is] made for an adequate amount of drill in reading, writing and arithmetic' (Board of Education, 1931, p.113). It went on to make the recommendation that 'the curriculum of the primary school is to be thought of in terms of activity and experience, rather than knowledge to be acquired and facts to be stored' (Board of Education, 1931, p.140).

Activity

As you read through this section, consider the extent to which the issues raised in the various decades resonate with what you hear about education today. Are there any issues that you thought were relatively new, but you now see have been a topic of debate or focus for development since before you, or even your parents, were born? How have they developed? Why are they still important aspects to consider in education?

1940S–1950S

The Second World War was in full swing in 1942 when William Beveridge chaired the committee that penned the report, *Social Insurance and Allied Services* (Beveridge, 1942). The report identified five 'giant evils' in society: disease (requiring improved health care), ignorance (requiring improved education for all), squalor (requiring adequate housing for all), idleness (requiring all to be in full employment) and want (to be addressed by welfare for children, the elderly and unemployed). As a result of this report, several reforms were developed, including the expansion of National Insurance, the creation of the National Health Service, and the introduction of the 1944 Education Act.

For the first time, the 1944 Education Act provided free education for all children aged 5 to 15. It introduced transport, free milk, medical and dental treatment and free school meals to all children who wanted them. It required all schools to begin each day with an act of worship and it recommended that local authorities educate children with special educational needs in 'ordinary' schools wherever possible. Local education authorities (LEAs) were set up, and these were required to appoint a Chief Education Officer who consulted with the Minister of Education.

Given the significant welfare change that was happening during this time, it may be surprising to you that in the early 1940s many forms of corporal punishment were legal, and the 1944 Education Act did nothing to change this. Therefore children were often physically and mentally injured or tortured (McKenzie, 2001).

For primary schools, the next significant document was published at the end of the 1950s: *Primary Education* (Board of Education, 1959). It clearly set out for the first time primary education as a very particular stage in the national system. It published inspection findings from Her Majesty's Inspectors (HMI), and was based on 'discussions with teachers about their work and about the principles on which they act and the standards they achieve' (Board of Education, 1959, p.vi).

It focused on children, and considered them as individuals with interests. There was a clear strand running through about children's learning alongside ways of teaching. Containing information about the expected development at various ages through the primary age range, it explored issues of providing for a wide range of ability, able children and those with special educational needs (referred to at the time as 'handicapped'). There was a section titled 'The fields of learning' (encompassing religion; physical education; language; mathematics; art, craft and needlework; handwriting; music; history; geography and natural history) in which the curriculum was explored. This document set the context for the Plowden Report, published in 1967.

1960S–1970S

The 1960s and 1970s saw a number of big changes within primary schools (Galton et al., 1980, p.156).

Although the 1944 Education Act introduced the opportunity for all children aged 5 to 15 to a free education, it was the 1962 Education Act that legislated that parents would become legally obliged to ensure that their children were educated (at school or elsewhere). Alongside this, LEAs were made responsible for ensuring that children attended school.

In the 1960s increasing numbers of immigrants were coming into the country and in 1965 local authorities were advised to avoid heavy concentrations of immigrants in any one school. Circular 7/65 stated that a group containing up to one fifth of immigrant children can fit in a school with reasonable ease, but if the proportion goes beyond a third, serious complications occur.

In the following year, Section 11 of the Local Government Act of 1966 provided for a payment to Local Authorities, a grant that was designed to

> *address disadvantage – brought about by differences of language or culture – that is experienced by members of any ethnic minorities in accessing education, training, employment and a wide range of other opportunities, services and facilities that are available to other people... {in order to} enable members of ethnic minorities {from the New Commonwealth} to overcome such disadvantage, and thereby to play a full part in the social, economic and political life of the country*

> *(Home Office, 1960)*

It was only in the 1993 Local Government (Amendment) Act that the scope was widened to all minority ethnic people.

Research Focus: The Plowden Report

In 1963 the Education Minister, Sir Edward Boyle, commissioned a report that would 'consider primary education in all its aspects and the transition to secondary education' (Plowden, 1967, p.1) and in 1967 the Plowden Report: *Children and their Primary Schools* was published. It focused on a child-centred approach to education, stating that 'at the heart of the educational process lies the child' (p.7). Among many other things, it considered:

- Child growth and development (including gender differences, cognitive, physical, emotional, behavioural and intelligence development);

- Increased communication with parents;

- A national focus to positively discriminate towards schools in the most deprived areas to receive extra help, termed 'educational priority areas';

- The need to re-examine the books schools use and the curriculum they teach, overcoming language barriers and educating immigrant children and their parents;

- The need for an 'integration of the social services' so that trained social workers can collaborate with schools;

→

- That continuity across education stages was required, including that teacher trainees should be trained in more than one stage, and that documentation should accompany children to the next school;

- Some changes in the way subjects are taught (e.g. mathematics and a second language) were 'taking place unusually rapidly';

- Aspects of the curriculum, stressing that 'children's learning does not fit into subject categories' and that the younger the child, the less differentiation should be made between the subjects. These were: religious education, English, modern languages, history, geography, mathematics, science, art and craft, music, physical education, sex education;

- That decisions on punishment should be left up to the teacher, within the school's policy; the infliction of physical pain should be forbidden;

- A recommendation on using a combination of individual, group and class work was made but it also welcomed the trend towards individual learning;

- The education of 'handicapped children in ordinary schools', suggesting that

  – society has created new stresses and strains
  – the term 'slow learner' should be substituted for 'educationally sub-normal'
  – trainee teachers should be equipped to help handicapped children as far as they can;

- The importance of the education of gifted children should be acknowledged, and that there was a need for further research;

- The suggestion that head teachers should have more say over their schools.

The Plowden Report was welcomed by most educationalists but there were a minority who loudly opposed the 'progressive' education being promoted in primary schools (see, for example, Bennett, 1976). In order to address the growing debate, on 18 October 1976 the Prime Minister James Callaghan made a speech that publicly launched what became known as The Great Debate.

The goals of our education, from nursery school through to adult education, are clear enough. They are to equip children to the best of their ability for a lively, constructive, place in society, and also to fit them to do a job of work. Not one or the other but both. The balance was wrong in the past. We have a responsibility now to see that we do not get it wrong again in the other direction. {...} I have outlined concerns and asked questions about them today. The debate that I was seeking has got off to a flying start even before I was able to say anything. Now I ask all those who are concerned to respond positively and not defensively. It will be an advantage to the teaching profession to have a wide public understanding and support for what they are doing.

(Callaghan, 1976)

The 1970s saw an increase in the legislation that was passed that had a direct influence on primary schools. For example, The Education (Handicapped Children) Act of 1970 transferred the responsibility for education of severely handicapped children from health authorities to LEAs, The Education (Milk) Act of 1971 limited the provision of free milk in schools, The 1975 Sex Discrimination Act affected school admissions, appointments and curricula and The 1976 Race Relations Act also impacted on the way schools operated. The school leaving age was raised to 16 in 1973.

Alongside the current sociological climate schools were in, other influences were beginning to drive government policy. For example, in 1974 the Assessment Performance Unit (APU) was established in order to promote assessment and monitoring methods in order to track children's achievement.

Additionally, a number of seminal reports with a focus on subjects and pedagogy were written in this decade. These included the Durham Report (1970) *The 4th R: Church of England report on church schools and religious education*, the Bullock Report (1975) *A Language for Life* related to the teaching of English, the Warnock Report (1978) *Special Educational Needs* that considered provision for children and young people with special needs, and the survey by HMI (1978) *Primary Education in England* that reported some aspects of the work of 7, 9 and 11 year old children in over 1,100 classes.

To inform the 'great debate', in the late 1970s LEAs were required to review and report on their curriculum policies. These events were the beginning of the 'process of reaching a national consensus on a desirable framework for the curriculum and consider the development of such a framework a priority for the education service' (HMI, 1980, Foreword).

1980S

A View of the Curriculum (HMI, 1980) called for a lengthy process of consultation in order to establish a curriculum. It reflected the principles of the Plowden Report and placed the Warnock Report explicitly and firmly at the heart of the process. This was followed by further support and advice for LEAs on curriculum development. One such source was a series entitled *Curriculum Matters* by HMI, which was published between 1984 and 1989, covering 17 subjects and other areas of importance in education from 5–16 years of age.

1985 saw the publication of the White Paper *Better Schools*. Among other things, it continued the focus on the national agreement about the purposes and content of the curriculum, it took steps to reduce under-achievement and to address truancy.

Later in the decade, a consultation document (DES, 1987) was published. This outlined the proposed ten subjects of the National Curriculum, comprising of three core (English, mathematics and science) and seven foundation (geography, history, technology, a foreign language (for secondary school pupils), art, music, and physical education) subjects, alongside the percentage of time to be allocated to each subject or group of subjects. It identified a need to assess children's attainment at 7, 11, 14 and 16 and it stated that most assessment would be carried out by teachers, with national tests supplementing their work. The latter was followed up in 1988 when the National Curriculum Task Group on Assessment and Testing (TGAT) identified how tests and school league tables would be structured. The report stated that one advantage to operating a national testing regime would be to apply a common set of benchmarks across the age ranges, and acknowledged the key role moderation would play to ensure consistency of judgements (Green, 2002).

Further reports were written into core areas of education provision, such as the Cockcroft Report (1982) *Mathematics Counts*, the Swan Report (1985) *Education for All*, and the Elton Report (1989) *Discipline in Schools*. Another key document to be reported was the ORACLE survey (Galton et al., 1980), which published findings including how, where the curriculum is broadened (beyond literacy and numeracy), children do better (Ross, 1999).

Furthermore, during this period a number of Education Acts were passed, including the two 1986 Education Acts. In the latter, LEAs were required to publish their curriculum policies, governors were required to publish annual reports, and schools were required to hold parents' evenings. Schools were no longer allowed to undertake corporal punishment. Additionally, they were inhibited from indoctrinating children into any political viewpoint. In 1988, the Education 'Reform' Act, which was the most significant Act since 1944 (Ross, 1999), was passed. Among other things, it legislated for the introduction of Key Stages, the National Curriculum and its accompanying testing regime with league tables. This meant that for the first time since the abolition of the *Elementary Code* in the 1920s teachers were required by law to teach a prescribed curriculum. More power over education was handed over to central government and the functions of LEAs were limited (Alexander, 2010).

The development of the National Curriculum was overseen by the National Curriculum Council and the School Examination and Assessment Council. The programmes of study were handed over to individual subject working groups and perhaps this is why the final documentation was 'substantial and set out in considerable detail the subject content that schools should be required to cover' (House of Commons, 2009, p.13).

The National Curriculum was introduced into schools in 1989 and implementation occurred over the next few years.

Early 1990s

After the introduction of the 1988 National Curriculum and the associated unrest related to unreasonable workload, the government commissioned Ron Dearing to review the National Curriculum. The Dearing Review (1994) suggested that the curriculum be slimmed down, time given to testing should be reduced, and around 20 per cent of teaching time set aside for the use of schools to design their own curriculum. This led to a revised National Curriculum in 1995 which saw a significant reduction in content and the introduction of eight level descriptors across the key stages.

The seminal report *Curriculum organisation and classroom practice in primary schools* (Alexander et al., 1992) (often referred to as the 'three wise men report') reviewed the delivery of education in primary schools. Reporting on it ten years later, Hofkins (2002) explained how many teachers rejected it at the time, but its influence on today's classrooms is clear. Although it was used in a 'back to basics' election campaign after the progressive years of the 1970s and 1980s, the report itself was calling for a balance in the way teachers taught, using whole-class teaching, group and individual work to teach subjects and topics. It also suggested teachers use questioning and explaining skills more effectively, and focused on teachers having higher expectations of all children.

Late 1990s–2010

National Curriculum reviews

1997 saw the first full review of the National Curriculum and as a result a revision of the National Curriculum occurred again in 1999. It was significantly slimmed down and was the first curriculum to provide underpinning values, aims and purposes. The three core subjects remained the same as the 1988 curriculum. The non-core foundation subjects were: design and technology, information and communication technology, history, geography, art and design, music and physical education. There were also non-statutory guidelines for personal, social and health education, citizenship, and modern foreign languages (MFL). Since then, *Languages for All: Languages for life* (DfES, 2000) included the directive for all KS2 children to learn a modern foreign language. Additionally, religious education was a statutory subject, supported by non-statutory guidance. Finally, the National Curriculum outlined a number of general teaching requirements: inclusion, the use of language (writing, speaking, listening and reading), ICT across the curriculum, and health and safety.

Literacy and mathematics

In 1997 the White Paper *Excellence in Schools* announced that at least one hour a day would be spent on English and on mathematics, and that schools were to have targets given to them in order to raise standards. Following this, in 1998 the schools standards minister, Stephen Byers, declared that literacy targets would raise standards so that 80 per cent of children would attain Level 4 or above in English, and 75 per cent of children Level 4 or above in mathematics by 2002 (although these targets were not met until later).

The late 1990s saw a distinct shift in governmental leadership of schools. Its focus turned from *what* to teach, to *how* to teach and the introduction of the first National Literacy Strategy was soon followed by the National Numeracy Strategy. Both produced frameworks for teaching literacy and mathematics and, while they were non-statutory, the vast majority of schools adopted their teaching methods.

2006 saw the Renewed Primary Framework for Literacy and Mathematics come out as an online resource and in the same year the *Review of the Teaching of Early Reading*, the Rose Report (2006), was published to address the debate about the place of phonics in the teaching of reading. In 2008, the Williams Report *Independent Review of Mathematics Teaching in Early Years Settings and Primary Schools* was published.

Although the National Strategies and the DCSF (House of Commons, 2009) emphasised that the National Strategies guidance was non-statutory, there was a widespread perception among teachers that National Strategies guidance was mandatory, and that they could be penalised by their local authority or school improvement partner, or through Ofsted inspection, for not following that guidance (Alexander, 2010).

Formal prescription did ensue when, in 2007, the government required phonics to be taught in the early stages of learning to read. This was built on in 2010 when it was announced in the White Paper that all children would be taught systematic synthetic phonics and children would be tested in Year 1 to 'confirm whether individual pupils had grasped the basics of phonic decoding [and] identify those pupils who need extra help, so the school can provide support' (DfE, 2010c).

Government intervention in relation to the guidance provided to schools about how to teach the curriculum continued (Wyse et al., 2008); the number of publications in primary literacy and mathematics alone totalled 769 (Hansen, 2012), and many more for other aspects of the curriculum were also produced. In a fairly damning indictment of the way National Strategies' non-statutory guidance was interpreted by schools, formal minutes of the House of Commons (2009) stated: 'We are concerned at the growth of centrally-produced curriculum-related guidance, and we believe that the National Strategies should be discontinued.' This was actioned, and as a result the National Strategies ceased to be in April 2011, following the QCDA that was one of the first government quangos to be axed in sweeping cuts in 2010.

Activity

Reflect on the planning and teaching that you have undertaken to date. To what extent did you use published materials from this period to support your planning? Who were they published by? What proportion were government based, and what proportion were private enterprise?

Every Child Matters

Another key development during this period was the Every Child Matters agenda. In 2003 the government published the Green Paper of the same name and the following year the Children Act 2004 became law, providing the opportunity to put into place a more integrated children's workforce focused on the needs of children, young people and their families.

Central to *Every Child Matters* were five aims that were designed to give all children the support they require in order to:

- be healthy;
- stay safe;
- enjoy and achieve;
- make a positive contribution;
- achieve economic wellbeing.

In the following years the Every Child Matters agenda was further developed and became the central tenet to the Children's Plan in 2007. Its launch presented a ten-year strategy to make England the best place for children and young people to grow up. This signalled the beginning of another curriculum reform.

A move towards creativity and personalisation

In addition to a continued focus on literacy and mathematics, the first decade of the new century renewed the focus on creativity and personalisation.

> *The new Primary Strategy will support teachers and schools across the whole curriculum, building on the lessons of the Literacy and Numeracy Strategies, but moving on to offer teachers more control and flexibility. It will focus on building up teachers' own professionalism and capacity to teach better and better, with bespoke support they can draw on to meet their particular needs.*

> *Primary National Strategy (2003)*

Creativity

The National Advisory Committee on Creative and Cultural Education's (NACCCE, 1999) report *All Our Futures: Creativity, Culture and Education* triggered the government to call on the (then) QCA to lead a three-year research project *Creativity: finding it, promoting it* (QCA, 2004), which investigated how teachers could promote children's creativity across the National Curriculum (NC).

The findings of the project found enhanced levels of children's literacy and numeracy skills, self-esteem, motivation and achievement, individual talents, and life skills.

The 2002 Education Act gave permission for schools to move away from the NC in order to enable 'development work or experiments to be carried out' (2002, Section 90). The government was signalling to schools that they did have more autonomy than many interpreted.

Personalisation

The 2005 White Paper *Higher Standards, Better Schools for All* encouraged schools to focus on individual children. In the same year, Ofsted were required to report on the extent to which schools take account of the views of the children. This led to most schools setting up School Councils, if they did not already have one.

Furthermore, *2020 Vision*, the report of the Teaching and Learning in 2020 Review Group (2006), placed personalising learning and teaching and pupil voice central to teaching in the future. It identified that personalising learning is 'learner-centred and knowledge-centred, and assessment centred' and outlined the importance of personalisation (Teaching and Learning in 2020 Review Group, 2006, pp.6–7).

Research Focus: The *Cambridge Primary Review*, the Rose Review and the 'new' primary curriculum

The *Cambridge Primary Review*, launched in 2006, was an independently-funded enquiry into the condition and future of primary education in England. This was the most comprehensive review since Plowden. The process involved the publication of 29 interim reports, two special reports on the primary curriculum and a final report, *Children, Their World, Their Education* (Alexander, 2010). The review addressed ten themes: purposes and values; learning and teaching; curriculum and assessment; quality and standards; diversity and inclusion; settings and professionals; parenting, caring and educating; children's lives beyond school; structures and phases; and funding and governance. The final review contained 75 recommendations (compared with 197 in Plowden and 333 in Bullock) that were signposted in the following summarising headings:

- Respect and support childhood
- Narrow the gap
- Review special needs
- Start with aims

⟶

- New structures for early years and primary education

- A new curriculum

- A pedagogy of evidence and principle

- Reform assessment

- Strengthen accountability, redefine standards

- Review primary school staffing

- Leadership for learning

- Reform teacher education

- Schools for the community

- Schools for the future

- Reform school funding

- Reform the policy process

- A new educational discourse

At around the same time as the Cambridge review, Sir Jim Rose was commissioned by the government to lead *The Independent Review of the Primary Curriculum*. It focused on curriculum design and content, highlighting that the primary phase of education was unique and that children had different and developing abilities during their time at primary school. It stated that literacy and numeracy remained central, but other aspects included ICT, personal development, transition and progression, and MFL at KS2. It suggested that the curriculum should be organised into six areas of learning:

- Understanding English, communication and languages;

- Mathematical understanding;

- Scientific and technological understanding;

- Historical, geographical and social understanding;

- Understanding physical development, health and wellbeing;

- Understanding the arts.

The Rose Review led directly into the development of the new National Curriculum primary handbook (DCSF, 2010) which was published in February 2010. It set out, for the first time, statutory aims which were to enable all young people to become successful learners, confident individuals and responsible citizens. The 1999 National Curriculum stated that its values 'do not change over time', and this proved to be correct in the new version. However, the values were amended to reflect the 'values in our society that promote personal development, equality of opportunity, economic wellbeing, a healthy and just democracy, and a sustainable future' (DCSF, 2010, p.4) which were resonant of the Every Child Matters outcomes.

However, three months after its publication, a pending election meant that it did not pass into law and as a result, another National Curriculum review was launched early in the new coalition government's term.

Where are we now?

The 2014 National Curriculum

Following a relatively short curriculum review process, the 2014 National Curriculum in England (https://www.gov.uk/government/publications/national-curriculum-in-england-primary-curriculum) became statutory for all state-funded schools from September 2014. The 2014 curriculum aims to introduce pupils to the

> *essential knowledge that they need to be educated citizens ... {to} engender an appreciation of human creativity and achievement ... {It} provides an outline of core knowledge around which teachers can develop exciting and stimulating lessons to promote the development of pupils' knowledge, understanding and skills as part of the wider school curriculum.*
>
> *(DfE, 2013, p.6)*

The core subjects are English, mathematics and science and these are accompanied by the foundation subjects: art and design, computing, design and technology, languages (KS2 only), geography, history, music and physical education. All schools are also required to teach religious education and should make provision for personal, social, health and economic education (PSHE). Furthermore, cross-curricular skills of numeracy and mathematics, and language and literacy (including spoken language, reading and writing, and vocabulary development) should be developed in all relevant subjects across the curriculum.

Inclusion issues are addressed in the new curriculum: teachers are expected to have high expectations of every pupil and set suitable challenges and ambitious targets for every pupil, including those of high attainment, those with low levels of prior attainment or those from disadvantaged backgrounds.

Alongside teaching the *National* Curriculum, schools are expected to design a *school* curriculum which they should publish on the school's website. 'The school curriculum comprises all learning and other experiences that each school plans for its pupils. The national curriculum forms one part of the school curriculum' (DfE, 2013, p.5).

Activity

The National College (2015) states:

It is useful to think of the National Curriculum as a set of ingredients that can be included in a school curriculum. A school should decide how the ingredients can be put together in the most exciting and effective way. A school should also consider what other ingredients are required to make a really outstanding curriculum that will inspire and challenge all children and prepare them for the future.

Look at the National Curriculum. What further ingredients would you add to a school curriculum?

Case Study: One school's curriculum

Samir was on a final block placement in a two-form entry primary school during a period when the staff were reconceiving their school curriculum in light of the new National Curriculum. She wrote a reflective piece on the way the school was changing in preparation for an end-of-course viva she was required to undertake after the placement. Here is an excerpt:

I was really surprised that the school even wanted to change anything. It is a lovely school with great children and teachers and they seem to do everything well. But in the first staff meeting we had about this the teachers were talking about how they felt that something was missing from their teaching and that they were fed up with being so prescriptive in their work with the children. The deputy head, who is new to the school and led the staff meeting, suggested that they come up with a 'bucket list' of what they wanted the children to have experienced by the time they left school. This included going to the beach, rolling down a hill, visiting the theatre and going on a bug hunt. This list then informed the themes of the new school curriculum. Between this meeting and the second, parents were asked to talk to their children about what they really wanted to learn about and this was also fed in to the themes list.

In the second meeting there was so much enthusiasm and excitement as the teachers divvied up the themes between year groups. They realised how the old themes had been around for ages and that they didn't really excite the teachers or children. They also decided to try a few new ideas. Sometimes 'expert teachers' might teach both year groups in the hall altogether, with the other teacher supporting them. They reasoned that if one teacher is really knowledgeable in a particular area it stands that they will be able to excite the children more than another teacher. They also agreed that a lesson doesn't have to be an hour and that a theme might last anywhere between one day and a whole term. Previously, their themes always lasted for half a term and this led to

→

struggling to keep the children excited or it meant finishing something earlier than the children wanted to.

In the third meeting the new themes were broadly compared with the new national curriculum. Any areas that were not covered were included or written on the 'assembly list' where, for example, some history topics would be taught as one-off inputs within assemblies.

I feel honoured to have been part of this process and although I didn't see the school as broken before, I can see how these changes that are putting the children's needs first before the national curriculum's – although hard work – will reignite a passion for learning within the school.

There is a job going in the school, I'm definitely applying! I'd like to explore further in the school how flipped classrooms and other technological innovations can enhance the exciting work the school is beginning.

Where are we going?

Transforming teaching: the current debate

It appears that one significant source for current debate in primary teaching is the ongoing tension between teachers having legislative autonomy, but the practical realities of governmental intervention through testing, inspection and non-statutory guidance are causing many teachers to become 'de-skilled' (House of Commons, 2009, p.33). While many (Alexander, 2010; House of Commons, 2009) have called for changes in arrangements for testing and inspection, the government are reforming the curriculum, testing and inspection concurrently, so only time will tell how comfortably these sit alongside each other.

What is clear is that the teaching profession is potentially on the cusp of a significant period of change (see the White Paper *The Importance of Teaching* (DfE, 2010a)). From every direction there is a call for a genuinely renewed curriculum. There is now a new National Curriculum that provides a slimmed down statutory requirement compared to the previous curriculum. *How* schools decide to engage and motivate their learners will be a decision led by the head teacher, giving back to schools a potentially higher degree of professional freedom (Bew, 2011; DfE 2011a, 2011b; Tickell, 2011). As a trainee teacher, your role will be crucial in seeing this change through.

Changes in the current landscape have:

- established a set of future-facing aims, values and principles;
- continued to address the gap in attainment between various groups of children;
- been shaped through the learner's perspective;

- shown a journey from birth (or 5) to 19;
- scaled down the content of the National Curriculum;
- required local ownership of the National Curriculum;
- challenged the decrease in the overall quality of primary education experienced due to the narrowing of the curriculum and impact of test preparation (Wyse et al., 2008);
- required teachers to become critical and reflective practitioners, basing their professional decisions on sound evidence and data;
- maintained subject knowledge as an essential component of high quality teaching;
- maintained testing as central to a standards agenda.

Activity

Make a list of the skills, knowledge and attributes a good teacher needs to possess when teaching children for their future. Then watch Sir Ken Robinson's talk (24 minutes) at https://www.thersa.org/discover/videos/event-videos/2013/07/how-to-change-education---from-the-ground-up/. Sir Ken lists what he thinks teachers need to be able to do. Compare your list to that of Sir Ken. Are your views forward thinking for preparing children for the twenty-first and twenty-second centuries, or are they formed using the older, industrialised view of education? How do you think you can you influence education from the ground up as a trainee teacher and beginning teacher?

Learning Outcomes Review

Thinking about the school in which you are working or have recently worked, respond to the prompts after each intended learning outcome, to identify your knowledge and understanding of the issues covered in the chapter.

- **Review the development of teaching and learning in English primary schools since the 1940s:**

  - Identify as many issues as you can that have continued to be central to educational debate in the last 80 years.
  - Which issues do you feel have been satisfactorily resolved in that time?

- **Reflect on how this development impacts our current teaching and learning practices in primary schools:**

  - Reflect on the different schools you have visited as a trainee teacher. Try to write a short paragraph about each school that summarises a) the teaching practices and b) the learning practices of the schools. What does this tell you about primary schools?

– What published documentation do you currently use to inform your planning in school? Which of this is statutory/non-statutory guidance/other published material? Why do you use these?

- **Consider your own professional knowledge and competence, by reflecting on how you are contributing to the 'transformation' of teaching and learning:**

  – What autonomy do you feel you have as a trainee teacher in supporting the development of your school's planning and delivery of the curriculum?
  – What strengths do you bring as a trainee teacher who will be contributing to the 'transformed' teaching profession? What personal/professional aspects of your skills, knowledge and understanding will you need to develop before you qualify or in your NQT year?

Further Reading

Derek Gillard's History of Education website (www.educationengland.org.uk/index.html) contains the text of most of the historical documents discussed in this chapter. It is also a good source of the governments in power.

The Cambridge Primary Review. A very readable booklet bringing together the key messages from the Cambridge Primary Review can be downloaded from http://www.primaryreview.org.uk/downloads/CPR_revised_booklet.pdf

The Framework for the National Curriculum can be found at: https://www.gov.uk/government/publications/national-curriculum-in-england-primary-curriculum

References

Alexander, R. (ed.) (2010) *Children, Their World, Their Education: Final report and recommendations of the Cambridge Primary Review.* London: Routledge.

Alexander, R., Rose, J. and Woodhead, C. (1992) *Curriculum Organisation and Classroom Practice in Primary Schools: A discussion paper.* London: Department of Education and Science.

Bennett, N. (1976) *Teaching Styles and Pupil Progress.* London: Open Books.

Beveridge, W. (1942) *Social Insurance and Allied Services.* London: HMSO.

Bew, P. (2011) *Independent Review of Key Stage 2 Testing, Assessment and Accountability: Final report.* London: DfE.

Board of Education (1931) *The Primary School.* London: HMSO.

Board of Education (1959) *Primary Education: Suggestions for the consideration of teachers and others concerned with the work of primary schools.* London: HMSO.

Bullock, A. (1975) *A Language for Life.* London: HMSO.

Callaghan, J. (1976) *The Ruskin Speech*. Available from http://education.guardian.co.uk/thegreatdebate/story/0,9860,574645,00.html accessed 07/12/10.

Cockcroft, W.H. (1982) *Mathematics Counts*. London: HMSO.

DCSF (2010) *The National Curriculum: Primary Handbook*. London: QCDA.

Dearing, R. (1994) *The National Curriculum and its Assessment*. London: School Curriculum and Assessment Authority.

DES (1987) *The National Curriculum 5–16: A consultation document*. London: HMSO.

DfE (2010a) The Importance of Teaching: Schools White Paper. Available from www.education.gov.uk/schools/teachingandlearning/schoolswhitepaper/b0068570/the-importance-of-teaching/ accessed 9/12/10.

DfE (2010b) Important information on the primary curriculum and Key Stage 3 level descriptions. Available from www.education.gov.uk/curriculum accessed 15/07/10.

DfE (2010c) Synthetic phonics will drive up basic literacy standards. *Govtoday*. Available from www.govtoday.co.uk/Education/Early-Years/synthetic-phonics-will-drive-up-basic-literacy-standards.html accessed 14/12/10.

DfE (2011a) *The Framework for the National Curriculum. A Report by the Expert Panel for the National Curriculum Review*. London: DfE.

DfE (2011b) *Independent Review of Key Stage 2 Testing, Assessment and Accountability: Government Response*. London: DfE.

DfE (2011c) *Teachers' Standards.* Available from www.education.gov.uk/publications

DfE (2013) *The National Curriculum in England: Key Stages 1 and 2 Framework Document*. London: DfE.

DfEE (1999) *The National Curriculum: Handbook for primary teachers in England*. London: QCA.

DfES (2000) *Languages for All: Languages for life*. London: DfES.

Durham Report (1970) *The 4th R: Church of England report on church schools and religious education*. London: National Society.

Elton, R. (1989) *Discipline in Schools*. London: HMSO.

Galton, M., Simon, B. and Croll, P. (1980) *Inside the Primary Classroom*. Australasia: Law book company.

Gillard, D. (2006) 'The Hadow Reports: an introduction', *The Encyclopaedia of Informal Education*. Available from www.infed.org/schooling/hadow_reports.htm accessed 15/07/10.

Green, S. (2002) Criterion referenced assessment as a guide to learning: The importance of progression and reliability. Paper presented at the Association for the Study of Evaluation in Education in Southern Africa International Conference. Johannesburg,

10–12 July 2002. Available from www.cambridgeassessment.org.uk/ca/digitalAssets/ 113775_Criterion_Referenced_Assessment_as_a_Guide_to_Learning_The_pdf accessed 09/12/10.

Hansen, A. (2012) Transforming teaching and learning. In A. Hansen (ed.) *Professional Studies* (2nd edition). London: Learning Matters/SAGE, pp. 5–23.

Her Majesty's Inspectorate (HMI) (1978) *Primary Education in England: A Survey by HM Inspectors of Schools*, London: HMSO.

Her Majesty's Inspectorate (HMI) (1980) *A View of the Curriculum*. London: HMSO.

Hofkins, D. (2002) Wise men's gift is lasting legacy. In *TES*, 8 February 2002. Available from www.tes.co.uk/article.aspx?storycode=359478 accessed 14/12/10.

Home Office (1960) *Section 11 Grant*. London: HMSO. Available from www.nationalarchives. gov.uk/ERORecords/HO/421/2/reu/grant.htm accessed 15/12/10.

House of Commons (2006) The Schools White Paper: higher standards, better schools for all. First report of session 2005–06. Vol. 1. Available from www.publications.parliament.uk/pa/ cm200506/cmselect/cmeduski/633/633.pdf accessed 14/12/10.

House of Commons (2009) *National Curriculum. Fourth report of session 2008–2009*. London: The Stationery Office.

McKenzie, J. (2001) *Changing Education: A sociology of education since 1944*. Harlow: Pearson Education.

National Advisory Committee on Creative and Cultural Education (1999) *All Our Futures: Creativity, culture and education*. Available from www.cypni.org.uk/downloads/alloutfutures. pdf accessed 09/12/10.

National College (2015) *A School Curriculum*. Available from http://apps.nationalcollege.org. uk/resources/modules/curriculum/Curriculum/Entries/2013/1/1_The_difference_between_ the_national_curriculum_and_a_school_curriculum..html accessed 26/04/15.

Plowden Report (1967) *Children and their Primary Schools*. London: HSMO.

Primary National Strategy (2003) *Excellence and Enjoyment: A strategy for primary schools*. London: DfES.

QCA (2004) *Creativity: Finding it, promoting it.* London: QCA.

Rose, J. (2006) *Independent Review of the Teaching of Early Reading*. London: DfES.

Rose Report (2008) *The Independent Review of the Primary Curriculum: Final report*. Available from www.education.gov.uk/publications

Ross, A. (1999) *Curriculum: Construction and critique*. London: Routledge.

Swan, M. (1985) *Education for All*. London: HMSO.

Teaching and Learning in 2020 Review Group (2006) *2020 Vision*. Available from http://publications.education.gov.uk/eOrderingDownload/6856-DfES-Teaching%20and%20Learning.pdf accessed 14/12/10.

Tickell, C. (2011) *The Early Years: Foundations for Life, Health and Learning. An independent report on the Early Years Foundation Stage to Her Majesty's Government*. London: DfE.

Warnock, H.M. (1978) *Special Educational Needs*. London: HMSO.

Williams, P. (2008) *Independent Review of Mathematics Teaching in Early Years Settings and Primary Schools*. London: DCSF.

Wyse, D., McCreery, E. and Torrance, H. (2008) The trajectory and impact of national reform: curriculum and assessment in English primary schools. Primary Review Research Briefings 3/2. Available from www.primaryreview.org.uk/Downloads/Int_Reps/7.Governance-finance-reform/RS_3-2_briefing_Curriculum_assessment_reform_080229.pdf accessed 09/12/10.

2. Curriculum approaches
Adrian Copping

Learning Outcomes

By the end of this chapter you will have explored:

- how beliefs about learning drive curriculum planning and teaching approaches;
- how children's learning and development is at the forefront of curriculum development;
- how a cross-curricular approach deepens learning through the joining of concepts and ideas;
- debates about integrated and single-subject learning opportunities.

TEACHERS' STANDARDS

A teacher must:

3. Demonstrate good subject and curriculum knowledge
- have a secure knowledge of the relevant subject(s) and curriculum areas, foster and maintain pupils' interest in the subject, and address misunderstandings
- demonstrate a critical understanding of developments in the subject and curriculum areas, and promote the value of scholarship
- demonstrate an understanding of and take responsibility for promoting high standards of literacy, articulacy and the correct use of standard English, whatever the teacher's specialist subject.

4. Plan and teach well structured lessons
- impart knowledge and develop understanding through effective use of lesson time
- promote a love of learning and children's intellectual curiosity
- contribute to the design and provision of an engaging curriculum within the relevant subject area(s).

8. Fulfil wider professional responsibilities
- make a positive contribution to the wider life and ethos of the school
- develop effective professional relationships with colleagues, knowing how and when to draw on advice and specialist support
- deploy support staff effectively
- take responsibility for improving teaching through appropriate professional development, responding to advice and feedback from colleagues.

Introduction

Chapter 1 outlined the statutory requirements and non-statutory components of the National Curriculum. For each subject in Key Stages 1 and 2, the National Curriculum programmes of study set out what children should be taught and it is for schools to choose how they organise their school curriculum to include the programmes of study (QCDA, 2010). Therefore, although teachers are statutorily obliged (that is, by law you are required) to teach the *content* of the National Curriculum (DfE, 2013), schools and teachers are not bound in any way as to *how* they should teach. One of the key principles of the National Curriculum is that it sets out only the essential knowledge that children require. This frees schools to design a school curriculum that meets the needs of the children in the school (DfEE, 2011a, p.6). In light of that, this chapter explores how schools and teachers might design their curriculum to include effective learning experiences for their children.

Theoretical approaches to curriculum design and designing learning

A curriculum, be it a national one or a derivative made for a specific context, is created based on a series of beliefs about learning, and the perceived purpose of the curriculum. This section discusses the impact that your own beliefs have on how you plan for learning. The case study below exemplifies how the National Curriculum for England reflects a theoretical framework of learning.

The National Curriculum for England (DfE, 2014) is based on the belief that in order for learning to occur, ideas and concepts should be re-examined and revisited over time. This has been termed a 'spiral curriculum' where 'students return again to the basic concepts, building on them, making them more complex and understanding them more fully' (Howard, 2007, p.1). Therefore, new learning builds on previous learning where the understanding of a concept is extended and enhanced through a process of *scaffolding*. This approach, outlined by Jerome Bruner, is rooted in the idea that learning is meaningful, has a purpose and that initial concepts have some validity and interest for the learner.

There are many other beliefs about how children learn and some of these are considered in Chapter 5, but it is important to remember as you read this chapter that a school's curriculum or scheme of work arises out of a belief in how children learn. The development of that curriculum, the activities contained therein, the progression of activities and teaching approaches indicated arise out of a particular belief about what learning is, how it happens and how children do it. The National Curriculum (DfE, 2013) provides broader statements of learning intent and curriculum coverage than its 1999 predecessor, especially for the foundation subjects, facilitating more local ownership of curriculum organisation.

Additionally, the way the curriculum is organised is shaped by how teachers perceive the wider curriculum itself. In light of this, the next section explores three ways of conceptualising a curriculum.

Conceptualising the curriculum

Activity
Read through the models below and consider to what extent they reflect how you see the curriculum. If appropriate, have a go at developing your own model that uses a metaphor to reflect your own perceptions.

The curriculum as a blueprint for learning

This belief suggests that the curriculum is a blueprint on which knowledge is built. Instructions for the building suggest that the preordained outcome must be reached and particular ways of working must be followed in order to get there. It is safe, secure and comfortable, provided the blueprint is accurate. It implies that there are no opportunities to explore alternative ways of constructing knowledge and is clearly focused on outcomes. This way of conceptualising the curriculum suggests a belief about knowledge which is propositional or declarative (knowing about facts, e.g. knowing the important events in Tudor England, how the water cycle works, or that Paris is the capital city of France) and that learning is procedural. Biggs (2003, p.41) explains that declarative knowledge 'is what is in libraries and text books, and is what teachers "declare" in lectures. Students' understanding of it can be tested by getting them to declare it back.'

While it could be argued that there is knowledge that should be known, it is limited in its use and application. Donald Schön, who developed the notion of reflective practice, explains how propositional knowledge or declarative knowledge is of limited value (Schön, cited in Brockbank and McGill, 2003). The implications of this belief are that learning could become rigid, concepts remain abstract and potentially irrelevant to the learner and that any learning that could take place through the process of an activity or created context is negated by the focus being on the arrival at the correct endpoint as provided by the instructions.

The curriculum as a set of outcomes to be able to quantify

This belief implies that a scheme of work (listing the statutory objectives, providing indicative activities that allow the learner to meet those and identifying suggested assessment designed to test the meeting of that outcome) can be tested, and the objective can be ticked off as having been taught and learnt.

This conceptualisation suggests something about how knowledge is gained. In this case, it is about knowledge being *procedural*. Biggs (2003) states that this procedural knowledge 'is a matter of getting the sequences and actions right having the right ... competencies' (2003, p.42). Just like the blueprint model, this is a very linear approach to the curriculum where the focus is on the outcome and passing the test which may indeed negate meaningful, constructed learning because in a sense this approach to curriculum is about the end result.

The curriculum as a map

This belief continues to use declarative knowledge as an end point. However, it may address the concerns of the models discussed above. The curriculum as a map model suggests that the curriculum is set within a particular environment and that participants within the environment are able to use a map to journey and explore within it. As long as a participant has the skills to be able to interpret the map, it is possible to reach a given destination using a number of possible routes. The route chosen will in turn offer new experiences and opportunities on the way to reaching the destination.

Boyle (2002, p.11) explains how a map metaphor can be used.

> *A map provides a systematic, integrated description of a particular geographical domain. This description, it should be noted, is both abstract and conventionalized. This knowledge base can be used to construct a route from any location on the map, through a series of 'valid steps,' to any other location on the map. This is far more powerful than any set of procedural descriptions.*

This belief builds on the notion that a curriculum should be designed to match the needs of the learners for whom it is intended because external guidance cannot be put into practice unless the context is considered. Boyle's map metaphor suggests a flexible and creative approach to learning knowledge and this places the learner (as the user of the map) and the teacher (as the expedition guide) in a position of being decision makers. Therefore, this takes into consideration the 'softer' skills a learner should possess, such as collaboration.

This approach reflects a belief that knowledge is useful and functioning. Biggs (2003) calls this 'functioning knowledge' (2003, p.42). However, in order for a functioning knowledge to exist, Biggs suggests that the learner must have high levels of both declarative and procedural knowledge. These types provide the learner with the *what* and *how*. Additionally, Biggs (2003, p.42) suggests that the learner needs a further type of knowledge which he terms 'conditional' that provides the learner with the *why* and *when*. As Biggs summarises, 'if the target is functioning knowledge, the declarative knowledge needs to be developed to relational levels in order to provide both the knowledge of the specific context, and the conditional knowledge that enable skills to be performed adequately' (2003, p.43).

Activity

Reflect on a recent school-based experience. Identify how the school's curriculum was designed. Which of the three beliefs about the curriculum, outlined above, were most prevalent in that design? Note down how the belief was exemplified in the learning and teaching. Also note what you consider to be the impact on children's learning.

Research Focus

In her work on trainee teachers' subject knowledge development in English, Twiselton (2006) identified three categories of trainee teacher: task managers, curriculum deliverers and concept/ skill builders. She suggests that trainee teachers pass through these stages on a continuum.

The stages are important in thinking about curriculum design and the nature of knowledge. The belief about curriculum as a set of outcomes is very much about teaching through delivering the curriculum. Twiselton's findings suggest that 'Curriculum Deliverers appeared unable to link concepts and skills. Instead they appeared to treat knowledge as isolated and atomised pieces. In this view learning can be represented as a series of "products" seen as ends in themselves' (2006, p.91). The implications for this approach to curriculum design are that the curriculum may lack cohesion and children may not be as able to make links between subject areas through the joining of concepts.

Because Twiselton's (2006) notion suggests that trainee teachers move through categories on a continuum, rather than stay within discrete categories, her research identified that ultimately trainee teachers should be aiming to develop into a 'concept/skill builder': a trainee teacher whose subject knowledge is not closed and who is able to link concepts and skills to situations outside of the classroom.

Earlier this section explored how Biggs suggests a joining up of knowledge types, and Twiselton (2006, p.93) supports this by stating that 'the bringing together of knowledge is the key to effective teaching'. It is also evident that this is one key to effective learning.

The implications for this research and the 'curriculum as a map' model above are significant. It allows children to explore, problem solve and investigate. It also suggests that the learning that takes place during the process of meaningful activity is as, if not more, important than meeting a prescribed objective. However, if this approach is the only one applied, a question must be asked about where does the solid foundation of declarative knowledge become built.

The case study below provides an example of how a trainee teacher on his final block placement planned and taught a lesson using Alfred Noyes' classic poem 'The Highwayman' as a stimulus.

Activity

As you read the case study, consider:

- Tom's beliefs about learning and teaching;
- how those beliefs may have directly impacted upon the children's learning and motivation to learn;
- where on Twiselton's continuum you would place Tom's subject knowledge.

Also consider your own response to the case study: would you be able to work in a similar way? As you read the case study, consider your own beliefs about learning and teaching and how they might impact upon how you would approach a similar unit of work.

Case Study: 'The Highwayman'

Tom, a trainee teacher working in a Year 6 class, planned an English unit for his placement class. The purpose of the unit was for the children to produce a news report about the two deaths that occur in the poem using processes such as enquiry, problem solving, reasoning and communication.

Prior to the children arriving, Tom had set the classroom up like a police murder scene using police cones and hazard tape to cordon off an area, taping outlines of two dead bodies on the floor and using anglepoise lamps to create subdued lighting. The chairs were arranged like a police investigation room, in pairs and in rows with police desk badges ready for the children to write their names on. A rolling slide presentation of images of highwaymen was playing on the interactive whiteboard and an action soundtrack supported this.

The effect was startling. The children came in for registration and were immediately asking questions about the classroom, investigating the artefacts, watching the slide show, discussing the images and there was an excited buzz of chatter and smiles and anticipation as to what would happen next.

Tom burst into the room in costume and introduced himself as the ghost of the highwayman lying dead on the floor and read/told the story from Noyes' narrative poem.

Tom then changed role to Detective Chief Inspector and charged the children with enquiring into the characters in the poem, what further information was needed to be found out, what might their motivation be for committing the murder and what questions might they like to ask the suspects. Tom used the dramatic technique of hot-seating and played the roles of the three main suspects. The children (in role as detectives) asked probing questions of the characters as to their motivation and 'where were you on the night of...' type questions while another child scribed useful information onto the board under a picture of each character. There was then an opportunity to share initial hypotheses and reflect on the views of others through small group discussion.

→

The children moved into role as journalists with the purpose of creating a news piece (a video presentation) in small groups. The teacher gave roles to each child (news anchor, camera operator, court reporter, crime scene reporter) and each group collated their ideas to form a news piece. A recording of a news programme was watched and the style analysed. A script was planned and prepared collaboratively in groups and then shared with the whole class. A 'good news report checklist' was used for evaluation purposes and each group had strengths and areas to improve to work on before final recording.

After recording, the class watched the news reports and assessed their performance in terms of news report criteria as well as understanding of the poem and story and a discussion about the key aspects of learning they had engaged in followed.

At the end of the unit some of the children made these comments:

- *I enjoyed being detectives, today we got be real police interviewing people.*

- *We were involved in everything.*

- *I learnt that English can be a bit like drama and acting.*

- *... that I'm more confident than I thought.*

- *... you got to do English physically as well as mentally.*

Interestingly, most of the comments came from the process of learning and were not particularly related with the end product of the video piece.

You are likely to have noticed that Tom was a very confident and creative trainee teacher. Crucially, he believed that children learn best from co-constructing their knowledge through experience and as a result he planned and taught in a way that reflected this. We see a social-constructivist belief (Lambirth, 2005), where, in small groups, children bring their ideas and expertise together, share it and in so doing jointly construct new knowledge and skills with their peers.

Research Focus

Vygotsky (1978) and Bruner (1983) both emphasise the role of talk in learning. They claim that discourse can enhance thinking and support learning. Vygotsky even suggests that thinking and learning can come into existence through the act of talking, taking the idea that the verbal expression of a thought brings it into being. Both believed that learning was socially constructed. Firstly that new learning is built upon previous learning and experience and secondly that this construction process can occur through social discourse, a process that Bruner termed 'scaffolding'.

Models of designing learning opportunities

This section focuses on the ways that you might design learning opportunities for the children you teach on placement. Regardless of the ways you conceptualise the curriculum, it is possible to approach planning the curriculum in several different ways.

Fogarty's models of curriculum design

Robin Fogarty has been writing about curriculum integration since the early 1990s. She has developed ten models for how school curricula may be conceived. This section considers four of these, but if you want to read more, see the further reading section at the end of this chapter.

Fogarty suggests that curriculum areas, knowledge, skills and understanding can be integrated in meaningful ways and that different models can be used by different teachers and in different times of the school year.

Shared

The shared approach is concerned with looking at two particular subjects and emphasising the common skills and concepts in them. Fogarty (1991, p.62) explains how the model 'views the curriculum through binoculars, bringing two distinct disciplines together into a single focused image'. For example, let's take English and history. Each circle in Figure 2.1

Figure 2.1 Example of shared integration: English and history

represents selected subject specific elements from the National Curriculum, and the area of overlap contains elements that appear in both. Therefore these can be shared when curriculum planning.

This approach has many advantages. It ensures that there is a strong link between two subjects and that any links made are meaningful and purposeful. It means that ideas and concepts can be applied easily and is relatively easy to organise. It does, however, mean that the rest of the curriculum might remain fragmented.

Threaded

The threaded approach is concerned with emphasising particular skills that can run through a subject and draws attention to the value of the process of learning, in particular thinking, social and study skills that can be threaded through a particular subject. Fogarty (1991, p.63) likens this model to viewing the curriculum 'through a magnifying glass: the "big ideas" are enlarged throughout all content with a meta-curricular approach'. Let's take design and technology as an example (see Figure. 2.2).

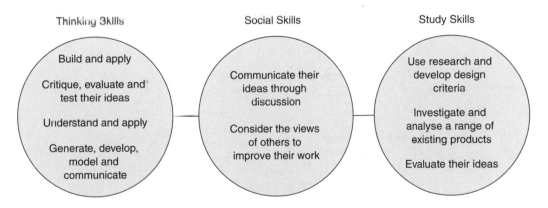

Figure 2.2 Example of threaded integration: Key Stage 2 design and technology

This list is by no means exhaustive but it does demonstrate how skills in different areas can be considered through a subject, meaning that as a subject is taught or a curriculum area covered, key process skills can be threaded through to make learning more meaningful and coherent. With this approach there is the explicit teaching of thinking skills and the explicit consideration of multiple intelligences. It means that the transfer of skills is easier and provides opportunity for children to gain insights into their own skills, strengths and weaknesses. Brown and Campione (1998, cited in Watkins et al., 2007, p.72) suggest that these insights, known as *meta-cognition* are where 'effective learners operate best'. This approach does however mean that subjects remain separate and meaningful links may not be fully exploited and therefore arguably the full learning potential may not be fully realised.

Integrated

With the integrated approach there is a common theme and subjects are not explicitly emphasised. Fogarty (1991, p.63) likens this to looking through a kaleidoscope where 'interdisciplinary topics are rearranged around overlapping concepts and emerging patterns and designs'. The theme may be a curricular topic such as 'The Victorians' but the emphasis is on the joining up of skills, concepts and attitudes rather than a focus on the subjects themselves. Let's use the theme of 'The changing power of monarchs using case studies such as Victoria' as an example (see Figure 2.3). This is a non-statutory theme from within history KS2 from the National Curriculum 2014. The skills, concepts and attitudes are derived from the general descriptors.

With this approach the interdependence of knowledge, skills and attitudes is clearly mapped out. This is the main advantage of this approach as learning is clearly identified as more than just knowledge being gained but to do with transferable skills and underpinning concepts as well as recognising that developing attitudes is a major part in learning. This

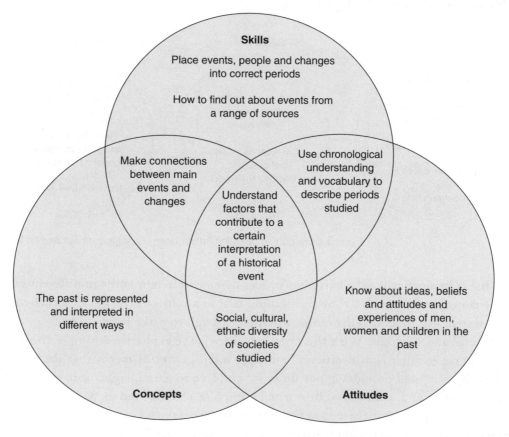

Figure 2.3 Example of 'integration' approach using a KS2 non-statutory unit
'The changing power of monarchs using case studies such as Victoria'

approach emphasises whole child development and the role that these different elements play in learning.

Webbed

Within the webbed approach a central theme or topic is identified, subjects treated separately but the consideration is what skills and concepts can each of those subjects contribute to the central theme. Fogarty (1991, p.63) suggests that this is like viewing the curriculum through a telescope, 'capturing an entire constellation of disciplines at once'. As an example let's take a Key Stage 1 focused topic, 'The Seaside' (Figure 2.4).

The purpose of this approach is to consider the skills that can be taught through the theme. The advantages of this are that the central theme or hub pulls everything together and integrates the content. It also provides a holistic approach to learning and allows children

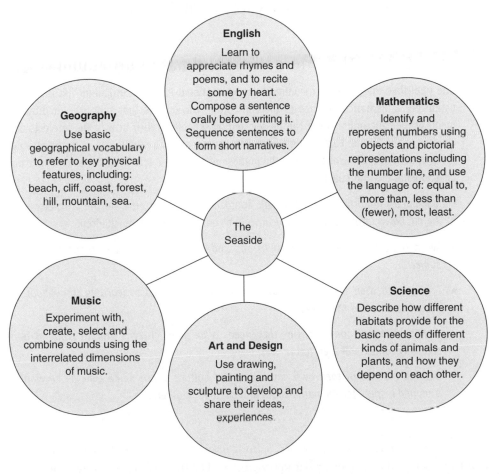

Figure 2.4 Example of webbed approach using a topic heading and KS1 curriculum objectives

to see links between concepts whilst also providing an opportunity for concepts, skills and content to overlap and be reinforced. However, its success is dependent on an appropriate theme and avoiding tenuous links. The content must also be relevant and meaningful.

Activity

Consider a plan for a unit of work you have undertaken. Which of Fogarty's models of integration do you see and how did your planning in these ways impact on the children's learning? Now that you have read about Fogarty's models of curriculum design, how might you amend the unit of work?

Integration versus single subject curriculum design

Case Study: The International Primary Curriculum

One published integrated curriculum is the International Primary Curriculum (IPC). The IPC is ostensibly a thematic approach to the curriculum. For schools that subscribe, it provides a menu of thematic units. These can be selected by schools so they best fit the interests of the children in the school. Each unit includes learning outcomes, a stimulus or entry point activity, tasks or activities, an explanation of the purpose of the theme and ideas for extending learning beyond what the unit suggests.

Fundamentally important to the thematic approach the IPC presents are the principles behind it. The IPC (www.internationalprimarycurriculum.com) aims to ensure children:

- *Learn the essential knowledge, skills and understanding of a broad range of curriculum subjects.*

- *Engage with their learning so that they remain committed to learning throughout their school careers and their lives.*

- *Develop the personal qualities they need to be good citizens and to respond to the changing contexts of their future lives.*

- *Develop a sense of their own nationality and culture at the same time as developing a profound respect for the nationalities and cultures of others.*

This, like all other curriculum approaches, is built upon a strong set of beliefs about how children learn best and also about what knowledge is. For the IPC, knowledge is not just about the acquisition of sets of facts but about the desire to learn, to become life-long learners with a thirst for knowledge. Their approach is also more global, on two levels. The first level is about a more international perspective, with children recognising and understanding the culture in which they live which will help them understand and develop a respect for the cultures of others. There is also a recognition that learning is about developing personal qualities such as flexibility, tolerance, resilience, interpersonal and intrapersonal skills essential in preparing them for jobs that may not yet exist. The IPC is also designed to take into account the idea that intelligence is multi-faceted.

There are other approaches and models to curriculum design. Although this chapter has focused on Fogarty's curriculum approaches that support ways of integrating subjects and consider the process of learning, Fogarty also identified as a curriculum approach a traditional, single subject design for organising the curriculum, which she called the 'fragmented' model (Fogarty, 1991, p.61).

There is some debate to be had around many of the ideas suggested in this chapter. This debate primarily concerns two arguments: an integrated approach with the joining up of concepts from subjects and a single subject approach. The first argument is that an integrated approach to curriculum encourages the joining up of subjects, concepts, skills, knowledge and understanding and so, the proponents of this approach suggest, makes learning more coherent.

An integrated approach

A *fully* integrated approach to the curriculum by its very nature suggests that all subjects, including daily mathematics and English lessons will be absolutely amalgamated. It is interesting to note that the IPC does not include mathematics within its units and it also provides complex mapping guides for schools for them to identify where they need to address potential gaps in their bespoke unit choices in relation to statutory National Curriculum content. The question therefore must arise about what drove most schools to make the decision to have each morning dominated by these two subjects.

Alexander (2009) suggests that the government's drive to have schools demonstrate high standards in these subjects is likely to be the reason. This concerns government targets for schools at the end of Key Stage 2 to achieve certain levels in Standard Assessment Tests (SATs). The publication of schools' results to the public, parents and Ofsted means that schools strive to get the best results possible. This in turn often gives rise to extensive preparation and a lot of test anxiety. Despite changes to the government's policy around statutory assessment and the removal of levels (in force in 2015/16), there is little evidence that this will change. Alexander (2009, p.22) explains that this approach to curriculum and assessment compromises children's entitlement:

The most conspicuous casualties are the arts, the humanities and the kinds of learning in all subjects which require time for talking, problem-solving and the extended exploration of ideas. A policy-led belief that curriculum breadth is incompatible with the pursuit of standards in 'the basics' has fuelled this loss of entitlement.

This illustrates the two main elements in the debate: curriculum breadth and pursuit of standards. Alexander reminds us that these do not have to be two opposing sides but that curriculum breadth can facilitate higher standards, but higher standards of what? This debate can only really have meaning once the question of the purpose of primary education is considered. If primary education is about enabling 'pupils to think creatively and critically, to solve problems, to make a difference for the better … to become creative, innovative, enterprising and capable of leadership to equip them for their future lives as workers and citizens' (Alexander, 2009, p.11) then it seems that an integrated approach that supports the development of these in a joined up way may be more effective in achieving this first aim of the National Curriculum.

A single subject approach

One concern with an integrated approach to the curriculum is that individual subjects may lose some of their integrity. Indeed, Ofsted's summary of evidence related to improving primary teachers' subject knowledge across the curriculum begins: 'The Independent Review of the Primary Curriculum accents the importance of subjects in primary education and the need for high quality teaching to ensure that pupils make all the progress that they are capable of' (2008, p.l). Additionally, it is not possible to ignore statistics about more students taking A-level mathematics in 2010 than ever before (STEM Advisory Forum, 2010) and how this is being linked to the implementation of the National Numeracy Strategy (NNS) which occurred when those students were in Year 2. This suggests that the NNS was a success in improving attitudes towards the subject. Furthermore, 80 per cent of children in Year 6 achieved expected levels or above in 2010. This is difficult to ignore when the proportion was a mere 54 per cent in 1997 (DfE, 2010).

Therefore, a single subject approach to curriculum design can also be highly effective. However, a clear progression of skills should be identified, planned for, and linked together in a structured way so that learners can gain initial skills and then learn how to use them effectively, particularly where an end product is identified. However, this does not mean that links cannot be made to other curriculum subjects. Designing the curriculum in this way allows the teacher to use the skills, knowledge and understanding gained through one subject to transfer them to another.

Figure 2.5 shows an example of a term's worth of work in art. As you look at it, consider the build-up of skills taught working towards the final product. You may notice opportunities for critical thinking, creative thinking, problem solving and also opportunities for developing meaningful cross-curricular links.

Medium-term plan checklist: Art and Design: Year 5

Learning objectives – linked to NC: skills, vocabulary, concepts and knowledge	Learning experiences	Resources
To understand that landscape painting involves viewing from a single point and using perspective and scale according to distance. (4a, 5a, 1b)	Children look at a range of landscape paintings: Constable, Monet, Cezanne, African landscapes in photographs and paintings, discuss similarities and differences. Look at colours: intense colours in foreground and paler colours further away. Look at scale and diminishing size.	Examples of landscapes by various artists and photographers
To have an appreciation of the use of colours to blend in paint and pastel. (2a,b,c)	Experiment mixing paler colours and intense colours and making patterns. Experiment with blending colours for African landscapes and creating vivid coloured skies and land with 'overpainting' areas, use pastels and watercolours in conjunction and blend together.	Paints, pastels, paper Mixing trays Pencils, paper
To use colours, lines and 3D materials to create an impression of texture. (4b, 5b,c)	Experiment sketching a landscape with diminishing features in the distance, looking at landscapes by a range of artists. Put painting and sketching together to produce an African landscape focusing on African prints and photographs.	As above and examples of African landscapes
Outcomes • To make detailed observations of African landscape paintings. • To imitate African landscapes taking into account colours used, blending and moods created. • To make 3D African landscapes, using papier mache, vivid colours and hot air balloons.	In small groups, use papier mache to make landscapes of Kenya based on pictures and photographs. Cover balloons with papier mache to produce hot air balloons to fly over African landscapes. Paint the papier mache when dry. Use mixed media to create banners depicting people, flags, animals and symbols of Kenya, use different textures, threads, embroidery in small groups.	Papier mache, balloons, wire, card Paint, fabrics, thread, other media such as dried pasta and printing blocks. Canes to hang work

Figure 2.5 Medium-term plan for Art (single subject approach), outcomes and objectives, derived from National Curriculum for Art and Design KS2, 2014

Activity

Using the Art medium-term plan in Figure 2.5, add any cross-curricular links you think are appropriate. Despite this being a plan for a single subject, can you integrate any concepts and skills using any of Fogarty's models for integration? Use this to see how these different approaches to design are not incompatible.

During the activity you may have been able to pull in lots of ideas and thoughts and used the ideas in the plan as a central hub for other ideas around, perhaps a topic of Africa, continents or more specifically, 'Kenya'.

Now let's step back and consider what beliefs about learning drove this plan. First, a belief in scaffolding: children need to have a purpose and then be taught the skills necessary to achieve that purpose. Each skill is then followed by an opportunity to try out, practise and explore. Just as in Tom's case study, we see a social constructivist belief (Lambirth, 2005) where, in small groups, children bring their ideas and expertise together, share it and in so doing jointly construct new knowledge and skills with their peers. Through this activity it is also possible to see how an integrated approach to curriculum design and a single subject approach do not have to be mutually exclusive. A skills-based art and design plan can certainly provide stimulus for an integrated approach to curriculum; similarly an integrated, perhaps webbed curriculum approach can facilitate a deep and exciting single subject plan. As stated before, subject knowledge is very important to success as a teacher, but it is what you do with that knowledge that is more important.

The case study below provides an example of how a group of trainee teachers in a Year 3 class on a creative themed week placement planned and taught a series of lessons around the theme of enterprise.

Activity

As you read the case study, consider:

- the trainee teachers' beliefs about learning and teaching;
- how those beliefs may have directly impacted upon the children's learning and motivation to learn;
- what learning took place and how this was scaffolded for the children.

Also consider your own response to the case study: would you be able to work in a similar way?

Thematic approaches

Case Study: Enterprise week

A small group of PGCE trainees were planning a week on the theme of 'enterprise'. Their placement was undertaken as part of a module in their training and involved planning with members of staff in the school. The group began with a main end product: creating a podcast to help raise money for an appeal important to the children in the school. The idea was to post it on the school website and sell a CD of the podcast at the school fair.

The week began with a role play and subsequent hot-seating and discussion about what it may have been like to be in the situation for which the appeal was raising money. It allowed children to respond physically, verbally and emotionally and begin to understand the world in someone else's shoes. This provided an excellent stimulus for the week as the children could mind map their thoughts and ideas and share them with others. The trainees brought in a range of subjects to their theme, providing subject knowledge in geography and science, marketing, persuasive writing and design. They were in role as rappers as well as business executives over the course of the week. The children had a large variety of learning opportunities not always measured in National Curriculum outcomes. The children learned how to make fruit smoothies, the technology behind making a podcast, the business of marketing and recording music using a mixing desk. They also had the opportunity to learn to express their thoughts, feelings and emotions and experience to a degree life in the shoes of people much less fortunate than themselves. While some of the outcomes of this learning were

Figure 2.6 Theme map: enterprise

demonstrated in more traditional acts of writing, drawing and mathematics, the main learning was taken from the processes the children went through and the shared experiences they had during the week of activities.

The class teacher commented that the children were more enthusiastic and engaged to work hard and the children's knowledge and understanding of issues outside their locality was definitely heightened. Interestingly the activities the children enjoyed most and articulated most learning from were those which they got practically involved in and made or created something. There was also a definite purpose to this week of work, raising money for people less fortunate than themselves, and this purpose captured the enthusiasm and imagination of the children. This purpose was enabled by the theme of enterprise and all the learning opportunities derived from the activities shared that common goal. Figure 2.6 is a theme map such as the trainee teacher group used.

You are likely to have picked up on the children's comments about learning best and enjoying most the activities where they could get practically involved. When planning this themed week of work, the trainee teachers were keen to promote practical and purposeful activity, believing that the children would learn most if they could engage in a full experience that involved not just their minds but their bodies too. The children gained a lot from experiences not traditionally associated with school work such as making smoothies and making a podcast. The trainee teachers believed that purposeful activity that was relevant and useful promoted learning and that the children would gain from it. They were able to define learning in broad terms.

This varied range of experiences and broad definition of learning encouraged more of the children to be successful and not 'turn off' those who found more traditional school work activities a challenge. Their planning demonstrates that they believed in the value of a range of different intelligences and that a child's intelligence is not defined by their ability in literacy and mathematics. The following research focus explains this in terms of 'multiple intelligences'.

Research Focus

Howard Gardner (2006) recognised that intelligence should not just be measured in terms of being literate and numerate but in many other areas too. Alongside more 'traditional' intelligence, Gardner places spatial intelligence, interpersonal and intrapersonal intelligence, kinaesthetic intelligence and musical intelligence as part of a child's unique blend of intelligence, which should not be ignored or allowed to stagnate at the expense of literacy and mathematics. This approach is clearly a way to provide children with the National Curriculum's aim of a broad, balanced and relevant curriculum through the profile raising of foundation subjects and mirroring the blending of intelligences with the blending of subjects through a themed approach. Perhaps this approach can offer an alternative to the government's standards agenda and assist in looking at education and approach to curriculum design and assessment in a more holistic way.

Activity

Examine the thematic web in Figure 2.6. Plot onto it opportunities for developing Gardner's intelligences: visual/spatial, bodily-kinaesthetic, musical, interpersonal, intrapersonal, linguistic, logical/mathematical. More information on each of these is available at www.tecweb.org/styles/gardner.html. Consider whether you think the above approach is an effective approach to planning.

Now go to this website: www.infed.org/thinkers/gardner.htm. This article presents more information on Howard Gardner and on his multiple intelligences theory and identifies some additional intelligences for consideration. Towards the end there are some key questions or problems with his theory, surrounding his criteria for deciding on a particular intelligence, his conceptualisation of intelligence and a lack of empirical evidence. Read these carefully and add the information gained to your thinking about whether considering these intelligences is an approach to planning to which you will subscribe.

Learning Outcomes Review

From your reading and from thinking about the school in which you are currently placed, or in which you most recently undertook a placement, respond to the questions that follow each of the intended learning outcomes, as a means of identifying your knowledge and understanding of the issues covered in the chapter.

- **How beliefs about learning drive curriculum planning and teaching approaches: Give some reasons why some of the class teachers you have worked with have**

  - organised their classroom in a certain way;
  - used particular teaching approaches;
  - used particular resources.
  - Look at the planning that the class teacher uses for their teaching. Identify the main learning theory(ies) that underpin this planning. Find the evidence in the plan.

- **That children's learning and development is at the forefront of curriculum development:**

  - What can you do in your planning for teaching to ensure that children's learning is at the forefront of all that you do?
  - Think about a class you have recently taught. How did they learn best? How did you know? What will you do in the future?

- **How a cross-curricular approach deepens learning through the joining of concepts and ideas:**

  - What different approaches could you use in your planning to join skills, concepts and ideas across subjects? Using the National Curriculum, devise some examples.

> • **Debates about integrated and single subject learning opportunities:**
>   - Reflect on and evaluate your own planning on placement. Did you use integrated and/or single subject? Why? What was the impact on the children's learning and on your own subject knowledge understanding?

Further Reading

The texts below relate directly to the research foci outlined throughout this chapter. They will provide you with more knowledge and understanding of some of the key principles that have been outlined.

Brown, A. and Campione, J. (1998) Designing a community of young learners: theoretical and practical lessons. In Lambert, N. and McCombs, B. (eds) *How Students Learn: Reforming schools through learner-centred education.* Washington, DC: American Psychological Association.

Cordon, R. (2000) Chapter 1 in *Literacy and Learning through Talk: Strategies for the primary classroom*, pp.7–10. Buckingham: Open University Press. In Lambirth, A. (2005) *Reflective Reader: Primary English.* Exeter: Learning Matters, pp.72–5.

Fogarty, R. and Stoehr, J. (2008) *Integrating Curricula with Multiple Intelligences: Teams, themes, and threads* (2nd edition). Thousand Oaks, California: Corwin Press.

Gardner, H. (2006) *Multiple Intelligences: New Horizons.* New York: Basic Books.

References

Alexander, R. (2004) Still no pedagogy? Principle, pragmatism and compliance in primary education. *Cambridge Journal of Education* 34(1) pp.7–33.

Alexander, R. (2009) *An Introduction to the Cambridge Primary Review.* Available from www.primaryreview.org.uk/DownloadslFinalreportlCPR-booklet_low-res.pdf accessed 22/07/10.

Arthur, J. and Cremin, T. (eds) (2010) *Learning to Teach in the Primary School* (2nd edition). London: Routledge.

Biggs, J. (2003) *Teaching for Quality Learning at University* (2nd edition). Maidenhead: Open University Press.

Boyle, T. (2002) Towards a theoretical base for educational multimedia design. *Journal of Interactive Media in Education* 2. Available at http://www-jime.open.ac.uk/2002/2 accessed 14/05/08.

Brockbank, A. and McGill, I. (2003) *Facilitating Reflective Learning in Higher Education.* Buckingham: SRHE.

Brophy, J. and Good, T. (1986) Teacher behaviour and student achievement. In Wittrock, M.C. (ed.) *Handbook of Research in Teaching.* London: Macmillan.

Brown, A. and Campione, J. (1998) Designing a community of young learners: theoretical and practical lessons. In Lambert, N. and McCombs, B. (eds) *How Students Learn: Reforming schools through learner-centred education.* Washington, DC: American Psychological Association.

Bruner, J.S. (1983) *Child's Talk: Learning to use language.* Oxford: Oxford University Press.

DfE (2010) *Analysis of Year 6 Attainment in Maths by Level.* London: National Strategies.

DfE (2011a) *The Framework for the National Curriculum.* London: DfE.

DfE (2011b) *Teachers' Standards.* Available from www.education.gov.uk/publications

DfE (2013) *The National Curriculum in England: Key Stages 1 and 2 Framework Document.* London: DfE.

DfEE (1999) *The National Curriculum: Handbook for primary teachers in England Key Stages 1 and 2.* London: HMSO.

DfEE (2002) *The National Curriculum: Handbook for primary teachers in England Key Stages 1 and 2* (2nd edition). London: QCA.

Fogarty, R. (1991) Ten ways to integrate curriculum, *Educational Leadership* 49(2) pp.61-5

Gardner, H. (2006) *Multiple Intelligences: New horizons.* New York: Basic Books.

Howard, J. (2007) *Curriculum Development.* Available from http://org.elon. edulcatlldocumentslcurriculum%20development.pdf accessed 20/07/10.

Lambirth, A. (2005) *Reflective Reader: Primary English.* Exeter: Learning Matters.

Ofsted (2008) *Improving Primary Teachers' Subject Knowledge Across the Curriculum.* London: Ofsted. Available from http://dera.ioe.ac.uk/305/1/Improving%20primary%20teachers%20 subject%20knowledge%20across%20the%20curriculum.pdf

QCDA (2010) *The Structure of the National Curriculum.* London: QCDA.

STEM Advisory Forum (2010) *Maths A-level Numbers Increase.* London: National Strategies.

Twiselton, S. (2006) The problem with English: the exploration and development of student teachers' English subject knowledge in primary classrooms. *Literacy: Teacher Education and Development* 40(2) pp.88–96.

Vygotsky, L. (1978) *Thought and Language.* Cambridge, MA: MIT Press.

Watkins, C., Carnell, E. and Lodge, C. (2007) *Effective Learning in Classrooms.* London: Paul Chapman.

3. Children's learning and development in the early years
Sally Neaum and Rebecca Walters

Learning Outcomes

By the end of this chapter you will have had the opportunity to:

- develop your understanding of the difference between learning and teaching at Foundation Stage and later Key Stages;
- understand the principles that underpin teaching and learning at Foundation Stage;
- reflect on the place of the child, and the role of the adult at Foundation Stage;
- consider the learning environment at Foundation Stage;
- learn about the Early Years Foundation Stage (EYFS): the statutory framework in early years;
- know how children's learning is assessed at Foundation Stage;
- become aware that there are significant debates about the content and purpose of early years education.

TEACHERS' STANDARDS
A teacher must:

1. Set high expectations which inspire, motivate and challenge pupils
- establish a safe and stimulating environment for pupils, rooted in mutual respect
- set goals that stretch and challenge pupils of all backgrounds, abilities and dispositions.

2. Promote good progress and outcomes by pupils
- be accountable for pupils' attainment, progress and outcomes
- be aware of pupils' capabilities and their prior knowledge, and plan teaching to build on these
- demonstrate knowledge and understanding of how pupils learn and how this impacts on teaching.

5. Adapt teaching to respond to the strengths and needs of all pupils
- demonstrate an awareness of the physical, social and intellectual development of children, and know how to adapt teaching to support pupils' education at different stages of development.

6. **Make accurate and productive use of assessment**
- make use of formative and summative assessment to secure pupils' progress.

8. **Fulfil wider professional responsibilities**
- deploy support staff effectively
- communicate effectively with parents with regard to pupils' achievements and wellbeing.

Introduction

The Early Years Foundation Stage (EYFS) is the statutory framework for the Foundation Stage. The Foundation years are the years between birth and 31 August following a child's fifth birthday. The Foundation Stage is delivered in schools, preschools and by childminders in England. However, this chapter considers the delivery of the Foundation Stage in school: nursery and reception class or a Foundation Stage unit.

There are significant differences between teaching, learning and assessment at Foundation Stage and at later Key Stages. These differences reflect our understanding of how very young children learn, and the adult's role in supporting and assessing their learning. So imagine opening the door to a nursery or Foundation Stage unit. What do you see? In what ways does it look and feel different from a typical school classroom? How are the spaces organised? How do the children spend their time? What is the role of the adults?

Open the door and you will see children playing. The children will be moving between activities, indoors and outdoors, choosing what to do next, playing at the activity individually or in small groups. Some children will be playing alone, some children will be playing alongside one other, and others will be playing together. Some children will be standing and watching, observing what is happening.

Some adults will be engaged with the children, playing alongside them at their chosen activity, using commentary to articulate what the child is doing, discussing, questioning and teaching. They will be following the children's ideas and interests, as well as making suggestions, modelling language and how things are done. They may record what the children are doing and saying, to inform later planning. Other adults will be observing the activities; watching and listening, noticing what the children are doing and what they are interested in, making a judgement about what learning is possible before joining in. Other adults may be watching, listening and then recording what they observe, to provide evidence of children's learning to inform planning, and EYFS observation based summative assessments.

The learning environment will be organised to encourage children to engage in a wide range of activities, both indoors and outdoors: sand and water, paints and crafts, small world play, role-play, large and small construction, table-top games and activities, wheeled toys, balls, bats, climbing and scrambling equipment, activities on computers, tablets and interactive whiteboards, CDs to listen to, and books to enjoy. Most of these activities will be available every day, varied from week to week to maintain the children's interest, but continuously available. For example, the role-play area may be a home, a hairdressers, a builders' yard, the Gruffalo's wood, or a spaceship. Other activities will be provided to enhance this continuous provision. These activities are often adult led and focused on a particular outcome. For example, children and staff playing with a farm set, working together to solve a series of problems for the farmer focused on maths; counting to ten, finding a total number by counting two groups, using the language 'more' and 'fewer' to compare groups, and beginning to use the vocabulary used in addition and subtraction (Early Education, 2012).

Most of each session will be free-flow, child initiated activity. However, you may also observe short whole group sessions for discussion, storytelling or singing; all the children in small groups for short adult led focused activities; or snack time when the children sit to eat, all together or in small groups.

In addition to free-flow play and group times, you will observe children involved in daily routines that embed learning: finding their name to hang up their coat, counting pieces of fruit for snack time, making a mark on a chart to indicate that they have had a go at a computer game, or solving a problem of how to fit things into a box when putting things away.

Clearly this provision and teaching differs significantly from a typical school classroom. So what are the principles that inform this pedagogical approach? What do we know about how young children learn, and how is this reflected in the statutory Early Years Foundation Stage Curriculum?

Principles and practice

The child

The early years of a child's life is a distinct developmental stage. We know that a child's experiences in this phase of their life have a profound and lasting impact on their future attainment and life changes (Sylva et al., 2009). The opportunities, relationships and experiences that are available to a child in the early years of education should therefore provide solid foundations for their life, as well as for the more formal approaches of learning in later phases of education. A child in the early years brings with them a unique range of experiences, interests and abilities that need to be supported and developed through a play based approach to learning: 'play is without a doubt the most natural way children learn all over the world ... this is why children need to have every opportunity to engage in play and playful experiences' (Moyles, 2010, p.1).

Play is a spontaneous and natural activity for most young children, and for young children their play is their work. Play is driven through a child's intrinsic motivation to become involved and absorbed in activity. It is the way in which young children learn and develop, and the possibilities for children are endless. They are able to take risks and attempt challenges that push boundaries as well as extending their experiences (Canning, 2011). It enables them to challenge their thinking and test out ideas, to build new understandings, discover, imagine and create. A supportive early years environment enables the child to ask questions, and engage in critical thinking to develop positive dispositions towards learning. Play provides opportunities for children to learn in a holistic and active way; children can actively explore their environment and make sense of the world around them, developing language, emotions, creativity, social and intellectual skills. Through a play based, child centred approach children's natural curiosities and interests are developed, and children are able to learn at their own pace, and in ways that make sense to them.

Well-planned and purposeful play in the early years enables young children to learn across all domains: physical, intellectual, social, emotional and linguistic. Abbot and Langston (2004) describe this as a holistic approach to learning when all of the domains are integrated in learning. Play supports this holistic approach to learning; children do not divide learning into separate subject domains such as mathematics or science. They do not experience the world like this: these are adult distinctions; they approach a task as a whole. This holistic approach to learning is an important aspect of the EYFS, and is embedded in how we see the child, the role of the adult and the learning environment in the learning process.

Many of our ideas about the value of play come from pioneers such as Froebel (1782–1852), Steiner (1861–1925), McMillan (1860–1931) and Montessori (1870–1952). All talked about a play based curriculum with the child at the centre, recognising that every child brings with them a unique range of interests, experiences and abilities, to be captured and used the starting point for planning playful learning activities and experiences. Therefore, provision in early years needs to be built around a play based child centred approach, supporting the child through play opportunities that start from the child's interests and experiences. This requires a particular pedagogical approach, one that is distinctively different from other phases of learning.

Research Focus: Playful pedagogies

In her paper *Understanding playful pedagogies, play narratives and play spaces* Goouch (2008) constructs a powerful argument for a play based pedagogy in early years. She notes that in spite of central government demands, many of those working with the youngest children in schools and nurseries have tried to define an alternative pedagogy, 'not technicist but human, not delivery but engagement' (2008, p.94). She argues that teaching and learning

⟶

with young children does not fit neatly into pre-formed moulds or packages, that there are levels of 'unpredictability, spontaneity, unique response, innovation, subversion and challenge' (2008, p.94).

This means that young children demand a specialised pedagogy, and adopting playful pedagogies enables this to happen. Playful pedagogies involve teachers creating contexts that enable them to follow children into play, co-constructing the activity, narrative and resources, 'working together to draw the child into a more mature understanding linked to what the child already knows' (Goouch, 2008, p.95). This is important; playful pedagogies require that teachers are able to forgo preordained curricular objectives and pursue children's play objectives, without any need for 'contrivance, hijacking or subverting children's intentions' (2008, p.95).

Goouch (2008, pp.96–7) observes that playful pedagogies are often evident in storying activities, in which teachers and children

> construct narratives without instruction, without coercion, without the conventional use of paper and pencil, for children's own purposes, in play, either alone or in the company of selected others. The pedagogy then is organic, developing out of the moment and in intimate conversation between teacher and child.

She argues that in these moments teachers need to possess the skill of 'catching the inner gleam' of children (2008, p.49), they need to trust the children and their own intuitive responses, and they need to be confident in the knowledge that cognitive development will occur in these kinds of play contexts and playful interactions.

Spaces for learning need to reflect this approach, and Goouch (2008, p.97) describes these as 'settings where children can shape and construct their own worlds and develop a sense of self as a creator, managing and controlling the space themselves, rather than being controlled by the environment'.

The adult

> *The greatest resource available to a child as a learner is the adult who understands their learning and development journey and how to support it.*
>
> *(Drake, 2014, p.xv)*

Children's play can be complex and so too can the role of the adult in supporting a child at play. The EYFS highlights three different types of play opportunities for young children: child initiated, adult led and adult initiated (DfE, 2014).

Child initiated play is also known as free play, in which the child independently chooses what, where and how they want to play. It is through this type of play that children are able to spend time exploring and developing their own ideas and interests, while developing their creativity and imagination and taking ownership of their learning. This type of play allows children to practise and refine skills that they have been introduced to, at their own pace and in a way that enables them to make sense of them.

Adult led play is the opposite of child initiated play. In adult led play the adult plans, organises and tells the children what they need to do. It is planned with a specific learning outcome for the child to work on. It is through adult led activities that we can introduce children to new materials, skills or ideas, develop their language, and engage in activities that they would not be manage by themselves, such as playing a new board game, baking or retelling a story using the small world people.

From adult led activities, play opportunities are often created for children to return to the activity or skill independently, to develop and explore their ideas further, and to practice and refine the new skill. This is an adult initiated approach that enables the adult to step in to support the child's learning at appropriate points while also giving the child opportunities to freely explore independently, thus bridging the gap between adult led and child initiated play.

Focusing on just adult led and directed play can cause us to limit children's learning and their opportunities to actively engage with their environment. On the other hand, leaving the child to direct their own play with limited or no adult intervention can cause them to miss out on valuable learning opportunities. It is useful, then, to consider play as a continuum that considers varying degrees of adult involvement and recognise that a balance of the different approaches can enhance and create more challenges for greater learning.

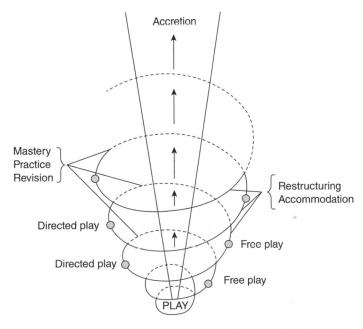

Figure 3.1 The play spiral (Moyles, 1999, p.16)

Moyles (1999) introduces the concepts of the play spiral in which she demonstrates the importance of balancing child initiated and adult led play to ensure learning is developed. Through opportunities for the child to freely explore and develop confidence in the activity or resource, the play should be directed by the teacher to expand their skills and develop a deeper understanding of the concepts. This is followed by further opportunities for free play and adult led play to practise and revise the skill, presented in a cyclical ongoing process, widening experiences through the accretion knowledge (Figure 3.1). It is through practising and refining skills that children develop confidence and are then able to apply the learning to other situations, such as learning to use scissors in an adult directed activity then using the skill in a child initiated activity, when playing at offices when they need to cut paper for a letter. Moyles (1999) refers to this as 'mastery' of learning.

One of the difficulties in ensuring that children have a balance of these three approaches is recognising when it is appropriate to support a child's play, and when it is appropriate let the child lead the play. This is not always an easy balance to achieve. It can be easy to misjudge and direct the learning inappropriately, denying children the opportunities to make mistakes, learn from them, solve problems creatively and negotiate solutions to social conflict (Hohmann and Weikart, 1995). However, by not stepping in at times to direct play, opportunities to extend and support the learning can be missed.

Case Study: Adult initiated play

A police officer had visited the nursery and following the visit a group of children had been playing at being police officers. They ran around arresting other children and taking them to gaol. The staff observed how much the children were enjoying the play. On the third day, Lois, one of the teachers, noticed that the play had become repetitive and the children were beginning to lose interest. She decided to join in the play to re-engage the children. Observations of the children had shown that some of them were beginning to give meaning to the marks that they make, and count saying one number name for each item (Early Education, 2012). Lois joined in as one of the police officers, asking questions at the crime scene, and at the gaol, making notes of what had happened and what was said, taking pictures of the crime scene, and counting and categorising the prisoners. The following day Lois left notebooks, pencils and cameras in the play areas. She noticed that the children were carrying the notebooks and cameras around with them, and some had begun to model their play on hers, taking pictures, making marks in the notebooks as they asked the suspects questions, and counting their prisoners.

By joining in the play Lois was able to use and develop the children's interests and ideas to extend their learning. She was able to re-engage them in their play and introduce new vocabulary, mark making, and counting to enhance their learning. Lois planned to observe the children further, to see how they developed the play, before she joined in again.

For young children to be able to engage effectively in these varied play opportunities, they need to feel secure and safe in their environment. When a young child leaves their parent or carer at the door of the Foundation Unit it can seem like a big, busy and daunting place. They are leaving the familiarity of the adult they have relied upon to meet their needs. This is recognised in the EYFS through the 'key person approach'. This approach advocates the forming of close attachments between the child and a teacher or teaching assistant (Goldschmied and Jackson, 2004). The key person will get to know the unique qualities of each child, they will monitor their learning and development through observation, and play and spend time with them. They will 'look out for' and pay attention to each child, greeting them at the start of the day as they arrive, and be there at the end of the day to meet the parents or carer to discuss any key moments. Their role is not to follow the child around the environment but to ensure that the child feels that they have someone they can rely on, so that they are happy and enjoying their experiences. The key worker will also make relationships with the key adults from the child's home environment, as it is through building positive relationships with both the child and parents and sharing of information that everyone can work towards the best outcomes for the child (Ahnert and Lamb, 2003).

Case Study: Starting from the child

Neve arrived at nursery each morning clutching a soft toy dinosaur. She had recently started nursery, and was becoming upset when her dad left. In order to help her transition into nursery Neve's key worker, Fahima, spoke with her dad to find out what she was interested in, so that she could plan activities that would interest and engage her. The following day the staff had set up small world play of a landscape with dinosaurs. As Neve arrived Fahima met her at the door and said that she had something to show Neve. Neve and her dad spent 10 minutes playing together at the dinosaur activity, then, as he left, Fahima stepped in and showed Neve a story book about dinosaurs and suggested that they read it together. Neve remained anxious as her dad left but settled quickly as Fahima began the story.

Research Focus: How do practitioners' understandings of play influence pedagogy?

If we accept that pedagogy, 'the art of teaching' (McInnes et al., 2011), is at the heart of early years practice, it is important that we understand the relationship between what we know and what we do; what is the impact of our understanding of how young children learn on what we do?

McInnes et al. hypothesised that differences in practitioners' understanding of play would be associated with differences in pedagogic interactions. Their small-scale study, undertaken as

→

part of a larger study on playful practice, looked at this relationship. The settings in their study had an expressed commitment to a play based approach to learning, which was confirmed with a 'photographic sorting task' (2011, p.124).

They found that there were differences in pedagogical approach, flowing from practitioners' understandings of play. Staff who had developed a clear understanding of play, and the adult role in children's play, adopted a pedagogical approach in which staff planned for a range of adult led and child led activities, and participated with the children in all activities. Their pedagogical interactions involved sharing choices and control of the play. In contrast, where staff had not yet developed a clear understanding of play and their role in it, they planned both adult and child led activities, but generally participated in the adult led activities. Their pedagogical interactions in these activities tended to involve adult directed choice and control within the activity.

What was particularly interesting was an emerging understanding of the impact of these pedagogical practices on children's understanding of what constituted 'play and not-play activities' (McInnes et al., 2011, p.121). They argue that previous research shows that children can distinguish between activities that are regarded as play activities, and those that are regarded as not-play activities, and they do this according to different cues that they pick up from the staff and the learning environment. They suggest that where practitioners interact in a range of activities, and share choice and control within the activity, children are less likely to use the cue of adult presence to differentiate between play and not-play activities. However, where practitioners focus on adult led activities, and give children minimal choice and control, children are more likely to use the cue of adult presence to differentiate between activities they regarded as play activities, and those they regarded as not-play activities.

In conclusion, McInnes et al. (2011) argue that a pedagogy founded on a clear understanding of both play and learning, their relationship to one another, and the role of the practitioner, means that children are less likely to differentiate between play and not-play activities. Where children make less distinction between activities the effect is that they are likely to approach more activities in a playful manner which, as previous research has shown, can improve performance and result in behaviours that facilitate learning.

The early years environment

A Foundation Unit will look and feel very different from the Key Stage 1 and 2 classrooms you may have worked in. Our understanding of how young children learn needs to be reflected in the organisation and presentation of the environment. Young children learn through a practical, play based approach. The early years environment is often referred to as the 'third teacher', highlighting the important role it plays in facilitating the learning and developing of young children. In school, learning is predominantly classroom based, while in early years the learning environment encompasses any space that can support learning for young children.

Indeed, one of the distinct features of the early years environment is the requirement for children to have access to both indoor and outdoor spaces, ideally giving children freedom to move fluidly across both areas throughout the day.

The focus across the environment should be to promote an investigative approach and learn through first-hand experiences. Children are encouraged to move around activity areas, both indoors and outdoors, making independent choices as to where, what and how they want to play. The EYFS calls this an enabling environment, one which is rich and varied, supporting children's learning and development while giving them the confidence to explore and learn in a secure and safe, yet challenging, space that responds to their experiences and needs. Provision will be both continuous and enhanced: learning resources that are available every day are the continuous provision, for example, of a sand and water tray, role play, writing area, maths area, malleable materials, construction, art and craft. This is enhanced by specific activities that are planned in response to children's interests, or learning needs identified through observations.

Indoor and outdoor spaces may reflect similar resources; for example, a sand pit that children stand next to and play with indoors, and outdoors a large sand pit that children can climb in and sit in the sand while playing, but the learning opportunities are different. The outdoor affords children the opportunity to explore on a large scale as well as enhancing physical activity, risk taking, creativity and language, opening up opportunities that the indoor space cannot.

All these spaces are carefully arranged, with some offering children the opportunity to be quiet and reflective, while others may be busier and more active. The environment needs to be a flexible and responsive space that evolves and adapts to meet the needs, interests and abilities of individual children.

Activity

Think about a school classroom that you know.

Bring to mind:

- how the children spend their time;
- what the adults do;
- who determines what happens next;
- who leads the learning, who follows;
- how the room is set out;
- what resources are available for the children.

Consider the differences between the description of practice at Foundation Stage and the classroom that you imagined.

(Continued)

(Continued)

- What are the implications of this for young children's learning?
- What questions does it raise about our approach to teaching and learning as children move from Foundation Stage into Key Stage 1?

Research Focus: Learning outdoors

There is evidence to suggest that learning outdoors can have a range of impacts including cognitive impact, affective, interpersonal/social and physical behavioural impacts.

(Dillon et al., 2005, in O'Brien, 2009)

This research aimed to understand the impact of Forest Schools on children's learning. Forest Schools are defined as an 'inspirational process that offers children, young people and adults regular opportunities to achieve and develop ... through hands on learning experiences in a woodland environment' (Murray and O'Brien, 2005, and Forest Education Initiative, 2007, cited in O'Brien, 2009). O'Brien (2009) states that this involves a type of learning approach that focuses on learning by doing, with teachers posing questions while children are engaged in activities to promote thinking and reasoning, and experimentation and problem solving in which children actively make meaning. As Kahn (1999, p.50, in O'Brien, 2009, p.47) observes, 'whilst knowledge entails facts and behaviour ... [this] ... more fundamentally entails understanding, and children actively construct their understandings through interaction with the physical and social world'.

O'Brien (2009) argues that Forest Schools have developed as part of a response to concern that children are not able to access the outdoor environment as freely as past generations (Kahn and Kellert, 2002, Bell, Ward Thompson and Travlou, 2004, Thomas and Thompson, 2004, Louv, 2005, DEMOS 2007, all cited in O'Brien, 2009). She cites multiple reasons for this; for example, concerns about safety because of increased traffic and fear of abuse and assault by strangers, and increased use of computers, games consoles and television.

The study used a variety of methods: workshops to establish shared understandings and to reflect on learning; observation on site; reflection tools based on propositions developed in the workshops; and questionnaires for children, parents and teachers.

Eight themes emerged from the data that demonstrated positive outcomes from engagement with outdoor learning. Significantly, O'Brien (2009) reports that many of the improvements took weeks to occur, highlighting the need for repeated and regular contact with outdoor learning spaces.

Reported positive outcomes for the children were:

- increased self-esteem and self-confidence;

- improved social skills;

- contribution to the development of language and communication skills;

- improved motivation and encouragement of concentration;

- contributed to children's knowledge and understanding;

- improved motor skills.

In addition, the study participants noted

- new perspectives gained by the practitioners on seeing the children in a different environment;

- ripple effects beyond the Forest School – the children took their experiences home and told family and friends.

O'Brien (2009) concludes that learning outside the classroom is an important part of children's learning, and the Forest School is an excellent example of this, that has been shown to have positive benefits for the children involved.

Statutory frameworks and assessment

The Early Years Foundation Stage (EYFS) sets the standards that all early years providers must meet to ensure that children between the ages of 0 and 5 in Ofsted registered settings learn and develop well, and are kept healthy and safe. It promotes teaching and learning to ensure a broad range of knowledge and skills that provide the right foundation for good future progress through school and life.

The role of the EYFS is to ensure that there is the same focus on quality and consistency across all early years settings (DfE, 2014). It is recognised that the early years of a child's life have a profound and lasting impact on children's future attainment and life chances (Sylva et al., 2004), and the early years provide a secure foundation for later learning. Importance is placed on partnership working, with a strong focus on engaging with parents, carers and other agencies to meet the individual needs of the child. Every child is valued as an individual and practice needs to demonstrate an inclusive approach that supports all children's learning.

The EYFS is a framework that combines the statutory requirements for both the care and education of young children, promoting a holistic approach to early learning. A framework is different from a curriculum. A curriculum focuses on the standards children need to meet in each subject area. This framework adopts a more holistic approach. It is based on a series of principles about the child, the adult and the learning environment.

The EYFS has four overarching principles (DfE, 2014, p.6):

- Every child is a **unique child**, who is constantly learning and can be resilient, capable, confident and self-assured.

- Children learn to be strong and independent through **positive relationships**.

- Children learn and develop well in an **enabling environment**, in which their experiences respond to their individual needs and there is a strong partnership between practitioners and/or parents.
- **Children develop and learn in different ways and at different rates.** The framework covers the education and care of all children in the early years provision, including children with special educational needs and disabilities.

These principles underpin the three sections of the EYFS statutory framework: learning and development; assessment; safeguarding and welfare requirements.

Learning and development

The learning and development section considers seven areas of learning that are used to shape activities and experiences. The areas are separated into Prime and Specific areas; the areas are connected as learning and development in each area contributes towards that of the others. The Prime and Specific areas provide the basis for the planning of activities and experiences that cumulate at the end of the reception year with the early learning goals. The goals represent the knowledge, skills and understanding that all young children should achieve at the end of the reception year.

Prime areas are seen as crucial and are expected to be the main focus for practitioners working with the youngest children. These areas are considered to be the basis for successful learning in the other four Specific areas. The balance between Prime and Specific areas will shift as children move through the Foundation Stage. The Prime areas are:

- Communication and language
- Physical development
- Personal, social and emotional development. (DfE, 2014)

Knowledge and skills in the Prime areas are of particular importance as they can impact on children's development later in school. The Prime areas underpin successful learning in the Specific areas. The Specific areas provide the range of experiences and opportunities for children to broaden their knowledge and skills. It is through the Specific areas that the Prime areas are strengthened and developed. The Specific areas are:

- Literacy
- Mathematics
- Understanding of the world
- Expressive arts and design.

The Prime and Specific areas highlight *what* children need to learn, but the EYFS also places great emphasis on understanding the ways *in which* young children learn. The characteristics of learning are as follows:

- **Playing and exploring** are the key ways that children learn. Play should be the basis for planning all activities in the early years. Children need opportunities to investigate and experience things and 'have a go'.

- **Active learning** is the second characteristic of learning. This is not about being physically active but about having an active and enquiring mind. Children need to have opportunities to become deeply involved in their play, developing concentration and persisting in solving problems. It is through play and exploration that children are able to be active learners, to make their own choices, follow their curiosities and ideas and become engaged in their play. We need to support children to persist in solving problems and developing a 'have a go' attitude, and to enjoy their achievements.

- **Creating and thinking critically.** This characteristic of learning is not about creativity in the sense of arts and crafts, but more about the thinking processes children go through when using their imagination and engaging in activities that encourage them to think flexibly, and to develop their own ideas. Children can achieve this through their explorations, thinking about the experiences that enable them to make sense of their world, making links between ideas, and developing strategies for doing this.

These characteristics are integral to the Prime and Specific areas, and need to be embedded through the planning and implementation of activities. They reflect the different ways that children learn, and describe the attitudes, skills and approaches to learning that need be nurtured in the early years.

Assessment

Assessment in the Foundation Stage is different from assessment that you may be familiar with at Key Stages 1 and 2. It is less focused on an end product and more about the learning that is evidenced through a child's play. Assessment is predominantly done through observation of children. Formative (ongoing) assessment to inform planning involves observations of children to identify their interests, how they approach learning, and the progress that they are making in the Prime and Specific areas. All staff are involved in observing all children but the key worker may take a prominent role in this.

In addition to these formative assessments, the EYFS has one statutory summative assessment between the ages of 2 and 3 years, and, depending on how a school opts to be assessed, a baseline assessment at the beginning of Reception year (FS2).

The progress check takes place between the ages of 2 and 3 and focuses on the prime areas of development highlighting the child's strengths as well as areas in which the child is not making expected progress. This must be shared with parents in the form of a written report. If at this stage concerns about a child's development are identified then the setting must develop a target plan to support the child's future learning and development. This must be shared with parents and, with consent, any other appropriate services to support the child, such as a health visitor or speech therapist.

From September 2016 there is also the possibility of a baseline assessment at the beginning of Reception year (FS2). This is because of changes in school's accountability measures. Schools will have to choose to be accountable for children's learning in one of two ways: attainment or progress. They must opt for one of these two measures:

1. Attainment: 85 per cent of pupils must achieve the expected standards in reading writing and mathematics at the end of Key Stage 2.

2. Progress: A school's pupils must demonstrate satisfactory progress in reading, writing and mathematics given their starting point in Reception.

If a school opts to be assessed on progress (and it is anticipated that most will) this will require that each child is assessed as they enter school, so that there is a starting point for measuring progress by the end of Key Stage 2. A baseline assessment will therefore be completed at the beginning of Reception year (FS2). Individual children's baseline scores will be used at the end of Key Stage 2 to calculate how much progress they have made compared to others with the same starting point. The outcomes of the baseline assessment will have to be communicated to parents, within the context of other teacher-based assessments. Baseline assessment for schools who have opted to be assessed on progress will begin in September 2016.

The current Early Years Foundation Stage Profile will no longer be statutory. However, settings and schools can continue to use it as a way of monitoring children's progress internally.

Safeguarding and welfare requirements

Children learn best when they are healthy, safe and secure, when their individual needs are met, and when they have positive relationships with the adults caring for them.

(DfE, 2014)

As the EYFS is delivered in settings other than school, it incorporates statutory welfare requirements. However, when the EYFS is delivered within the context of a school, existing policies will cover these areas.

Activity

Reflect on what you have learned about teaching and learning at Foundation Stage and what this might mean for young children's transition to KS1.

Read the research focus below. Why do you think that Whitebread and Bingham (2011) argue that schools should be ready for children, rather than children being made ready for school?

Research Focus: School readiness

In their paper Whitebread and Bingham (2011) challenge the current emphasis on school readiness. They argue that there is now extensive evidence that does not support a curriculum centred approach, and an emphasis on formal learning at an ever younger age. This approach, they conclude, leads to a situation where children's basic emotional and cognitive needs for autonomy, competence and relatedness, and the opportunity to develop meta-cognitive and self-regulation skills are not being met.

Whitebread and Bingham observe that all children at all ages are 'ready to learn', so the significant question is not *whether* children are ready to learn but *what* a child is ready to learn (2011, p.2). They argue that the current model of readiness is expedient in that 'it is attractive to governments as it seemingly delivers children into primary school ready to conform to classroom procedures and even able to perform basic reading and writing skills' (2011, p.4).

There are, they argue, increasing concerns that

> *stem from a mismatch between increasingly evidence-based pedagogical understandings within the early years sector and the curriculum required to be delivered within Primary schools in England, arising from and compounded by the continued intervention of recent Governments.*

> *(Whitebread and Bingham, 2011, p.1)*

They note that in its attempts to 'raise standards' the government has encouraged the introduction of formal curricula at ever earlier points in a child's schooling. But, in contrast to this focus on early, didactic instruction, current research into early emotional and cognitive development suggests that long term wellbeing and success at school are most powerfully supported by opportunities for multisensory, active learning, and repeated practice. Play, they argue, is the central vehicle for such learning, and 'both free play and guided play are linked to social and academic development' (Whitebread and Bingham, 2011, p.3).

They conclude that the problem is that schools are not ready for children, rather then children not being ready for school.

Conclusion

Teaching and learning at Foundation Stage are distinctly different from teaching and learning at later Key Stages: the place of the child, the role of the adult and the learning environment create a distinctive early years pedagogy. This pedagogy emphasises a fluid response to children as individuals, starting from what they know and can do, and with a focus on learning as a shared, socially constructed endeavour. The EYFS provides a framework for early years provision. It is underpinned by an evidence-base about how young children learn. The EYFS outlines developmental trajectories in Prime and Specific areas of learning, against which children's learning is mapped. Assessment of learning at Foundation Stage is predominantly observation based. These differences in approach at different Key Stages has resulted in a lively debate about the relationship between Foundation Stage and later Key Stages.

Learning Outcomes Review

This chapter has enabled you to explore the differences between learning and teaching at Foundation Stage and later Key Stages. It has supported your understanding of the principles that underpin teaching and learning at Foundation Stage. You have been able to consider the place of the child, the role of the adult, and the learning environment. You have learned about the EYFS including how children's learning is assessed. You have been asked to consider current debates about the content and purpose of early years education.

Further Reading

Broadhead, P., Howard, J. and Wood, E. (eds) (2010) *Play and Learning in the Early Years: From research to practice.* London: Sage.

Brooker, L. and Edwards, S. (eds) (2010) *Engaging Play.* Berkshire: McGraw-Hill.

Dahlberg, G., Moss, P. and Pence, A. (1999) *Beyond Quality in Early Childhood Education and Care: Postmodern Perspectives.* London: Falmer Books.

Gulberg, H. (2009) *Reclaiming Childhood: Freedom and play in an age of fear.* Abingdon: Routledge.

House, R. (ed.) (2011) *Too Much Too Soon: Early learning and the erosion of childhood.* Stroud: Hawthorne Press.

Miller, L. and Hevey, D. (eds) (2012) *Policy Issues in the Early Years.* London: Sage.

Miller, L. and Pound, L. (eds) (2011) *Theories and Approaches to Learning in the Early Years.* London: Sage.

Moss, P. (ed.) (2012) *Early Childhood and Compulsory Education: Reconceptualising the relationship.* London: Routledge.

Moyles J. (1999) *Just Playing.* Maidenhead: Open University Press.

Moyles, J., Georgeson, J. and Payler, J. (eds) (2014) *Early Years Foundations: Critical issues* (2nd edition). Maidenhead: Open University Press.

References

Abbot, L. and Langston, A. (eds) (2004) *Birth to Three Matters: Supporting the Framework of Effective Practice*. Maidenhead: Open University Press.

Ahnert, L. and Lamb, M.E. (2003) Shared care: establishing a balance between home and child care settings. *Child Development* 74, pp.1044–9.

Canning, N. (2011) *Play and Practice in the Early Years Foundation Stage*. London: Sage.

DfE (2014) *Statutory Framework for the Early Years Foundation Stage*. Available from https://www.gov.uk/government/uploads/system/uploads/attachment_data/file/335504/EYFS_framework_from_1_September_2014__with_clarification_note.pdf accessed 02/03/15.

Drake, J. (2014) *Planning for Children's Play and Learning: Meeting children's needs in the later stages of the EYFS* (4th edition). London: Routledge.

Early Education (2012) *Development Matters in the Early Years Foundation Stage*. Available from http://www.foundationyears.org.uk/files/2012/03/Development-Matters-FINAL-PRINT-AMENDED.pdf accessed 27/02/15.

Goldschmied, E. and Jackson, S. (2004) *People Under Three: Young children in day care* (2nd edition). London: Routledge.

Goouch, K. (2008) Understanding playful pedagogies, play narratives and play spaces. *Early Years: An International Research Journal* 28(1) pp.93–102.

Hohmann, M. and Weikart, D. (1995) *Educating Young Children*. Ypsilanti, MI: High/Scope Press.

McInnes, K., Howard, J., Miles, G. and Crowley, K. (2011) Differences in practitioners' understanding of play and how this influences pedagogy and children's perceptions of play. *Early Years: An International Research Journal* 31(2) pp.121–33.

Moyles J. (1999) *Just Playing*. Maidenhead: Open University Press.

Moyles, J. (ed.) (2010) *The Excellence of Play*. Maidenhead: Open University Press.

O'Brien, L. (2009) Learning outdoors: the Forest School approach. *Education 3–13. International Journal of Primary, Elementary and Early Years Education* 37(1) pp.45–60.

Siraj-Blatchford, I., Sylva, K., Muttock, S., Gilden, R. and Bell, D. (2002) *Researching Effective Pedagogy in the Early Years*. London: DfES.

Sylva, K., Melhuish, E., Sammons, P., Siraj-Blatchford, I. and Taggart, B. (2004) *The Effective Provision of Pre-School Education (EPPE) Project*. Final Report. London: DfES.

Whitebread, D. and Bingham, S. (2011) *School Readiness: A critical review of perspectives and evidence*. TACTYC Occasional Paper 2. Available from http://tactyc.org.uk/occasional-paper/occasional-paper2.pdf accessed 09/02/15.

SECTION 2
THE DEVELOPING CHILD

4. Child-centred teaching and learning
Denis Hayes

Learning Outcomes

By the end of this chapter you will:

- be aware of the multi-dimensional nature of learning;
- understand different theories of child development and their implications for teaching;
- recognise the significance of memory and memorising for learning;
- identify different learning styles and their implications for teaching;
- understand the place of learning through experience;
- be able to distinguish between individualised and personalised learning.

TEACHERS' STANDARDS

A teacher must:

1. **Set high expectations which inspire, motivate and challenge pupils**
- establish a safe and stimulating environment for pupils, rooted in mutual respect
- set goals that stretch and challenge pupils of all backgrounds, abilities and dispositions
- demonstrate consistently the positive attitudes, values and behaviour which are expected of pupils.

2. **Promote good progress and outcomes by pupils**
- be accountable for pupils' attainment, progress and outcomes
- demonstrate knowledge and understanding of how pupils learn and how this impacts on teaching
- encourage pupils to take a responsible and conscientious attitude to their own work and study.

3. **Demonstrate good subject and curriculum knowledge**
- demonstrate a critical understanding of developments in the subject and curriculum areas, and promote the value of scholarship.

4. **Plan and teach well structured lessons**
- promote a love of learning and children's intellectual curiosity
- contribute to the design and provision of an engaging curriculum within the relevant subject area(s).

5. Adapt teaching to respond to the strengths and needs of all pupils
- have a secure understanding of how a range of factors can inhibit pupils' ability to learn, and how best to overcome these
- demonstrate an awareness of the physical, social and intellectual development of children, and know how to adapt teaching to support pupils' education at different stages of development
- have a clear understanding of the needs of all pupils, including those with special educational needs; those of high ability; those with English as an additional language; those with disabilities; and be able to use and evaluate distinctive teaching approaches to engage and support them.

8. Fulfil wider professional responsibilities
- make a positive contribution to the wider life and ethos of the school
- develop effective professional relationships with colleagues, knowing how and when to draw on advice and specialist support
- deploy support staff effectively
- take responsibility for improving teaching through appropriate professional development, responding to advice and feedback from colleagues.

Theories of learning

For further information about theories of learning, see also Chapters 5 and 9 of this book.

Definitions of learning

The nature of learning and how it takes place has dominated the education debate in recent years. The term is normally used to describe any situation in which the brain assimilates knowledge but the processes that combine to produce a learning outcome (i.e. the thing being learned) are difficult to define and explain. One of the challenges for primary teachers is to know when it is correct to claim that a child has 'fully' learned something and, in due course, to formally register the achievement.

Learning can be defined in various ways, including:

- the process that helps the learner to make sense of information and create something new from it;
- the means of sharpening current understanding;
- utilising knowledge and insights gained from earlier experiences to respond effectively to new ones;

- the ability to step back from the security of familiar knowledge to explore less familiar areas;

- the ability to think and reason.

With respect to the last point, Robson (2006, p.3) suggests that learning is a necessary *consequence* of thinking, 'which includes use of the imagination, a playful disposition, persistence and the ability to learn with and from others'. It is therefore important for you to be aware that children are not merely recipients of learning but active partners and initiators of it.

Learning can also be broadly classified into *functional* (immediate use) or *transferable* (usable in other contexts). Take, for instance, a situation where children are learning to use a software program. Some children will doubtless become adept at using the program (functional) and may even be called upon by the teacher to act as tutor to other children. However, only a proportion of the same group of well-informed children will make connections with the implications for using other, similar programs, and transfer their knowledge to the new situation. Again, children who learn a set of spellings for a test may get them all correct (functional learning) yet misspell some of the words in free writing. The aim is, of course, to ensure that children not only master the word list but also utilise their learning in a variety of active, writing situations where spelling is only one of the required skills. Both of the above examples illustrate that apparent 'mastery' of the immediate knowledge is far from being the end of the process.

One explanation about learning is that different forms of it are associated with the right and left parts of the brain. The left part deals principally with language acquisition, sequences and number; it works to analyse information and responds best to structured and sequenced learning. The right part interprets images, looks for patterns, creates metaphors (figures of speech) and strives to synthesise (pull together) and consolidate information. Interplay between the left side and right side of the brain is necessary for the development of deep understanding, creative expression and problem solving. To speak of a person solely as 'left-sided' or 'right-sided' is simplistic, though one dimension is normally prominent.

Research Focus: Bloom's taxonomy

To explain the functions of learning, Bloom and his colleagues developed what came to be known as Bloom's taxonomy in the 1950s (Bloom, 1956). Taxonomy simply means 'classification', so the taxonomy was an attempt to classify forms of learning. The team suggested a hierarchy of six major classes of learning, supposedly moving from simple learning (knowledge) to very complex forms of learning (evaluation), as follows:

1. knowledge;

2. comprehension;

3. application;

$\longrightarrow$

4. analysis;

5. synthesis;

6. evaluation.

The taxonomy is of interest when you are planning and teaching or evaluating children's work because it offers a yardstick against which to monitor the level of demands that are being placed on them and what level of difficulty they can handle. However, as in all models of learning, it is important to appreciate that Bloom's taxonomy is meant to be a guide and not a rigid formula. The same applies to Piaget's model (see next section under 'Child development') and any other model applied to education.

Activity

Use Bloom's taxonomy to evaluate the sorts of demands you are placing on a group of children during a lesson or series of lessons. Consider whether there are ways in which more capable children can engage with the higher order demands, notably levels 4, 5 and 6.

The learning process

Whichever learning theory is in vogue, it is a fact that children of similar age take varying amounts of time to absorb information and grasp concepts (ideas). Children do not learn in a smooth, uninterrupted fashion with bits of knowledge added in a neat, efficient way like engine parts on an assembly belt. Their experience of learning is more akin to the movement of the tide up and down the beach – sometimes gaining ground, sometimes falling back and occasionally surging forward. Learning has also been likened to a spiral staircase, as a pupil returns to the same point to reinforce and deepen his or her existing understanding but 'higher up' the stairway. The spiral staircase analogy is helpful to illustrate the fact that the learner not only needs to 'look down' to see where he or she has come from but also 'look up' to gain an idea of what comes next (see Chapter 2 for further discussion of spiral learning and the spiral curriculum). Skilful teachers encourage children to make such links by asking them to recall previous learning and introduce them to the hoped-for 'next step' in the learning process.

Child development

Interest in the field of child development grew significantly in the early twentieth century, with particular attention being paid to children and young people who exhibited abnormal behaviour. Only later were these ideas applied to all children.

Theories about child development

There were a number of key theories proposed to explain development, including those by Sigmund Freud, who stressed the importance of *childhood events and experiences*. Erik Erikson was a Danish/German/American developmental psychologist and psychoanalyst, famous for his theory on social development of human beings and coining the phrase 'identity crisis'. He suggested that life could be organised into eight stages that extend from birth to death, the first four stages of which have some applicability to the primary phase.

1. *Infancy:* from birth to 18 months – children learn to trust.

2. *Early childhood:* from 18 months to 3 years – children build self-esteem and autonomy.

3. *Play age:* from 3 to 5 years – children try to copy the adults around them and take the initiative in creating play situations.

4. *School age:* from 6 to 12 years – a social stage of development during which we master many new skills and increase our knowledge.

By contrast with Freud, Erikson claimed that each stage of development is dependent on *overcoming conflict* – because success or failure in dealing with the conflict impacts on the child's future development. For instance, if children aged 3 to 5 years are not given opportunities to play and deal with the social and emotional issues attached to this activity, they may struggle later in life when required to show initiative and relate to others.

Theorists such as the Russian psychologist Ivan Pavlov and the American Burrhus Frederic (B.F.) Skinner dealt only with *observable behaviour* rather than the thinking and reasoning that underpinned it. In their view, development was a spontaneous reaction to rewards, punishments, stimuli and other reinforcing behaviours (such as praise).

John Bowlby was an English psychiatrist who developed *attachment theory*, one of the century's most influential theories of personality development and social relationships. Bowlby believed that early relationships with caregivers, especially parents, play a major role in child development and continues to influence social relationships throughout life.

The work of the Swiss/French biologist and psychologist Jean Piaget has significantly influenced the way that learning is organised in school. Piaget's approach is central to the school of cognitive theory known as *cognitive constructivism*. He suggested that children think differently from adults and proposed a *stage theory of cognitive development*. Piaget was among the first people to promote the idea that children play an active role in gaining knowledge of the world. He considered the most critical factor in children's cognitive development to be interaction with their peers. Most famously, Piaget stressed the role of maturation (growing up) in children's increasing capacity to understand their world.

He also proposed that children's thinking does not develop smoothly but rather that there are certain points at which it moves into completely new areas and capabilities, as described in the following model:

- sensori-motor stage: birth to 18 months/2 years;

- pre-operational stage: 2 years to 7 years;

- concrete operational: 7 years to 11 years;

- formal operational stage: 11 years and beyond.

By the 1950s Piaget's ideas had become world renowned, especially in the field of early childhood education where they were seen as legitimising the idea of learning through play that was free from direct adult influence, thereby reflecting the nursery school tradition (Penn, 2005).

Initially, teachers interpreted the model to mean that children are not capable of understanding certain things before they reach specific ages and it was therefore used as the basis for organising the school curriculum on an age-based structure. However, experience with children shows that Piaget's model is too rigidly structured. For example, some children manage concrete operations earlier than the Piagetian model suggests and even some adults don't function at the level of formal operations or are not called upon to use them, so lose the ability to do so. You should be careful therefore not to make too many assumptions based on the child's age; it is only one indicator of likely capability.

Piaget is associated with *cognitive* constructivism. Cognition is defined as the mental process of knowing, including aspects such as awareness, perception, reasoning and making judgements. More simply, it is the process of perceiving, thinking, reasoning and analysing. Cognitive functions deal with logic, rather than with areas of the emotions. However, theorists such as Lev Vygotsky (Russian) and Jerome Bruner (born 1915 in the USA) are known as *social constructivists* because they placed considerable emphasis on the part played by language and the influence of others in facilitating learning. Vygotsky argued that mature mental activity involves 'self-regulation' through social interaction, which affects thought, language and reasoning processes. Consequently, instruction and schooling play a central role in helping children to discover how to pay attention, concentrate and learn effectively. Vygotsky claimed that a more experienced partner (buddy), such as another child or a teaching assistant, can provide help to the less knowledgeable partner in the form of an 'intellectual scaffold', which facilitates more rapid progress than would be possible alone.

Jerome Bruner's theories are based upon the premise that the process of constructing knowledge of the world happens within a social context and argues that 'there is no unique sequence for all learners and the optimum progress in any particular case will depend upon a variety of factors, including past learning, stage of development, nature of the material and individual differences' (Bruner, 1966, p.49). Bruner emphasised his opposition to the theory of 'readiness' espoused by Piaget, arguing that any subject can be taught effectively in some intellectually honest form to any child at any stage of development. He also insisted that interest in the material to be learned provides the best motivation, rather than external goals such as grades, being top of the class or merits. From the wide range of explanations above, you can see that there are many factors influencing individual development; no single theory explains everything that happens in education.

Significance of the emotions

In recent years there has been a growth of interest in the way that learning is affected by the emotions and the concept of *emotional intelligence.* The study of emotional intelligence evolved from theorists such as Howard Gardner (1983) – who worked with Bruner for a time – and Williams and Sternberg (1988). However, Salovey and Mayer are credited with coining the expression 'emotional intelligence' (Salovey and Mayer, 1990). Daniel Goleman popularised emotional intelligence in the business realm by describing its importance as an ingredient for successful business careers and as a crucial component for effective group performance (Goleman, 2005). However, whereas Goleman equated high emotional intelligence with maturity and character, Salovey and Mayer firmly resisted making such a link.

Claude Steiner coined the term *emotional literacy* during the 1970s, defined broadly as being aware of your own emotions and understanding the emotions being experienced by others. He went on to develop his ideas about emotional literacy as 'emotional intelligence with a heart'. It is worth noting that emotional literacy is a term that is often used interchangeably with *emotional intelligence* (Steiner, 2000). Hein (2008) claims that emotional literacy is the ability to express feelings with words that convey specific feelings in three-word sentences; for example, *I feel confused*; he argues that the purpose for developing our emotional literacy is to precisely identify and communicate our feelings. In England and Wales, emotional literacy is commonly linked with the Social and Emotional Aspects of Learning (SEAL) initiative in the belief that by assisting children to articulate their feelings and negotiate with peers and adults – a process formerly known as 'assertiveness' – their confidence will grow and they are more likely to take a positive approach to learning.

Note that another expression, *emotional education*, is also entering the education lexicon, loosely defined as understanding others and understanding ourselves in a deeper and more insightful manner. Emotional education draws on the research from emotional intelligence and emotional literacy and is said to improve our life chances, health and wellbeing, in addition to reducing conflict in social interactions.

Memory and remembering

It is common to hear teachers telling children that they must remember a fact, way of working/behaving or a procedure. However, memorising is a complex phenomenon, the most familiar aspect being an *active working memory* that children can use immediately after they see, hear or otherwise experience something. The active working memory provides a mental 'jotting pad' to store information for everyday activities such as remembering times, following instructions and keeping track of lists of things to do. A working memory allows children to hold information in their heads and manipulate ideas mentally; for example, adding up numbers without a calculator or doing the summation ('sums') on paper.

Research Focus

Gathercole and Alloway (2008) found that the majority of children with poor working memories are slow to learn in the areas of reading, mathematics and science. Children with memory strengths are easy to identify because they can accommodate large amounts of information and retain it effortlessly from a variety of sources. By contrast, children who struggle with memory weaknesses need a considerable amount of repetition, careful explanation and opportunities to explore ideas through problem solving and investigations.

Weak memory

You will be alerted to a pupil's weak memory when written work is characterised by poor sequencing, missing words and inadequate grammar, despite the fact that they may be able to explain their ideas in speech. If children have problems in absorbing verbal information or are poor listeners they need to have directions explained and visually reinforced (with a diagram, for instance). If children have poor visual recall they may forget what they have read or been shown and need to have their learning supported through careful explanation and 'hands-on' experiences. See VAK types of learning, later in this chapter.

Memory and learning

One of the teacher's most important roles is to ascertain what children have learned after exposure to a planned educational experience, drawing on observations, talking with children, asking questions and marking their completed tasks. In doing so, it quickly becomes apparent that memory affects learning, such that something may be:

1. learned for now but likely to be forgotten very soon;

2. learned, never to be forgotten;

3. learned within defined limits;

4. learned but requiring updating and reinforcement to be secure;

5. learned and understood so thoroughly that the learning can be used successfully in different situations.

Memory and knowledge

The *retention of knowledge* through memorising is a key factor in learning; for example, it is possible for children to master words from a modern foreign language early in the school year but forget them after a short time unless they are regularly practised. In this instance, the learning has been temporary and functional and the fourth of the above statements is relevant. Again, a child may learn how to multiply two numbers by using a certain technique but flounder when given the same problem in a different form – for example, to know that 5 times 8 is 40 but struggle to understand that 8 items at 5 pence each costs 40 pence. In such cases, the third statement above is relevant.

Effective learning

Learning that consists of memory *without understanding* has limited value. For example, children might be systematically taught to read words correctly, recite multiplication tables or chant a religious creed, but unless they grasp their meaning and significance, the depth of learning remains shallow. Furthermore, learning that is purely functional, such as knowing how to subtract two numbers, has limited usefulness unless it can be employed in a genuine life situation (such as shopping). Watkins (2003) argues that characteristics of effective learning implies that the learner is:

- active and strategic;
- skilled in cooperation, dialogue and creating knowledge with others;
- able to develop goals and plans;
- able to monitor his or her own learning and is versatile across contexts (different life situations).

Consequently, children need to reflect on their own learning as an essential ingredient in their development, assisted by talking to peers or adults, a point emphasised by both Vygotsky and Bruner (see earlier).

The ideal is for children to have such a grasp of knowledge, skills and understanding that they can use their existing abilities to forge ahead confidently and apply their existing knowledge in unfamiliar situations, as noted in the fifth option listed on p. 77. This deep and expansive type of learning, involving *long-term memory*, extends beyond the boundaries imposed by a task or technique and allows knowledge and understanding to be applied more widely. You cannot rightly claim that children have learned something until these conditions apply.

Classroom practice

Helping children learn

Although learning is taking place continuously, it is in a formal educational setting (such as a school) that it is structured and closely monitored through the curriculum, programmes of study, levels of attainment and so forth. Whatever the specific nature of these imposed structures, educationists agree that the process benefits from well-informed and capable teaching. In other words, though children are capable of learning without experiencing a formal period of education – you only have to observe children playing to realise that a great deal of learning takes place spontaneously during play and personal interactions – pupil progress can be enhanced by a teacher's understanding of how children learn, what they learn and how best to organise learning. MacGilchrist (2003) makes five important points about the nature of learning that have implications for classroom practice.

1. Learners construct and integrate new knowledge in a way that makes sense to them.
2. Learning about learning ('meta-learning') and making sense of experience is a hallmark of effective learners.
3. The relationship between learning and performance is complex and is influenced by motivation and self-image.

4. Learning can be enhanced through developing a variety of social skills and a willingness to persevere and stay on task.

5. The social contexts of the school and classroom are significant in promoting or inhibiting learning.

(Amended list)

Reinforcing learning

You cannot learn for the children but you can do a lot to assist them by providing the right resources, providing them with adequate information, enthusing them to find out more, encouraging them to ask questions and using every possible means to reinforce their learning. Ultimately, all significant learning must be embedded and etched in the mind of the learner (long-term memory) through repetition and reinforcement by means of discussion, problem solving and activities appropriate to the intellectual capacity and maturity of the child. For instance, memorising a poem 'off by heart' to present to an audience requires practice, rehearsal, coaching and the gradual development of natural speech as the words become more familiar and their significance comprehended. It is quite possible, however, that this mastery may be temporary and largely forgotten after a period of time has elapsed. Contrast this temporary sort of memorising with the ability to interpret words on a page for the purpose of reading, in which the regular use of the words in a variety of contexts (books, work sheets, text on a whiteboard, screen, etc.) will more or less ensure that they can be read at any time in the foreseeable future. Your task is to help children to maintain their understanding and capacity to handle ideas beyond the point at which they are needed for task completion.

Learning styles and preferences

One way in which you can assist the learning process is by taking account of the 'learning styles' or 'learning modes' of children. A widely used model is referred to as VAK, the three letters standing for: visual learning, auditory learning and kinaesthetic learning. *Visual* learners are those who learn best by seeing (e.g. pictures, graphs and diagrams). *Auditory* learners learn best by hearing (e.g. listening to a poem). *Kinaesthetic* learners learn best through practical work. Some educationists separate kinaesthetic from *tactile* (as a fourth category): kinaesthetic referring to 'constructing' (e.g. building kits; using computer programs) and tactile emphasising 'touch' (e.g. work with clay). Yet other educators include a fifth category of *written* learning style. None of the definitions is watertight and there is a degree of overlap between them but the basic principle is for teachers to take account of individual learning preferences as they prepare lessons and actively engage in teaching.

Another way of determining preferred learning styles is by allocating children into four basic categories: (1) innovative and imaginative learners; (2) analytical learners; (3) pragmatic learners; (4) dynamic learners. Thus, *innovative and imaginative* children seem to learn particularly effectively when they have opportunity to use the full range of their senses and ask questions about why things happen. Children with more *analytical* minds tend to process information by studying a range of possibilities closely, thinking deeply and reflecting on the issues involved, developing their own ideas and comparing them with what they observe happening. *Pragmatic* learners first speculate and make suggestions before finding out if their ideas work in practice, then adjust their ideas accordingly. *Dynamic* learners learn best when they have a chance to experiment with ways in which they can use their present level of information and probe other possibilities without fear of being rebuked for doing so.

In practice, the most effective learning takes place when children are given the opportunity to use a combination of tactile senses, visual stimuli, careful listening, enquiry based activities, conversation and paper and pencil exercises, supported by teacher explanation and reinforced through individual or group activities.

Differentiation

You will need to take account of these different learning preferences when you plan lessons, such that there is sufficient freedom to satisfy the innovative pupil; sufficient intellectual challenge to satisfy the analytical pupil; sufficient opportunity for practice to satisfy the pragmatic pupil; and sufficient investigative element to satisfy the inquisitive pupil. You also have to take account of the needs of children with special educational needs (SEN) and those for whom English is not the primary tongue. Cultivate the habit of speaking at a steady pace and articulating words carefully. Using 'street language' may be fine in an informal social setting but is inappropriate in class and can bewilder second language speakers. See Chapter 5 for further discussion on meeting individuals' needs.

Every class group contains children with different learning preferences and you cannot possibly hope to recognise, process and deliver them all. As a new teacher, the best you can manage is to organise learning situations using groups, varying the stimuli and providing differentiated tasks. For example, the stimuli might include pictures, discussions, making, doing, saying and hearing (Garnett, 2005). The more that children can see the relevance and usefulness of their learning, the more likely it is that they will engage enthusiastically with the lesson content, gain understanding and retain knowledge. Children also need to be given the opportunity to transfer what they have learned to new situations; this is often the acid test for whether or not deep learning has been achieved.

Jeffrey and Woods (2003) declare that real learning and children's personal knowledge are encouraged through hands-on, active engagements, through role-play and through generating positive feelings about learning. Learning then becomes exciting, fun, inspiring, rewarding and motivating. Teachers gain this information when they get alongside children, converse with them, ask questions, allow them to respond, offer advice and explanation and discuss the next steps in the learning process.

Differentiation is a term used to describe a means by which lessons and the associated questions, tasks and evaluation of achievement take close account of children's abilities and aptitudes. In practice, differentiated work often means that children engage with different tasks of varying degrees of difficulty. A teaching assistant will often support children who find learning a challenge. If children are all given the same work, teachers take account of their abilities when assessing work and offering feedback.

Important note: As meeting the high standards described above is a challenge for even the most experienced teacher, don't expect overnight success!

Child-centred education

Child-centred education is a term frequently associated with the American philosopher and educationist John Dewey to describe a teaching approach in which children actively construct knowledge by exploring the outside world through free-play, though in fact Dewey did not especially advocate such an approach. Teachers that motivate children to discover new skills and knowledge for themselves are sometimes referred to as 'child-centred teachers'. Such teachers do not favour transmitting facts to (largely) passive children through a 'lecture' style of teaching but prefer to facilitate the discovery of knowledge that is interesting to the children through (for instance) establishing areas around the room with different activities for children to access or assigning children to work together in groups on a chosen project. Relatively little whole class teaching takes place and limited systematic direct instruction (step by step) is employed in helping children to master basic skills. Rather, children discover for themselves through play, investigation and using adults as sources of information and guidance.

A key aim of child-centred learning is to empower children in the belief that a full education is not just about verifiable facts (information) but also about helping children to develop positive attitudes, sensitive judgement and thoughtful evaluation of evidence. Smith (2006) argues that pupil empowerment is a crucial factor in learning and that all children, regardless of ability, should be involved in decision making in two ways: first, and principally, by contributing to decisions about the effectiveness of their own provision, and second, by participating in decision making at a wider level and thus influencing school policy.

Supporters of a 'child-centred' approach claim that it helps children to develop greater social competency and creativity than in a more formal setting. However, sceptics point out that children need to be taught basic skills before they can employ them creatively, and consider child-centred methods to be unreliable. It is still common to hear sceptics refer to the damage caused by the emphasis on 'child-centred learning' in the Plowden Report, published as long ago as 1967 – though such allegations do not bear close scrutiny. In 2009, the Rose Review revived the fortunes of a child-centred philosophy by advocating cross-curricular links in learning (see Hayes, 2010). In addition, ICT was added to mathematics and literacy as the 'core' of the curriculum and spoken communication and personal development are to be developed intensively.

Experiential learning

Outside school, most learning is gained or enhanced by first-hand experience, for which no amount of direct teaching will substitute; for example, exploring a pond; absorbing the sights, scents and sounds in a wooded valley; or a visit to a local craft centre. Similarly, children benefit from listening to visiting poets and authors reading their own work; practical drama, playing with construction materials; handling unfamiliar objects; and shopping in the local market.

Schools that promote experiential learning encourage self-motivation, harmonious social relationships, spontaneous enthusiasm, sharing with others about the work in hand and 'learning about how they learn best' – sometimes referred to as 'meta-learning' or 'metacognition' (see Chapter 2 for further discussion). Children's learning is also improved through *investigations* such as science experiments; special effects through random mixing of paints; researching a topic; and creative computer simulations. These investigative approaches to learning assist children's conceptual understanding, skills acquisition and factual knowledge, and differ markedly from sterile approaches with set procedures and outcomes.

Research Focus: Meta-learning

The concept of meta-learning was introduced by Maudsley (1979) as the process by which learners become aware of and increasingly in control of habits of perception, inquiry, learning and growth that gradually become natural to them. Put simply, meta-learning is becoming more sensitive about and aware of the ways in which we learn.

Discovery learning

Discovery learning is an open-ended form of problem solving in which the teacher provides an introductory activity or stimulus on a relevant theme or topic to gain the children's interest, stir their natural curiosity and raise the level of enthusiasm and motivation. Children are then permitted considerable latitude to decide how they will proceed and shape the enquiry. When they have found out as much as they can in the allocated time, the children determine how they will present their findings – orally, formally written or presented diagrammatically. Younger children with limited ability to write, offer feedback about their discoveries through the spoken word or in the form of a drawing.

Discovery learning is closely associated to work by the French psychologist Jean Piaget and 'constructivist' theory (see earlier in this chapter), in which learners draw on their existing knowledge and past experiences to discover facts and relationships and insights. Robson (2006) refers to Penn (2005) and notes that by the 1950s Piaget's ideas had become known worldwide, especially in the field of early childhood education 'where they were seen as legitimising the idea of learning through "natural" or "free" play [i.e. free from direct adult influence], very much part of the nursery school tradition' (2006, p.13).

Proponents believe that discovery learning encourages active pupil engagement; promotes autonomy motivation, responsibility and independence; develops creativity and problem-solving skills; and offers an individualised learning experience. Critics cite disadvantages, such as the danger of cognitive overload (i.e. too much to think about at one time); the possibility of misconceptions (i.e. developing wrong ideas); and teachers failing to detect and correct mistakes and misconceptions (Learning-Theories.com).

In primary schools, discovery learning is normally carried out in pairs or small groups and a report of findings is then made to the rest of the class. Resources are provided by the teacher in advance or created by the children as they proceed with their investigations. The use of information technology (notably through computers) is particularly helpful where the discovery is factual, rather than practical knowledge from hands-on application using materials (kinaesthetic learning). Discovery learning has become more difficult to employ in recent years with the onset of timetabling and increases in curriculum content, with its accompanying time pressures. It is most effective when it is guided by a knowledgeable adult and used in conjunction with the more familiar direct instruction method.

Activity

Observe groups of children engaged in discovery learning and note: (a) which child or children dominate proceedings; (b) which children are passive; (c) how much genuine collaboration exists among the children; (d) the nature of the verbal and non-verbal interactions. Think carefully how your observations will affect the way that you organise such learning.

Case Study: Collaborative learning

Becky organised a collaborative learning activity based on four children per group. She provided the resources and explained broadly what she expected them to do, while stressing that they should discuss their decisions and actions with other members of the group. She was surprised about four things. First, some children were anxious to avoid 'mistakes' and so kept checking with her that they were doing the right thing. Second, some children were strongly dominant and insisted on 'taking charge'. Third, some children copied ideas from other groups instead of using their own. Fourth, the conversations were frequently 'off-task'. Becky soon realised that merely organising children into groups and giving them tasks without first educating them in ways to cooperate, discuss, resolve different viewpoints and reach decisions was unsatisfactory. Over the coming weeks, she spent time helping the children to improve these skills, which resulted in a noticeable improvement in their concentration levels, application to task and final results.

Individualised and personalised learning

The concept of 'personalisation' is based on the belief that it is possible to assess children's progress accurately and tailor-make teaching and learning in such a way that those needs are met. Personalised learning is seen as a highly structured and responsive approach to each child's and young person's learning in order that every pupil is able to progress, achieve and participate in the work (DCSF, 2008; see also Hargreaves, 2006).

Personalised learning should not be confused with the *individualised* learning of the past, characterised by each child engaged on solitary learning paths – often dominated by work sheets – or letting children choose what they want to do.

Research Focus: Personalised learning

In a major study of the ways that schools use personalised learning, Sebba et al. (2007) describe how schools were using their personalised learning approaches to target specific interventions that were then developed more widely. Thus, literacy interventions, programmes and support initially aimed at children with identified special educational needs and provision for gifted and talented children could be targeted at one group of children and gradually extended across the school. The case study schools seemed to have developed activities that reflected greater involvement of the parents through review days and use of ICT for linking home to school.

Some schools have created leadership roles or teaching posts to manage and disseminate best practice in support of the personalised learning agenda, including information to parents and opportunities for them to receive advice about how they may better contribute towards their children's education; see West-Burnham (2008). Schools now hold a lot of assessment information about children in their management systems that are available to staff and parents to provide information about measurable pupil attainment that can be valuable in planning for personalised learning. Hansen and Vaukins (2011) explore this further.

Concerns have been raised about the implementation of personalised learning. First, that it is an unattainable ideal because no teacher, however, skilled and knowledgeable, can offer a bespoke education to each child. Second, learning does not depend solely on teaching methods, so even the most carefully designed programme cannot guarantee outcomes. Third, personalised learning can become unduly rigid in format and thereby constrain creativity and innovation. Finally, a good education does not only consist of high attainment in measurable areas of learning but encompasses (for instance) the ability to relate well to others, act with integrity and make sensible decisions and appropriate choices, none of which can be identified through a specific grade or mark.

Learning Outcomes Review

Thinking about the school in which you are working or have recently worked, respond to the prompts after each intended learning outcome, to identify your knowledge and understanding of the issues covered in the chapter.

- **To be aware of the multi-dimensional nature of learning:**
  - What types of learning are likely to be taking place in the classroom?

- **To understand different theories of child development and their implications for teaching**
  - Make a list of the theorists referred to in the Child Development section and for each of them: (a) Write down a one-sentence summary of his principal belief about learning. (b) Suggest a classroom application for the idea.

- **To recognise the significance of memory and memorising for learning**
  - What part does memory play in learning?

- **To identify different learning styles and their implications for teaching**
  - What range of learning styles exist across a class of children?

- **To understand the place of learning through experience**
  - What benefits do children gain through experiential learning?

- **To distinguish between individualised and personalised learning**
  - What are the three distinguishing features of individualised and personalised learning?

Further Reading

Hayes, D. (2009) *Learning and Teaching in Primary Schools: Achieving QTS*. Exeter: Learning Matters.

Hayes, D. (2010) *Encyclopaedia of Primary Education*. London: Routledge.

Smidt, S. (2006) *The Developing Child in the 21st Century*. London: Routledge.

References

Bloom, B.S. (ed.) (1956) *Taxonomy of Educational Objectives, the Classification of Educational Goals – Handbook I: Cognitive Domain*. New York: McKay.

Bruner, J.S. (1966) *Toward a Theory of Instruction*. Cambridge, MA: Belknap Press of Harvard University Press.

DCSF (2008) *Personalised Learning: A practical guide.* London: HMSO.

Department for Children, Schools and Families (2009) *Independent Review of the Primary Curriculum: Final Report* (The Rose Review). Annesley, Nottingham: DCSF.

DfE (2011) *Teachers' Standards.* Available from www.education.gov.uk/publications

Gardner, H. (1983) *Frames of Mind.* New York: Basic Books.

Garnett, S. (2005) *Using Brainpower in the Classroom.* London: Routledge.

Gathercole, S.E. and Alloway, T.P. (2008) *Working Memory and Learning: A practical guide for teachers.* London: Sage.

Goleman, D. (2005) *Working with Emotional Intelligence.* New York: Bantam Books.

Hansen, A. and Vaukins, D. (2011) *Primary Mathematics Across the Curriculum.* Exeter: Learning Matters.

Hargreaves, D. (2006) *Personalising Learning 6: The final gateway – school design and organisation.* London: Specialist Schools Trust.

Hayes, D. (2010) 'Cross-curricular, Rose Review', *Education 3–13* 38(4) pp. 381–7.

Hein, S. (2008) *Emotional Literacy.* Available from http://eqi.org/elit.ht

Jeffrey, B. and Woods, P. (2003) *The Creative School: A framework for success, quality and effectiveness.* London: Routledge.

Learning-Theories.com: *Discovery learning (Bruner).* Available from http://www.learning-theories.com/discovery-learning-bruner.html

MacGilchrist, B. (2003) Primary learners of the future. *Education 3–13* 31(3) pp.58–65.

Maudsley, D.B. (1979) A theory of meta-learning and principles of facilitation: an organismic perspective, doctoral dissertation, University of Toronto (40, 8, 4354–4355–A).

Penn, H. (2005) *Understanding Early Childhood.* Maidenhead: Open University Press.

Robson, S. (2006) *Developing Thinking and Understanding in Young Children.* London: Routledge.

Salovey, P. and Mayer, J.D. (1990) Emotional intelligence. *Imagination, Cognition, and Personality* 9, pp.185–211.

Sebba, J., Brown, N., Steward, S., Galton, M. and James, M. (2007) *An Investigation of Personalised Learning Approaches used by Schools.* DfES Research Report RR843. Available from http://www.canterbury.ac.uk/education/tf-mentors/ActivitiesforMentoring/Personalised/documents/DfESReport.pdf accessed 17/12/10.

Smith, C. (2006) From special needs to inclusive education. In Sharp, J., Ward, S. and Hankin, L. (eds) *Education Studies: An issues-based approach.* Exeter: Learning Matters.

Steiner, C.M. (2000) *Emotional Literacy: Intelligence with heart.* Fawnskin, CA: Personhood Press.

Watkins, C. (2003) *Learning: A sense-maker's guide.* London: Association for Teachers and Lecturers.

West-Burnham, J. (2008) *Leadership for Personalising Learning.* National College for School Leadership. Available from http://www.ncsl.org.uk

Williams, W.M. and Sternberg, R.J. (1988) Group intelligence: Why some groups are better than others. *Ingelligence* 12, pp. 351–77.

5. Including all learners
Jonathan Glazzard

Learning Outcomes

By the end of this chapter you will be aware of:

- definitions of inclusion and associated issues;
- current over-arching policy agendas and legislation which regulate classroom practice;
- the characteristics of inclusive environments;
- the principles of inclusion in the statutory inclusion statement and ways in which these can be addressed in the classroom.

TEACHERS' STANDARDS

A teacher must:

1. Set high expectations which inspire, motivate and challenge pupils

- establish a safe and stimulating environment for pupils, rooted in mutual respect
- set goals that stretch and challenge pupils of all backgrounds, abilities and dispositions
- demonstrate consistently the positive attitudes, values and behaviour which are expected of pupils.

2. Promote good progress and outcomes by pupils

- be accountable for pupils' attainment, progress and outcomes
- plan teaching to build on pupils' capabilities and prior knowledge
- guide pupils to reflect on the progress they have made and their emerging needs
- demonstrate knowledge and understanding of how pupils learn and how this impacts on teaching
- encourage pupils to take a responsible and conscientious attitude to their own work and study.

5. Adapt teaching to respond to the strengths and needs of all pupils

- know when and how to differentiate appropriately, using approaches which enable pupils to be taught effectively
- have a secure understanding of how a range of factors can inhibit pupils' ability to learn, and how best to overcome these
- demonstrate an awareness of the physical, social and intellectual development of children, and know how to adapt teaching to support pupils' education at different stages of development

- have a clear understanding of the needs of all pupils, including those with special educational needs; those of high ability; those with English as an additional language; those with disabilities; and be able to use and evaluate distinctive teaching approaches to engage and support them.

6. **Make accurate and productive use of assessment**
- make use of formative and summative assessment to secure pupils' progress

8. **Fulfil wider professional responsibilities**
- make a positive contribution to the wider life and ethos of the school
- develop effective professional relationships with colleagues, knowing how and when to draw on advice and specialist support
- deploy support staff effectively
- take responsibility for improving teaching through appropriate professional development, responding to advice and feedback from colleagues.

Introduction

This chapter introduces you to the three principles of inclusion as outlined in the National Curriculum (DfE, 2013). The historical development of inclusion as a policy agenda is briefly addressed, and the underpinning statutory framework which guides practice is discussed. The chapter emphasises the importance of trainee teachers and teachers formulating a set of inclusive values upon which to base their practice.

Defining inclusion

According to Sikes et al. (2007, p.366) attempting to define inclusion 'is a thorny and controversial task which has occupied many commentators over the years'.

Activity

What is your own definition of inclusion?

What factors have helped you to develop that definition?

How important are values and attitudes in shaping inclusive practice and how important is knowledge?

Is knowledge more important than your personal values?

Personal interpretations of inclusion

It has been argued that 'inclusion is a bewildering concept which can have a variety of interpretations and applications' (Avramidis et al., 2002, p.158). Thus, your own interpretation of inclusion and inclusive practice will fundamentally affect the way you perform in the classroom. According to Sikes et al.:

> *Whilst policy, structure and culture might shape the broader social and institutional contexts in which teachers and teaching assistants operate, it is their personal interpretations and understandings, their day-to-day enactments, how they perform inclusion, their agency which determines how the policy is formulated and re-formulated in practice.*

> *(Sikes et al., 2007, p.366)*

On placements you will gain experience of working with several teachers in different schools and it is likely that you will witness a range of inclusion practices. Professional autonomy allows teachers a degree of freedom in translating policy into practice and teachers interpret policy frameworks in different ways. Inclusive classrooms are central to providing all children with high quality learning experiences and the school's interpretation of inclusion should be articulated within the inclusion policy and it is important that you read this carefully.

Including all learners

You might think about inclusion only in relation to the education of children with special educational needs and disabilities in mainstream environments. However, inclusion is a broad concept which embraces **all** learners. When you think about inclusion, reflect on how you are going to set suitable learning challenges, respond to children's diverse learning needs and overcome potential barriers to learning and assessment for all learners. This constitutes a minimum statutory entitlement for every child.

As a trainee teacher you will need to think about inclusion on different levels, such as:

- the needs of all learners when planning and teaching;
- how you might develop inclusive classroom environments;
- the ways in which you form effective, mutually respectful partnerships with parents, carers and other adults.

Personal values and inclusion

Before you can start to put inclusion into practice it is beneficial for you to reflect on your own values. These will inevitably shape and define your practice. A useful starting point is to reflect on whether you hold any prejudices towards specific groups. Negative stereotypes can lead to discrimination and therefore have no place in the modern world of education.

As a teacher you are a role model and you need to demonstrate that you welcome and respect all individuals and groups of learners.

Mainstream and special education

Earlier definitions of inclusion focused on the inclusion of all learners into mainstream schools. However, Warnock has argued that:

> *Inclusion is not a matter of where you are geographically, but of where you feel you belong. There are many children, and especially adolescents, identified as having special educational needs, who can never feel as though they belong in a large mainstream school.*

> *(Warnock, 2005, p.38)*

Warnock stresses that 'the idea of inclusion should be ... redefined so that it allows children to pursue the common goals of education in the environment within which they can best be taught' (2005, p.54). In this sense it might be useful for you to conceptualise inclusion in terms of inclusion into the enterprise of education rather than inclusion into mainstream environments. Special schools can and do create inclusive learning environments if the learners thrive, make progress, feel valued and feel that they belong. Despite this there has been a wealth of literature which has emphasised that special schools are exclusionary, oppressive and marginalise learners with special educational needs (see Barton, 1998a; Skrtic, 1991; Tomlinson, 1982). These writers have stressed the point that the education of all children in mainstream schools is part of an international human rights agenda which emphasises that any form of segregation is discriminatory.

Activity

Reflect on the above arguments relating to mainstream and segregated education.

- Do you agree with Warnock's perspectives on inclusion?
- What are your views on special schools?
- Do you think all learners can be educated in mainstream schools?

Inclusion as acceptance and respect for all

According to Farrell (2001) the term 'inclusion' refers to the extent to which a school or community values diversity and welcomes all people as full members of that community. Increasingly inclusion is defined as a broad concept which aims to eliminate social exclusion (Ainscow, 2007). Thus, inclusion embraces issues related social class, disability, gender, ethnicity, race, religion and sexuality. Corbett (2001) has stressed that inclusion should be thought of as an active rather than a passive process. It represents a continual commitment from all staff to challenge and eliminate all forms of discrimination. Inclusion demands a radical transformation of policies and practices within schools so that barriers to learning, participation and achievement are identified and removed. It represents a whole school commitment to the principles of social justice, equity and respect and it positively celebrates diversity. Inclusive schools challenge discriminatory attitudes which ultimately create barriers to learning, participation and achievement.

According to Giroux:

> *Educators should reject forms of schooling that marginalize students who are poor, black and least advantaged. This points to the necessity for developing school practices that recognise how issues related to gender, class, race and sexual orientation can be used as a resource for learning rather than being contained in schools through a systemic pattern of exclusion, punishment and failure.*

(Giroux, 2003, p. 10)

Activity

How does the current education system marginalise specific groups of learners? How can this problem be overcome?

Inclusion as a policy agenda: a critique

Inclusive schools enable all learners to thrive. However, recent and current governments in England have advanced a policy of *normalisation* under the umbrella of inclusion (Armstrong, 2005) which focuses on closing the achievement gap between different groups of learners. Inclusion policy has focused on the use of intervention and support programmes to maximise opportunities for all learners to achieve narrow performance indicators.

Inclusion as a process of normalisation

Research Focus

Christine Lloyd's critique of government policy in relation to inclusive education shows that current practices and policies focus on the normalisation of individuals and groups rather than the 'denormalization of institutions, systems and rules which comprise education and schooling' (Lloyd, 2008, p.228). Consequently, vulnerable learners are pressurised into achieving national performance indicators, regardless of whether these are appropriate.

Denormalising schooling involves the development of different curriculum frameworks and assessment systems to meet the needs of all learners. Lloyd emphasises the inaccessibility of the schooling system through a system which measures individual and school success through the achievement of norm-related standards. For Lloyd, the standards agenda and the way in which the education system currently measures success and achievement is exclusive rather than inclusive. The standards agenda therefore erects barriers to participation and achievement rather than breaking them down (Benjamin, 2002; Lloyd, 2008) through constructing vulnerable learners as failures.

According to Lloyd, inclusive education demands not only a radical transformation of classroom practice, but also a radical transformation of policy. She argues that:

> *Achievement conceived in this way can be seen to create the greatest barrier to success. To remove the barrier it is necessary to reconceptualize achievement in such a way that it is attainable and accessible to all.*
>
> *(Lloyd, 2008, p.229)*

Activity

What do you think Lloyd means by 'reconceptualising' achievement? Can you think of alternative approaches to measuring achievement so that all learners can experience and enjoy success?

Inclusion agenda versus standards agenda

Many have argued that there is an incompatible relationship between the standards agenda and the inclusion agenda (Warnock, 1996; Barton, 1998b; Armstrong, 1998, 2005; Lloyd, 2008).

Research Focus

According to Cole (2005), within the relationship between the standards agenda and the inclusion agenda 'there will be winners and losers and it is suggested that the losers will be the children who are deemed as having special educational needs' (p.334). Goodley (2007) supports this argument, explaining that 'educational environments, curricula content, teacher identities are all normatively associated with environments, standards and achievements that are at odds with the quirkiness of disabled learners' (p.319). He goes on to explain that 'academic excellence is troubled by those who might never be capable of (nor interested in) such achievements' (p.322).

Goodley (2007) argues that the marketisation of education constructs all learners as 'able', productive and skilled as current educational policy links education to entrepreneurship,

→

which is 'hugely problematic for students with disabilities and or special educational needs who require the support of others' (p.321).

Goodley (2007) encourages us to think of more socially just pedagogies which 'resist over coding and the subtle forms of segregation brought about by assessment' (p.324).

Activity

How can educational environments be more flexible to cater for a diverse range of learners? In what ways is the inclusion agenda incompatible with the standards agenda?

It could be argued that inclusive education demands a radical rethink of education policy. Current policies related to narrowing the achievement gap between learners with and without special educational needs, have resulted in the marginalisation and exclusion of some learners. Current policies which focus on closing the gaps uncritically assume that all learners are able to meet the same socially constructed norms. Such policies instrumentally fail the most vulnerable, thus resulting in further marginalisation and exclusion. Socially just or inclusive pedagogies celebrate differences and redefine achievement as a broad concept. Within a socially just inclusive education system learners should be empowered to develop strengths in areas which they are both interested in and feel confident in. Genuine child-centred education is the route to an inclusive education system which recognises that one curriculum and one assessment system cannot meet the needs of all learners.

The development of inclusive education

The documents in the research focus below mark milestones in the evolution of inclusion as a policy agenda. Current policy documents are also listed. It is important that you are aware of these and understand the impact their publication made on approaches to education for all after their publication.

Research Focus

- The Warnock Report (DES, 1978) introduced the terminology of *special educational needs* and recommended the *integration* of children with special educational needs into mainstream schools.

- The Salamanca Statement called on all governments in the United Nations to 'adopt as a matter of law or policy the principle of *inclusive* education, enrolling all children in regular schools, unless there are compelling reasons for doing otherwise' (UNESCO, 1994).

⟶

- Both the Green Paper (DfEE, 1997) and *Removing Barriers to Achievement* (DfES, 2004) emphasised the need for schools to plan for inclusion and to raise outcomes for children with special educational needs.

- The Green Paper (DfE, 2011) identified that the established system for meeting the needs of pupils with special educational needs and/disabilities in England was too complex, too bureaucratic and was characterised by a culture of low expectations for pupils.

- The revised National Curriculum (DfE, 2013) includes a statutory inclusion framework.

- The revised Code of Practice for Special Educational Needs and Disabilities (DfE, 2014), which replaces its predecessor (DfES, 2001), sets out a graduated response to support children with special educational needs and emphasises the importance of genuine consultation with learners and their parents or carers.

- The Equality Act (2010) identifies nine protected characteristics. Individuals with these characteristics must be protected from direct or indirect discrimination. The characteristics are age; disability; gender reassignment; marriage and civil partnership; pregnancy and maternity; race; religion and belief; sex; sexual orientation.

The Special Educational Needs and Disabilities Code of Practice

The revised Code of Practice for SEND identifies some fundamental principles which schools and teachers need to address. The key principles of the Code of Practice (DfE, 2014) are summarised below. The Code aims to ensure:

- greater participation of children, their parents and young people in decision making;

- early identification of children and young people's needs and early intervention to support them;

- greater choice and control for young people and parents over support;

- greater collaboration between education, health and social care services to provide support;

- high quality provision to meet the needs of children and young people with SEN;

- a focus on inclusive practice and removing barriers to learning;

- successful preparation for adulthood, including independent living and employment.

The definition of special educational needs has not changed. Within the context of the revised Code a child and young person has SEN if they have learning difficulty or disability which calls for special educational provision to be made. A child of compulsory school age or a young person has a learning difficulty or disability if they have significantly greater difficulty in learning than the majority of others of the same age or has a disability that prevents or hinders them from making use of facilities of a kind generally provided for others of the same age in mainstream schools. Statements of special educational provision for pupils with the most complex needs have been replaced by Education and Health Care plans. The revised Code has established one school-based assessment phase known as *SEN Support* for pupils who meet the criteria for special educational needs and/disabilities. This replaces the previous two-phased assessment process (*School Action* and *School Action Plus*). The aim is to reduce the proportion of pupils who were formerly identified as having SEN at the *School Action* phase where SEN resulted from weak teaching.

The Code challenges schools and teachers to have the highest expectations of pupils with special educational needs and/disabilities and to focus sharply on interventions that improve outcomes for these learners. The Code emphasises that quality first teaching at all phases of education should reduce the proportion of pupils identified as having special educational needs and that quality first teaching should be the initial response of schools rather than intervention.

Inclusive environments

Despite the issues associated with personal interpretations of inclusion there are several key characteristics of inclusive learning environments which you need to embed into your practice. Inclusive environments:

- value difference and celebrate diversity;
- recognise what each child can do and build on this by providing suitable learning challenges;
- respond to children's diverse learning needs;
- identify and remove barriers to learning and achievement;
- are warm, friendly and positive so that all adults and children feel as though they belong;
- demonstrate an ethos of mutual respect;
- value the views of all (child, parents, carers and all adults working within the school);
- create a climate of hope, success and possibility.

The statutory framework for inclusion

The National Curriculum (DfE, 2013) sets out a statutory framework for inclusion. This identifies key principles that schools must address in order to develop inclusive practices. All schools must:

- *set suitable challenges to respond to children's diverse learning needs;*
- *respond to pupils' needs and overcome potential barriers for individuals and groups of pupils.*

(DfE, 2013)

When you are undertaking placements ensure that you provide opportunities for all children to experience success in learning. To address these principles you will need to:

- plan appropriate learning objectives which match your learners' needs;
- use varied teaching styles to cater for your learners differing learning styles;
- plan access strategies to make learning accessible to all children.

Setting suitable learning challenges

As you move towards achieving the Teachers' Standards, you must demonstrate that you are able to provide suitable learning challenges for every child in your class. There is a clear expectation in both the National Curriculum (DfE, 2013) and in the Teachers' Standards (DfE, 2012) that teachers should have the highest expectations of all learners. This involves setting children challenging, ambitious targets that take account of prior assessments. There is an even greater focus in these documents on teachers demonstrating their abilities in setting stretching targets for the most able learners.

Know your learners
Spend time getting to know your learners before you start to teach them. Observe them in a range of curriculum areas. Talk to your mentor about their learning needs, and ask if you can have access to any prior assessment records which detail your learners' attainment. You will be able to plan for progression in learning once you have a clear understanding of your learners' starting points and prior attainment.

Subject knowledge
Only with adequate subject knowledge will you understand strands of progression in various aspects of learning in specific subjects. You will then be able to identify children's next steps in learning.

Using assessment to build on prior learning
You need to ensure that you assess your learners frequently. Much of the assessment you carry out will be informal and formative and help you to identify what children can do and whether they have any misconceptions. Read more about assessment in Chapter 16.

Identifying appropriate learning outcomes
In some instances you might be able to build in access strategies to enable all learners to achieve the same learning outcomes. In others it may not be appropriate to have all your learners working on the same learning outcomes, so differentiate the outcomes to match the needs of your learners.

Using appropriate grouping arrangements
Although your ability to influence grouping arrangements as a trainee teacher on placement will vary, the ideal situation is to operate flexible grouping arrangements so that children can

switch groups according to their needs. For example, a child may have specific difficulties with reading and writing but may excel in speaking and listening activities. Another child may struggle in mathematics with number and calculations but may excel in geometry. It is also important to remember that children respond differently to different areas of the curriculum. Mixed attainment grouping can often provide children with a suitable context for peer to peer scaffolding.

Personalised learning

When planning for children's needs, think carefully about setting personal learning targets for individuals if appropriate. Involve support staff in the assessment process and encourage them to suggest possible next steps for the learners they are supporting. Remember that you need to demonstrate that you are able to work collaboratively as part of a team. See Chapter 14 for planning for other adults.

Taking responsibility for all learners

You must take your responsibilities seriously in relation to planning for the education of *all* learners. The important point to bear in mind is that learners with additional needs should only be withdrawn when necessary. Additionally, ensure that the education of learners with additional needs is not left solely to support staff or specialist classroom assistants.

High expectations of all learners

It is your responsibility to ensure that every child makes progress. Planning for progression will help children move forward in their learning. You will be required to demonstrate that all of your learners have made good rates of progress in relation to their abilities and starting points. Maintain high expectations of all learners and track their progress regularly. You will also be able to forecast progress rates more accurately once you have a clear picture of their prior attainment and rates of progress.

The principle of high expectations for all learners means ensuring that learners who have been identified as gifted and challenged receive appropriate learning challenges. Ensure that these learners make rapid rates of progress and be confident that you have the necessary subject knowledge required to challenge learners who are working above age-related expectations. 'Target setting' for/with your learners is fundamental to securing the very best outcomes for all your children.

Using appropriate curriculum frameworks to aid differentiation

Schools have a statutory duty to teach all primary aged children the content of the National Curriculum (DfE, 2013). This entitlement ensures that all children have access to a broad and balanced curriculum. However, teachers have the flexibility to select programmes of study from earlier or later key stages to ensure that all children are provided with appropriately differentiated learning challenges.

Understanding child development

Chapter 4 outlines the need to ensure you have a very secure understanding of child development. Having a secure understanding of the steps children progress through, and knowledge of what stages children have reached in relation to those steps, is pivotal to planning appropriate learning challenges.

Activity

Imagine that you are teaching literacy to a Year 2 class. You are planning guided writing and the focus is to compose sentences using adjectives, verbs and nouns for precision, clarity and impact. Adam finds literacy difficult and is not yet able to write in sentences. Beth is able to cope with this task and needs to be challenged further.

- Identify a more suitable learning objective for Adam.
- Identify a learning objective that will challenge Beth.

Responding to pupils' needs and overcoming potential barriers to learning

The National Curriculum (DfE, 2013) emphasises the need for schools to comply with their duties under the Equality Act, 2010. There is a clear expectation in the National Curriculum that pupils with special educational needs and/disabilities are entitled to study the full breadth of the National Curriculum and that a *minority* of pupils will need additional resources and/interventions to enable them to do this. With the right teaching many pupils with special educational needs and/disabilities will not require additional resources and/or intervention (DfE, 2013).

Your learners may come from very diverse social and cultural backgrounds. During your teaching placements and teaching career it is likely that you will gain experience of teaching different groups of children. These may include:

- children with special educational needs and disabilities;
- children from different ethnic groups;
- travellers, refugees and asylum seekers;
- boys and girls;
- children from diverse linguistic backgrounds.

As Chapter 4 outlines, children have different interests and learning styles. To ensure that your curriculum engages all children, think about the resources you use to support your teaching and the extent to which these reflect children's diverse backgrounds. Try to draw on children's social and cultural experiences in your teaching. You must challenge any form of bullying or harassment, including racial harassment.

Children's interests can often be used as a starting point for learning in the classroom. Boys and girls may have different interests so reflect these interests in:

- the books available for children to read;
- the writing tasks you present;
- the topics and themes you plan.

You will need to respect children's cultural beliefs. Additionally you must ensure that all children have the opportunity to participate in the learning experiences that you have planned. Think carefully about:

- your classroom environment reflecting aspects of social, linguistic and cultural diversity;
- images around your classroom reflecting positive images of disability;
- the choice of famous people that you choose to study in history;
- how you present other countries in geography to avoid stereotypical views.

Think about how you might embed aspects of social and cultural diversity through art, dance, music or drama. Try to be creative in your approach. Think carefully about your word choices and avoid generalisations. Children do not all live in houses, they do not all live with a mum and a dad and they do not all celebrate Christmas or shop in the local supermarket. Although this is obvious, teachers may inadvertently transmit white middle class values onto learners. You should demonstrate your sensitivity to the diverse backgrounds of the learners in your class.

Prejudice-based bullying: race, homophobia, biphobia and transphobia

The Equality Act (2010) clearly states that schools must be proactive in promoting positive relationships between different groups of pupils. Additionally the legislation protects individuals with specific characteristics from direct or indirect discrimination. This legislation places a duty on schools to take a proactive stance towards race equality. It is not sufficient just to address racist incidents as and when they occur (Knowles, 2006). Children need to be educated about race equality. The same is also true of other forms of prejudice-based bullying including homophobic, transphobic or biphobic bullying. The government in England and school inspectors are concerned about the extent of homophobic, transphobic and biphobic bullying in schools (including primary schools) and particularly about the unchallenged use of homophobic language ('that's so gay!'). Stonewall have produced some superb training materials and information for schools to help them in addressing this issue (see http://www.stonewall.org.uk/).

The way in which schools promote positive attitudes about race, disability and sexual orientation is now a significant focus of school Ofsted inspections. Schools need to address issues proactively by educating pupils about diversity as a positive aspect of our society. Additionally, inspectors will request to view documentary evidence of incidents of bullying or harassment in order to check that all incidents have been addressed appropriately. Try to demonstrate your commitment to diversity by embedding every aspect of it into your planning, teaching, classroom environment and ethos.

Activity

When on placement, discuss with your class teacher how their planning responds to the diverse needs of the children in their class and more broadly in their local community.

Case Study: Gender differences

Jane was on placement in a mixed R/Y1 class. She created a writing area to support children's independent writing. Over a period of several weeks Jane began to notice that many of the boys in her class were reluctant to enter the writing area in self-chosen activities. The boys often chose to play in the outdoor area or in the construction area. If they did go in the writing area they did not persist with activities for any length of time.

Jane decided to carry out a small-scale action research project. The aim of the research was to improve boys' motivation in writing. She initially observed a small group of boys during independent play. Jane noticed that the boys frequently played at being superhero characters that they had watched on television. Jane informally asked them about the characters they were playing and she discovered more about the characters they liked. Jane decided to capitalise on the boys' interests in developing the writing area to reflect these.

She focused on a 'Superman' theme and put resources (pictures, comics and stationery) into the area to reflect this character. After the writing area had been enhanced Jane immediately noticed that the boys wanted to use it, and continued to do so.

Activity

- How might Jane use the children's diverse learning styles to develop other areas of the classroom?
- Can you think of any dangers with this approach?

You play a major role in raising achievement in school. You are responsible for identifying vulnerable groups: these are children who are likely to under-achieve. You will need to monitor achievement carefully and plan for individuals and groups of learners to help them make further progress. You will need to be prepared to justify the progress of all of your learners. There is a clear expectation in the Code of Practice (DfE, 2014) that schools should focus more sharply on raising outcomes for pupils with SEND rather than focusing exclusively on the provision that is being offered. Interventions that are not successfully improving outcomes for these learners should be replaced with more effective interventions that accelerate achievement and thus close the achievement gap.

Groups of learners at risk of under-achievement include:

- travellers;
- children identified as being gifted and talented;
- children who are learning English as an additional language;
- looked after children;
- learners who experience prejudice-based bullying;
- children with special educational needs and disabilities.

To overcome barriers to learning you may need to:

- break tasks down;
- vary your teaching styles, e.g. by providing children with visual, auditory and kinaesthetic learning opportunities;
- build in access strategies to enable children to access a piece of learning.

Access strategies will vary depending on the specific barrier to learning but typically might include:

- use of additional support e.g. support staff and peer support;
- use of ICT;
- specific equipment;
- visual timetables.

Activity

The above list is not exhaustive. What strategies have you seen being utilised to support children with specific impairments, e.g. dyslexia, autism, speech and language, sensory difficulties and social, emotional and behaviour difficulties. Draw on your experiences from your school-based training to help you.

Working with travellers

Lloyd and McCluskey (2008, p.335) identify some of the key issues facing the education of children who are travellers. These include:

- *low educational participation/ attendance;*
- *high incidence of exclusion (DfES, 2003);*
- *low attainment;*
- *racist harassment, physical bullying, name calling;*
- *interrupted learning;*
- *inadequate support;*
- *failure of schools to pass on records;*
- *inappropriate identification of special educational needs.*

Travellers are entitled to a flexible system of education and the use of ICT/internet based home learning is having a positive impact on attainment. The Equality Act (2010) places a duty on schools to promote racial equality and challenge discrimination. Schools and teachers should embrace and accept the cultural differences between travelling and non-travelling children and offer differentiated and flexible provision accordingly. Inclusion necessitates additional and different provision, not provision which is the same. Schools should develop effective partnerships with the local Traveller Education Service to help develop inclusive ways of working. Above all, teachers should reflect on their own values and prejudices. Ignorance and negative teacher attitudes potentially result in the marginalisation of learners from this community. Teachers should celebrate the culture of travellers and use this as an opportunity to educate other children about the history of travellers and their cultural beliefs.

Gifted and talented children

> *Giftedness is usually seen as the potential a child may possess in any particular subject or area of human activity; it is characterised by the child's ability to learn in that area faster than its peer group. Talent is seen as the realisation of that giftedness; in effect, the performance of that giftedness.*
>
> *(Knowles, 2006, p.150)*

Essentially children in this category could be those who have advanced vocabularies or are able to reason. These children may master concepts, knowledge and skills at a quicker rate than their peers. These learners may disengage if the learning is not sufficiently challenging and they may be socially aloof. The term 'talented' is often used to describe children's abilities in sport, music or the visual/performing arts, while giftedness is often used to refer to ability in academic domains.

Children who are gifted and/or talented need access to:

- a differentiated and challenging curriculum;

- extension activities which advance learning;

- opportunities to think, problem solve, reason and evaluate (Bloom's taxonomy of thinking skills may help you to extend children's thinking skills further – see Chapter 4);

- opportunities to consider a range of perspectives/viewpoints;

- opportunities for learning through personal enquiry/research;

- a teacher with excellent subject knowledge who is capable of extending their learning within specific strands;

- regular assessments to identify their individual learning needs.

It is important that you abandon stereotypical views when identifying children who are gifted and talented. These learners may well come from working class backgrounds or socially deprived backgrounds. The Teachers' Standards (DfE, 2012) state that teachers must set high expectations which inspire, motivate and challenge pupils (TS1), and Ofsted inspectors are focusing on the level of challenge in lessons with particular attention on the level of challenge for the more able learners.

Research Focus

Porter's work (Porter, 1999) illustrates how children who are formally identified as gifted and talented are often punctual; attend school regularly; have parents who are interested in education; and behave. It is possible for a range of factors to mask a child's giftedness.

Children with English as an additional language, refugees and asylum seekers

During your course it is likely that you will work with children with English as an additional language (EAL). Children will need support to access the language across the curriculum and not just in English lessons. Environmental print should display children's first languages, so classroom labels, posters and displays need to include words using children's first languages as well as English. This will demonstrate that their first language is valued. First languages can be used during class greetings so that all children have opportunities to hear the language.

Encourage children to use both languages. Gardner (2006) recommends the use of dual language texts and the use of 'code switching' so that children can use both languages when writing if they struggle to write an English word. Teachers should celebrate the children's cultural backgrounds and use this as an opportunity to enrich their teaching.

You might wish to consider using the following strategies to support language development in these children:

- use of visual teaching strategies;
- use of tactile resources such as objects to represent words;
- use of puppets;
- use of bilingual support workers.

Instructions need to be precise and supported by visual stimuli as appropriate. Think carefully about how to develop partnerships with parents and carers and the use of family literacy programmes may be useful in helping to break down barriers. Letters and notes to parents and carers may also need to be translated.

Children with special educational needs and disabilities

Read the case study below.

- How did Sally help Sam to overcome any barriers to learning?
- In what ways did Sally minimise categorisation?
- What actions could have been undertaken by the head teacher in relation to Chris?
- How important are teacher attitudes in facilitating (or erecting barriers to) inclusion?

Case Study: Sam

Sam was a four-year-old child with Asperger syndrome or high functioning autism. In his previous school he had been labelled as a 'disruptive' child. Sam's parents decided that the case study school would be a better option for Sam, due to the fact that there was an autistic resource base on site and the mainstream teachers were experienced at including children like Sam in their classrooms. Sam's parents were keen that he was educated in mainstream provision, despite the fact that there was special provision for autistic children on the premises. Sam came to the school with 20 hours of support. He was immediately placed in the reception class (Sally's class) because of his age.

During Sam's first two days at the school he was accompanied by a member of staff from the Communication and Interaction Team from the Local Authority. His teacher commented that the member of staff:

→

… seemed to have 'textbook' strategies for dealing with autistic children. She insisted that he had a daily schedule, even though I thought that we should try him without one in the first instance. I was anxious not to make him feel different. She said that he had to be escorted to the toilet. She wanted him to go out to play before the others so that he was not distressed by being in a busy cloakroom. She said that he would need one-to-one support on the playground. She wasn't very happy because I said 'no' to all of her recommendations. These strategies would have isolated Sam and were not practical in a mainstream classroom and a mainstream school. There was simply no way that we could escort him everywhere and the bottom line was that his parents had chosen to send him to a mainstream school for a reason. They did not want us to operate a mini special school. She also wanted Sam to have one-to-one teaching which I am totally opposed to. I was glad when she left us alone. After a couple of days he settled brilliantly. He didn't need a schedule. He didn't need one-to-one supervision and he didn't need to be taught in a one-to-one situation. He coped with getting ready to play with the other children. He coped with our normal classroom routines. Sometimes I remember that he used to throw himself on the floor. This was often when he needed his own space. We used to withdraw him to give him the space he needed but not as a punishment. It allowed him to calm down. (Sally)

Sally was determined to avoid implementing strategies that would emphasise and draw attention to Sam's differences. Rather than using an individual schedule with Sam, Sally used a whole class visual timetable on a 'planning board' so that all the children could clearly see which areas of the classroom they were supposed to be working in. This also enabled all adults to identify where children were. Sally prepared Sam for changes in routine through pre-warning him. In addition she used social stories as an approach to talk him through new experiences in advance. Sally talked about his obsessions with books and computers:

I used them as a bargaining tool. If I wanted him to do a task I would tell him that he couldn't go in the book area or use the computers until he had done what I had asked him. It worked a treat! (Sally)

Sally recalled how Sam's mother was more relaxed about him being in mainstream provision than his father:

His father wanted us to watch him like a hawk. I told him that this was not necessary but he still wanted us to protect him more than the others. (Sally)

After a very successful year in Sally's class, Sam moved to another teacher (Chris). She explained that Chris operated a much more formal classroom and had very little patience for children who were not always able to behave in appropriate ways:

He had very low tolerance levels. He would shout at Sam all the time and Sam used to cry constantly. He used to send him out of class with his TA when he couldn't cope with him. Sam became a very distressed little boy. Chris just doesn't recognise that

→

children are not all the same and cannot be programmed to behave in the same ways. Children are not robots. I saw all my hard work going down the drain and it made me so angry. One day Sam was wailing and screaming because Chris had shouted at him. I was furious and so was Julie, the SENCO. Julie was deeply disturbed and she told Chris that it said more about him and his classroom ethos than it did about Sam. I asked the Head to move Sam to a teacher who would continue what I had started. The Head luckily agreed and within a matter of weeks, Sam's behaviour improved. (Sally)

This case study provides an example of successful inclusion. Barbara Cole's research with 'mother-teachers' (Cole, 2005) demonstrated that above all, the notion of being 'wanted' was an important factor in developing an inclusive ethos. For these parents, their overriding concern was that the teachers wanted their children. In the case study Sally clearly wanted to teach Sam but Chris was reluctant. Sam's case study illustrates that children with autism are capable of internalising negative teacher attitudes and this can affect their behaviour. In inclusive environments children need to feel that they are welcome in mainstream settings and have a right to be there. There is clearly a need for some practitioners to reflect on their own values in relation to the education of learners with special educational needs and until all teachers accept their shared responsibility for the education of all children, genuine inclusion will remain problematic.

Learning Outcomes Review

Thinking about the school in which you are working or recently worked, respond to the prompts after each intended learning outcome, to identify your knowledge and understanding of the issues covered in the chapter.

- **Definitions of inclusion and associated issues:**
  - How does the current focus on the attainment in the National Curriculum (DfE, 2013) exclude some learners?

- **Current over-arching policy agendas and legislation which regulate classroom practice:**
  - What is the significance of the Warnock Report and the Salamanca Statement in the movement towards inclusion?
  - Are you aware of school inspection frameworks? Researching the latest framework for school inspections will help you to understand what inspectors are looking for when they inspect schools. The current framework for school inspections can be found on the Ofsted website (www.ofsted.gov.uk).
  - How familiar are you with the Code of Practice (DfE, 2014)? What steps can you take to develop your understanding?

- **The characteristics of inclusive environments:**

  - What are the characteristics of inclusive environments? (reflect diversity and challenge discrimination and prejudice)
  - How can gender, class, race and sexual orientation be used as a resource for learning?

- **The principles of inclusion in the statutory inclusion statement and ways in which these can be addressed in the classroom:**

  - What are the statutory principles of inclusion within the National Curriculum?
  - What are the implications for you as a trainee teacher?

Further Reading

Billington, T. (2000) *Separating, Losing and Excluding Children: Narratives of difference.* London: Routledge Falmer.

Skidmore, D. (2004) *Inclusion: the dynamic of school development.* Maidenhead: Open University Press.

References

Ainscow, M. (2007) Taking an inclusive turn. *Journal of Research in Special Educational Needs* 7(1) pp.3–7.

Armstrong, D. (1998) Changing faces, changing places: policy routes to inclusion. In Clough, P. and Barton, L. (eds), *Managing Inclusive Education: From Policy to Experience.* London: Paul Chapman Publishing.

Armstrong, D. (2005) Reinventing 'inclusion': New Labour and the cultural politics of special education. *Oxford Review of Education* 31(1) pp.135–51.

Avramadis, E., Bayliss, P. and Burden, R. (2002) Inclusion in action: an in-depth case study of an effective inclusive secondary school in the south-west of England. *International Journal of Inclusive Education* 6(2) pp.143–63.

Barton, L. (ed.) (1998a) *The Politics of Special Educational Needs.* London: Falmer Press.

Barton, L. (1998b) Markets, managerialism and inclusive education. In Clough, P. and Barton, L. (eds) *Managing Inclusive Education: From policy to experience.* London: Paul Chapman Publishing.

Benjamin, S. (2002) *The Micropolitics of Inclusive Education.* Buckingham: Open University Press.

Cole, B. (2005) Good faith and effort? Perspectives on educational inclusion. *Disability and Society* 20(3) pp.331–44.

Corbett, J. (2001) Teaching approaches which support inclusive education: a connective pedagogy. *British Journal of Special Education* 28(2) pp.55–9.

Department for Education (DfE) (2011) *Support and Aspiration: A new approach to special educational needs and disability: a consultation.* London: DfE.

Department for Education (DfE) (2012) *Teachers' Standards: Guidance for School Leaders, School Staff and Governing Bodies.* London: DfE.

Department for Education (DfE) (2013) *The National Curriculum in England: Key Stages 1 and 2 Framework Document.* London: DfE.

Department for Education (DfE) (2014) *Special Educational Needs and Disability Code of Practice: 0 to 25 years: Statutory guidance for organisations who work with and support children and young people with special educational needs and disabilities.* London: DfE.

Department for Education and Science (DES) (1978) *Special Educational Needs: Report of the Committee of Enquiry into the Education of Handicapped Children and Young People* (The Warnock Report). London: HMSO.

Department for Education and Employment (DfEE) (1997) *Excellence in Schools.* London: DfEE.

Department for Education and Employment (DfEE) (1999) *The National Curriculum for England.* London: DfEE.

Department for Education and Skills (DfES) (2001) *Special Educational Needs Code of Practice.* Nottingham: DfES.

Department for Education and Skills (DfES) (2003) *Aiming High: Raising the attainment of Gypsy Traveller Children.* London: DfES.

Department for Education and Skills (DfES) (2004) *Removing Barriers to Achievement: The Government Strategy for SEN.* London: DfES.

Department for Education and Skills (DfES) (2006) *Primary Framework for Literacy and Mathematics.* Nottingham: DfES.

Department for Education and Skills (DfES) (2007) *The Early Years Foundation Stage: Setting the standards for learning, development and care for children from birth to five.* Nottingham: DfES.

Farrell, P. (2001) Special education in the last twenty years: have things really got better? *British Journal of Special Education* 28(1) pp.3–9.

Gardner, J. (2006) Children who have English as an additional language. In G. Knowles, Gifted and talented. In Knowles, G. (ed.) *Supporting Inclusive Practice.* London: David Fulton.

Giroux, H.A. (2003) Public pedagogy and the politics of resistance: notes on a critical theory of educational struggle. *Educational Philosophy and Theory* 35(1) pp.5–16.

Goodley, D. (2007) Towards socially just pedagogies: Deleuzoguattarian critical disability studies. *International Journal of Inclusive Education* 11(3) pp.317–34.

HMSO (2003) *Every Child Matters.* Norwich: The Stationery Office.

Knowles, G. (2006) Gifted and talented. In Knowles, G. (ed.) *Supporting Inclusive Practice.* London: David Fulton.

Lloyd, C. (2008) Removing barriers to achievement: a strategy for inclusion or exclusion? *International Journal of Inclusive Education* 12(2) pp.221–36.

Lloyd, G. and McCluskey, G. (2008) Education and Gypsies/Travellers: 'contradictions and significant silences'. *International Journal of Inclusive Education* 12(4) pp.331–45.

Porter, L. (1999) *Gifted Young Children: A Guide for Teachers and Parents.* Buckingham: Open University Press.

Sikes, P., Lawson, H. and Parker, M. (2007) Voices on: teachers and teaching assistants talk about inclusion. *International Journal of Inclusive Education* 11(3) pp.355–70.

Skrtic, T. (1991) *Behind Special Education: A critical analysis of professional culture and school organisation.* Denver: Love Publishing.

Tomlinson, S. (1982) *The Sociology of Special Education.* London: Routledge and Kegan Paul.

UNESCO (1994) *The UNESCO Salamanca Statement and Framework for Action on Special Needs Education.* Paris: UNESCO.

Warnock, M. (1996) The work of the Warnock Committee. In Mittler, P. and Sinason, V. (eds) *Changing Policy and Practice for People with Learning Difficulties.* London: Cassell.

Warnock, M. (2005) *Special Educational Needs: A new look.* Impact No. 11, Philosophy of Education Society of Great Britain.

6. Transitions and progression
Mary Briggs

Learning Outcomes

This chapter will introduce you to the topics of transitions and progression and what they mean for children, parents/carers, teachers and other adults working with children, schools and other settings. By the end of this chapter you will have:

- an understanding of the concepts of transitions and progression;
- an understanding of the relationship between transitions, continuity and progression;
- become aware of the need to plan for transitions in your teaching;
- an awareness of transitions as a continuous process rather than a one-off event and everyone involved needs time to adapt to new situation;
- an understanding that smooth transitions can ensure continuity and progression in children's learning.

TEACHERS' STANDARDS

A teacher must:

1. **Set high expectations which inspire, motivate and challenge pupils**
- establish a safe and stimulating environment for pupils, rooted in mutual respect
- set goals that stretch and challenge pupils of all backgrounds, abilities and dispositions
- demonstrate consistently the positive attitudes, values and behaviour which are expected of pupils.

2. **Promote good progress and outcomes by pupils**
- be accountable for pupils' attainment, progress and outcomes
- plan teaching to build on pupils' capabilities and prior knowledge
- guide pupils to reflect on the progress they have made and their emerging needs
- demonstrate knowledge and understanding of how pupils learn and how this impacts on teaching
- encourage pupils to take a responsible and conscientious attitude to their own work and study.

5. **Adapt teaching to respond to the strengths and needs of all pupils**
- have a secure understanding of how a range of factors can inhibit pupils' ability to learn, and how best to overcome these
- demonstrate an awareness of the physical, social and intellectual development of children, and know how to adapt teaching to support pupils' education at different stages of development

- have a clear understanding of the needs of all pupils, including those with special educational needs; those of high ability; those with English as an additional language; those with disabilities; and be able to use and evaluate distinctive teaching approaches to engage and support them.

8. Fulfil wider professional responsibilities

- make a positive contribution to the wider life and ethos of the school
- develop effective professional relationships with colleagues, knowing how and when to draw on advice and specialist support
- take responsibility for improving teaching through appropriate professional development, responding to advice and feedback from colleagues.

Introduction

Activity

Before starting to read this chapter think about the kinds of transitions that children experience. If possible discuss this with others on your training programme and/or school-based tutors/mentors or teachers.

Here are some of the ideas you may have thought about. It is not an exhaustive list but one just to get you started thinking about transitions:

- into play group/preschool/care outside the home;
- into school;
- between each Key Stage (KS1, Lower KS2 and Upper KS2);
- smaller transitions in relation to identity (e.g. arrival of brothers and sisters);
- between tasks;
- within settings/schools, e.g. for specific subjects within the curriculum or specific classes.

Defining transitions

Transitions are changes in the situation for children and those associated with them and can include the transition between home and a play group or preschool, or care outside the home particularly in the early years. We often just associate transitions with children's entry into formal school but there are other transitions for children. For example, there can be changes for children at home in relation to their position in the family when a new brother or sister arrives, which means children consider their role in the family, such as no longer being the baby and now a big sister or brother.

This section will begin to unpack some of the issues in relation to transitions in education between home and school, within school between key stages which may be in different buildings, within the class with transitions between tasks and groups, and between schools.

Research Focus

In her review of the literature related to transitions for children and young people Annmarie Turnball (2006) came up with the following list:

Starting nursery	Illness of family members	Changing friends
Starting primary school	Death of family members	Coming out as lesbian or gay
Starting secondary school	Separation from parents	Diagnosis of illness
Changing school	New siblings	Diagnosis of a disability
Moving house	Moving through year groups	Living with illness/disability
Puberty	Entering care	New step parents
First exams	First sexual experience	Living in a new country

(Turnball, 2006, p.2)

She describes how these transitions are 'potentially challenging episodes of change' which may be gradual or sudden and last for a short or longer period of time.

Transition between home and an educational setting

The first major transition that children and their families often experience is between home and an educational setting. This can be a source of stress and anxiety for all those involved partly as a result of not knowing what to expect. You may remember your first visit to a new school or more recently to university and the feelings you had about the event, which could help you begin to understand some of the anxieties around the situation. Any teacher working within this age range will want to establish a relationship with children and their families before the children start in the new setting. This can often involve home visits, with photographs being taken of the child at home (with permission) which are then used to identify drawers or pegs for the new child when they start attending the new setting.

Children or schools ready?

The NFER have carried out considerable research into the issue of transitions and particularly in relation to the school starting age in different countries. Caroline Sharp has been a key researcher of this early years issue. Over the years in the UK we have had varying policies for children starting school at different ages. At one point schools took children in three times a year, which meant that summer-born children always had less time in school before any assessments. This group have been seen as disadvantaged by their age. The following quotation from the conclusions of a presentation encourages us to consider the purpose of transitions and for whose benefit are all the activities associated with this area.

The challenge is to ensure that the system minimises inequalities due to relative age. We need to make schools ready for children, rather than focusing on making children ready for school.

(Sharp, 2009)

The case study of activities below is taken from a study in the USA by Kagan et al. (2010). This specific study is of 'Countdown to Kindergarten' in Boston, Massachusetts.

Case Study

The project is a non-profit collaborative effort of the City of Boston, Boston Public Schools (BPS), and more than two dozen public and community agencies. The programme engages families, educators and community members in a citywide effort to celebrate and support the transition into kindergarten, recognising it as a significant educational and developmental milestone for children and their families. The programme has developed a series of educational activities that create a continuum of services supporting families from birth through kindergarten entry. The aims of the project are to raise awareness within the community but particularly targeting parents/carers, of the importance and availability of kindergarten provision. This project wants parents and carers to know about:

- the kindergarten curriculum to ensure that families take advantage of the academic and social benefits kindergarten provides.

- the processes of choosing schools, registering, and entering kindergarten and that they are clear and welcoming to all families.

This project aims to lay the groundwork for primary caretakers to be active partners in their children's education in BPS elementary schools and beyond. They also coordinate and expand social and learning activities that help children transition from home or preschool into kindergarten. The kinds of activities that are offered are set out in a calendar of local events for children and families and include:

- an 'I'm Ready' DVD, Countdown to Kindergarten information sheets, registration guides and readiness activities;

→

- an 'I'm going to Kindergarten' T-shirt that allows children to access child-friendly community resources (e.g. museums) for free;

- School Preview Time: opportunities to visit schools and learn about how to choose and then register for school;

- School Welcome Sessions: opportunities for families to explore their newly assigned school and receive a 'Counting Down to Kindergarten' readiness guide;

- Neighbourhood Kindergarten Days: celebrations held at neighbourhood Boston Public Library branches for children and families entering kindergarten;

- Annual Kindergarten Celebration at the Boston Children's Museum: Boston's citywide celebration where children have the opportunity to meet teachers, sample typical kindergarten activities, climb on board a real school bus and receive free health screenings;

- a Countdown exhibit at the Boston Children's Museum;

- free Playgroups groups for families with children 1 to 3 years old.

Activity

After you have read the case study about early transitions in one US city, find out about the information and activities that are available for families in your area. Is there a children's centre where information and activities might take place?

Early Years Foundation Stage to Key Stage 1

This particular transition has become an international focus of attention for research with educationists concerned about providing the very best start for children as they enter school. This section looks at different approaches from a variety of countries.

Australia

Research carried out in Australia which was reviewed by Petriwskyj (2005) suggests that one of the major issues with the transitions at this point is around the conception of children's readiness for more formal learning and there are still tensions for teachers related to the academic expectations of the move from the Foundation Stage Curriculum to the National Curriculum and the overall approach taken. Peters (2000) found that teachers and parents viewed continuity between preschool and school as essential to successful transition into school, but that many saw increasing structure in preschool curriculum and pedagogy as providing this continuity.

Denmark

In Denmark, Broström (2000) describes the need to make the child feel 'suitable, that is to have a feeling of well being and belonging'. The argument for this is that research on starting school shows that children who feel suitable, relaxed and well adjusted in kindergarten are much more likely to experience success in school than children who do not feel well adjusted at the beginning (Margetts, 2006). In many ways this might appear to be common sense but as a trainee teacher you will need to be aware of the feelings of the children and parents as well as being versed in the routines and practices.

Whose perspective?

There can be a tendency to consider this very important transition purely from the adults' perspective, concentrating on what parents/carers and teachers need to know, and this has been a focus of much of the research. This is rather than focusing on what children may need and want to know. From Margett's (2006) work in Australia, asking children what they thought children needed or wanted to know about starting school, the following themes emerged: peer relationships; school rules; general procedures; classrooms; academic skills; and feelings.

It is not just the classroom and potential changes in practice that the children must learn to adapt to; negotiating the playground environment can be very daunting for the youngest children in school. Although they often have a separate space outside from the rest of the school, this is still a place to learn new things. These include learning about being friends, dealing with unfriendly behaviour and aggressive behaviour, fighting or quarrelling, sharing, turn-taking, being comforted, being lonely and telling a secret (Smith, 2003). Part of the role of being a teacher is to establish a purposeful and safe learning environment conducive to learning and identify opportunities for learners to learn in out-of-school contexts, which includes considering the playground and play times.

In *Excellence and Enjoyment: A Strategy for Primary Schools* (DfES, 2003) the government set out its intention to ensure continuity between the areas of learning in the Foundation Stage and the Key Stage 1 programmes of study. It also made a commitment to gaining a better understanding of whether there were still difficulties around transition and whether teachers need more support. Two major studies published by the DfES and Ofsted examined the transition from Reception to Year 1. Saunders et al. (2005) found that schools had adopted a variety of strategies aimed at smoothing transition. These tended to focus on three areas: induction of children into Year 1; continuity of practice between Reception and Year 1; and communication between staff, parents and children. The study found that: 'the best transitions for children take place where conditions are similar, communication is encouraged, and the process of change takes place gradually over time' (Sanders et al., 2005).

The other study was carried out by Ofsted (2004) and this found that there was an imbalance in the curriculum with a much stronger emphasis on numeracy and literacy than other areas of the curriculum. Since this study was published the curriculum balance has been reconsidered for the whole of the primary age range with a greater focus on creativity across the curriculum. Although from a professional perspective learning is very important in the dialogue between parents/carers and school, the key issue is the emotional wellbeing of the children from the parental perspective as indicated in the following quote from the report.

> *... a means of keeping in touch, not only with reading but other issues affecting their children. One father commented about his daughter: 'I want to know is she is settling in well and is beginning to start to read and write a bit as well as recognising numbers. But above all, I want to know if she is happy.'*

(Ofsted, 2004, p.16)

Activity

Discuss with your school-based tutor or mentor the school's approach to the transitions and the issues discussed between the staff at both ends of the transition. What do you notice about the tensions they experience? How do they support children and parents during this period? Do they have a specific programme of events for the children and their parents? Does this happen at specific times of the year or is this a continuous process?

Research Focus

One important aspect of transitions is how children feel about the changes to come, and this was a focus of research at the National Foundation for Educational Research (NFER) by Caroline Sharp and Gabrielle White in their 2005 paper 'How children make sense of the transition to Year 1'.

When asked about what they anticipated Year 1 would be like these are typical answers which illustrate how they are thinking about the changes to come:

Girl: *We will do all writing and stuff ... They don't have any toys, only some, not lots ...*

Boy: *When you go in Year 1 you get older so you will have to do harder work.*

Where children had visited the Year 1 classes previously they appeared to have a clearer idea of what to expect.

Girl: *I already know because I have been there because we had 'change over classes'.*

→

Sharp and White followed the children to ask them about what they noticed after the transition.

In Reception we used to dress up and we could play on the carpet with the dressing-up stuff. We can play in Year 1, but not lots of times any more.

You only go outside at playtime and lunchtime. They don't have any toys outside though.

Every time we do [work] sheets there is always a more difficult sheet to go on to next, and you can't go and play when you finish your work because there is always another sheet.

These comments illustrate a key and current approach in educational research that is including 'pupil's voice' in their work. This changes the focus of the research from looking at events or activities undertaken here as part of the transition to exploring the children's views of the process and their thoughts about the changes to come. 'Pupil voice' comes from a growing recognition that children and young people are not simply citizens of the future, but are capable persons willing and able to be involved in their communities and schools and perhaps above all as a teacher we can learn from children's views about improving the learning process. You can read more about pupil voice in Chapter 7.

Sharp and White's research demonstrated there was a clear distinction between the Early Years Foundation Stage and Key Stage 1 practice.

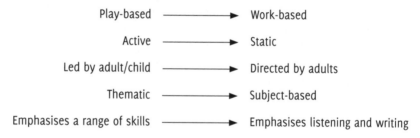

Play-based   ⟶   Work-based

Active   ⟶   Static

Led by adult/child   ⟶   Directed by adults

Thematic   ⟶   Subject-based

Emphasises a range of skills   ⟶   Emphasises listening and writing

Their conclusions were:

- most children coped well with the move to Year 1;

- school transition strategies were important;

- growing up brought new challenges and harder work;

- curriculum and pedagogy had a clear impact on children's enjoyment of learning.

As the issues identified in the research above have been a focus of continuous professional development and review in many schools, it would be worth exploring how much practices have changed since this research was undertaken.

The short case study below is drawn from information available on Teachers' TV and focuses on the transition between the children's centre just down the road and the primary school. Clapham Manor Primary School in London looked closely at the issues in relation

to transitions and some of their work can be seen on Teachers' TV (https://www.tes.co.uk/
teaching-resource/teachers-tv-building-on-learning-6043319). When reading this case study
consider what you have learnt about the school's approach to transitions and how this might
compare to your experiences so far.

Case Study: One school's approach

The staff reviewed the results of children's learning for end of Key Stage 1 and saw that they were
not as high as end of Key Stage 2. They drew the conclusion that they needed to improve on their
transition periods at Clapham Manor Primary School and Children's Centre in London. They identified relationships with parents as playing a key part during the transitional periods, especially in
the children's move from the nursery to reception. They developed a transitions policy for the
school that sees transition as a continuous process rather than a one-off event. This resulted in
more activities across the phases of the school and an acknowledgement that for some children
an individual transition plan was needed to further support the process and ensure progression
of children's learning. One unique aspect of the school is their use of learning partners, with each
class in the school linked with a class of older children, visits take place between the classes,
helping to establish friendships and mentoring. Staff and learning partners from the school visit
the nursery to make themselves familiar to the children and this goes on throughout the year
with longer visits each time. The children also keep a celebration book to highlight their achievements up to Year 1. All these activities have helped them to establish smooth transitions between
the nursery and school. One result of the review of transitions has resulted in staff development
and changes in practice in Year 1 to support the movement of children into Key Stage 1.

Activity

If possible, when you are on placement, observe in a Reception class and a Year
1 class during the morning sessions, as this is when you may see differences in
approach. Although you may find more similarities depending upon the school
philosophy and the teaching staff involved, what do you notice about the similarities
and differences in practice? You may also be able to talk to your school-based tutor/
mentor about the changes that may have occurred since this research was completed
and what the teachers, parents/carers and children think about the changes made.

Smooth transitions

Smooth transitions are essential for children to experience continuity and minimal disruption
to their learning and security. The recommendations from Sanders et al. (2005) for the
transition between the Foundation stage and Year 1 are:

- more play-based learning in Year 1;
- maintenance of friendship groups;
- good communication between staff and parents.

The key features of good transitions are around consistency.

- Consistency is important to and identifiable in young children (e.g. schemas).
- Effective educational provision needs consistency:
  - adults;
  - routines and information;
  - experiences and materials.
- Consistency enables children to be active and independent learners.

Transitions for individuals in the class

At a micro level there are a number of transitions for children within the classroom throughout the day and as the teacher you need to consider these when planning your lessons, activities and the use of resources.

Transitions between different phases of a lesson and location in the class

This can be a difficult activity for trainee teachers as some children can find it difficult to make transitions between activities or use this as the opportunity to behave inappropriately. Part of planning for the transitions often involves movement between activities and there is a need for quiet before instructions can be given to facilitate the movement. Trainee teachers have talked about the use of something like a rain stick to shake, making a relatively quiet noise to gain the class's attention, or children repeating a clapping pattern started by the teacher. You can read further strategies for managing behaviour in Chapter 15. These techniques help with transitions during teaching times and at the end of lessons.

Activity
Either through observation, or by reflecting on a previous experience in school, make notes about the following transitions and how teachers handle them.

- Entry to the classroom.
- Exiting the classroom.

- From carpet to table activities.
- Break and lunch times.
- Moving to assembly.
- Moving from the class to the hall or outside for PE/games.

Do teachers employ different techniques for different occasions, or do they have one method that they stick to? Do they use the transitions as a teaching activity, e.g. asking children to identify if they have lace up shoes or answer a spelling or a mental calculation in order to be able to leave the class?

Transitions between groups within the class

Sometimes you find that children are in different groups for different areas of the curriculum, particularly if grouping is based on attainment, so you may find that groups have names to distinguish them apart. There can be routines established in the class that assist the transitions between different groupings, which can involve the collection of books and the handing out of a different set, sometimes by 'book monitors'. With groups like guided reading groups this could include children collecting their copies of the book the group is working on.

Relationship between transitions, progression and guided group work

Children can be grouped in a number of different ways to ensure progress in their learning. *Progression* is seen in this book as the moving through the phases of education. It is often explicitly linked with continuity of experiences and learning. It can also be seen as progression in learning though this is more closely related to assessment and will be addressed in Chapter 13. It is also essential that you understand how *continuity* (how academic and pastoral arrangements are made in a way which ensures progression), is taken into account when planning provision for them. Guided group work can be one way of organising children for teaching purposes. Guided work is continued focused teaching designed to support children's learning. It can be used to move learning forward, to extend and challenge all learners, or to focus on a particular concept, skill or strategy that needs developing; or to develop the children's language and communication skills in order to express their ideas and build up their confidence. Guided group work can provide opportunities for:

- focused teaching, structured to address the shared needs of the group, identified by ongoing and periodic assessments;

- teaching core routines for tasks/games;

- interactive teaching and scaffolding;

- planned talk – opportunity for sustained discussion;

- assessing learning – to diagnose and address barriers to progress.

These are all part of the teacher's role in ensuring continuity and progression for all learners. One reason for discussing this under transitions is that children need to understand why they are being grouped in particular ways in the classroom and how they might use the learning that takes place in these guided groups in the usual teaching groups that might occur in the class. Teachers play a crucial role in helping children to make the transition between different groups in the class.

Activity

List the particular features of guided group work, and how this is different to self-facilitated work. Consider how guided group work would assist you to ensure pupils progress in their learning.

Transitions for setting within year groups or across years within the school

We don't always associate transitions from class to class with primary education but tend to think about this as a secondary school issue. However, many schools set within year groups or across years for English and mathematics and as a consequence children must move between classes, mostly in the mornings when these subjects are taught. This may be something you encounter when in schools on placement. If this is the case, think carefully about how they manage the transitions. For example:

- How much time is allowed for the transfer of children from class to class?

- How does the class teacher know about the children in their class's progression in learning if some are taught either or both subjects by another teacher?

- How can they build on the learning in those subjects when teaching the rest of the curriculum?

Transitions for groups between classes

This can be particularly important for children who attend intervention sessions within the school day or other special educational needs support groups. Transitions can also apply to children who take music lessons where they are out of a specific lesson and may miss explanations. When children return to the class, and make the transition into the class lesson, they will need guidance and support to take part in the learning. As the teacher you will need to ensure that their learning progresses in the same way as the rest of the class.

Think about how individual differences are taken account of in planning the timing of such sessions. What will you do about any work that is missed? It may be useful to talk to some of the children involved and ask about their feelings with regard to the transitions they need to make and what makes it easier or harder for them returning to the class. You can then use this information to help you plan your own actions for individuals/groups where this occurs.

Transitions between classes at the end of the school year

Most primary age children change classes at the end of the academic year, though you may find yourself in a school where there are classed of mixed ages. The short case study below, based in a primary school in the Midlands, details the kinds of activities that go on before, during and after transitions between classes in a primary school each academic year.

Case Study: Planning and preparing for transition and progression

Much of what happens appears to be behind the scenes. Teachers meet to look at the numbers of children within a particular year group and this can often make the difference between having a single year class or a mixed year class. For mixed year classes the discussion involves how the mix is to be decided. If it is just one or two classes that are mixed the decision can often be on age alone as this can be the easiest way to explain why some children may appear to have 'moved up' while others 'stayed down'. If there is more than one class in a year group the discussion can be about the grouping of children to allow all children to learn and maybe to separate those who don't always work well together. This discussion can also be influenced by the strengths and interests of the teachers who will teach the classes. Once the make-up of the classes is decided then parents and children are usually informed (a few weeks before the end of the term). Visits usually take place on the same day that the Year 6 visit their secondary schools, so all teachers can receive the next year's group. This can also be a time that NQTs are invited to meet their classes before taking up their appointments in the new academic year. Teachers can then receive internal records for the class they are going to teach to ensure continuity and progression in the children's learning.

Transition and progression to secondary school

Moving to secondary school is a challenging time for children. Children have a variety of concerns but those raised most often include concerns about bullying, queries about school uniforms, queries about discipline or queries about new subjects (Powell et al., 2006). A key to effective transition and progression from primary to secondary is the flow of information, and the following research highlights a number of specific issues in relation to ensuring that the information get to the right people involved in the process.

Research Focus: From primary school to secondary school

Powell et al.'s (2006) research focused on practice in Wales but many of the issues are the same for England. All the secondary schools organised parents' evenings to introduce the school to parents of Year 6 children, although the frequency and timing varied.

Powell et al. identified a number of activities that supported good liaison and therefore transition for children between primary and secondary schools:

- termly meetings between primary school head teachers and staff;

- meetings between primary school curriculum area leaders and the relevant staff in the secondary school;

- links between secondary learning support staff and the primary schools;

- pastoral links;

- more extra-curricular activities, for example sports and music. (Powell et al., 2006, p.38)

A key issue is the progression and continuity of learning between KS2 and KS3 and in this study of practice cooperating to develop schemes of work for the primary schools or to bridge the KS2/KS3 transition was seen as effective in maintaining the learning across the change of school.

It is worth considering the different perspectives of those involved in the transition process at this stage of a child's life. The information that parents/carers want can be different from that needed by their children. Secondary schools often provided parents the following kinds of information:

- a general introduction to the school, its staff and the National Curriculum;

- the school's results at GCSE and A level (where appropriate);

- registration procedures, including where to go at the start of the first day;

- information about the number of lessons each day;

- details of what equipment the children would require;

- lunchtime arrangements;

- what is needed in terms of school uniform and where it can be purchased.

Transitions to ensure progression in learning

In order to ensure that there is continuity and progression in children's learning between schools, information about prior learning across the curriculum and in and outside school needs to be passed between the schools. This would help you understand the requirements for Q6 related to collaboration. Typically the kinds of information on pupil attainment supplied by primary to secondary schools are:

- national KS2 test marks;

- teacher assessments for a range of subjects not just the core curriculum;

- reading ages and other information for children with SEN;

- teacher comments, which may include particular strengths or areas of concern.

In addition to data about academic subjects and attainment, schools find other information helpful in settling children into a new school and making decisions about form tutors or pastoral groupings as well as any early subject setting. The type of information passed on to secondary schools can include:

- information about children's strengths and weaknesses;

- attendance;

- extra-curricular activities;

- friends;

- language used at home;

- religious affiliation if appropriate;

- health;

- behaviour;

- potential for sport;

- musical or performing talents.

Activity

When you are in a primary or junior school, find out which Year 6 teacher is responsible for transfer liaison with the secondary schools. Find out what kinds of information is transferred between schools. How are the children supported in their transition to secondary school?

For certain groups of children transitions can be more problematic and this was highlighted by Robinson and Martin (2008). They reviewed the experience of Traveller and Roma communities, where at age 11 school and parental expectations and desires may come into conflict. The importance of specific outreach work was indicated as being the best way to work with these particular communities. Chapter 5 explores issues related to supporting all learners further.

Research Focus: The Strengthening Transfers and Transitions project (DCSF, 2008)

Seven local authorities selected families of schools to engage in action research to explore what strengthens transfers and transitions. The action research projects clearly identified seven key principles that underpin effective transfers and transitions for progress.

- Assessment for Learning (AfL) principles underpin progress across transfers and transitions.

- Transfers and transitions are key drivers in raising standards.

- Children need confidence, understanding and skills to advance their own progress across transfer or transition.

- Partnership working is essential for effective transfers and transitions for progress.

- Effective partnerships are built on a common vision, shared responsibility and trust.

- Partnership working requires mutual understanding through shared experiences and a common language.

- Sustained collaboration requires systems and structures that support formal and ongoing links between partners.

The following elements emerged in a number of the schools' projects as having particular leverage.

- Head teacher/SLT involvement. The crucial element here is a 'leader' with the status to give importance to transfers and transitions, but additionally able to align it with wider school improvement priorities.

- Ongoing collaboration before and after transfer in the context of both key stages.

- This has not been one key stage 'doing' transfer to the other, but an equal partnership that has professionally developed all stakeholders.

- Cross-phase network meetings whose agenda and discussions have focused on professional dialogue about teaching and learning within the contexts of transfers and transitions, and not about the cohort or individual children that are involved.

$\longrightarrow$

- The development of children's skills through a part- or full-time competency-based curriculum designed to build on prior learning and to facilitate successful movement to the following year/key stage.

- Building capacity and sustainability for ongoing improvement by involving children and parents in the monitoring, reviewing and planning process and strategically sharing effective practice through a planned process, both within an LA and a school.

Learning Outcomes Review

Thinking about the school in which you are currently placed, or in which you most recently undertook a placement, respond to the questions which follow each of the intended learning outcomes, as a means of identifying your knowledge and understanding of the issues covered in the chapter.

- **An understanding of the concepts of transitions and progression, and the relationship between transitions, continuity and progression:**
    - What do the terms transition, continuity and progress mean?
    - What transitions have the children in your class experienced?
    - Which of these are in school and which are out of school?
    - What features of the school's organisation and day-to-day operation provide children continuity with experience and ensure progression in children's learning?
    - What structures are in place in the class to ensure that there is progression of children's learning with each transition? How do you do this, and how effective is it?
    - What features or structures support continuity of learning in school?

- **Become aware of the need to plan for transitions in your teaching:**

Identify examples of planning for transition during your placement when:

    - you have planned lessons;
    - you altered your teaching strategies to ensure effective transitions as you were teaching;
    - you evaluated your lessons with a focus on transitions;
    - you have discussed transitions with your school-based tutor/mentor/class teacher when moving children around the school;
    - you assessed your learners to form guided groups for specific topics to ensure progression in learning.

- **An awareness of transitions as a continuous process rather than a one-off event and everyone involved needs time to adapt to new situation:**

    - What activities have you seen individuals or classes experience that supported an ongoing process of transitions across the school?

> – Identify ways of working/ideas for development that you want to develop to support transitions throughout your practice.
>
> • **An understanding that smooth transitions can ensure continuity and progression in children's learning:**
>
>   – In what ways have you seen individuals or classes experience activities that supported a smooth transition?
>   – Identify ways of working/ideas for development that you want to develop to support transitions in your practice.

Further Reading

Further issues associated with continuity and progression will be addressed in the assessment chapter of this book.

DCSF (2008) *Strengthening Transfers and Transitions: Partnerships for progress.* London: DCSF.

DfES (2006) *Seamless Transitions: Supporting continuity in young children's learning.* Norwich: DfES. This is a support pack including DVD for schools and early years settings.

Underwood, L. and Ward, L. (2004) *Staveley and Brimington Learning Community Community Transition Package* (http://www.ttrb.ac.uk/attachments/d34fa91d-6861-40a7-a620-b8a521445647.pdf). This is a package of ideas for teachers to use as part of the transition process at different stages.

References

Broström, S. (2000) Communication and continuity in the transition from kindergarten to school in Denmark. Paper related to poster symposium on 'transition' at EECERA Annual Conference, University of London, 29 August to 1 September.

DCSF (2008) *Strengthening Transfers and Transitions: Partnerships for progress.* London: DCSF.

DfE (2011) *Teachers' Standards.* Available from www.education.gov.uk/publications

DfES (2003) *Excellence and Enjoyment: A strategy for primary schools.* Nottingham: DfES.

Kagan, S.L., Karnati, R., Friedlander, J. and Tarrant, K. (2010) *Compendium of Transition Initiatives in the Early Years: A resource guide to alignment and continuity efforts in the United States and other countries.* Columbia: National Center for Children and Families/Teachers College.

Margetts, K. (2006) 'Teachers should explain what they mean': what new children need to know about starting school. Summary of paper presented at EECERA Annual Conference, Reykjavik, Iceland, 30 August–2 September.

Ofsted (2004) *Transition from the Reception Year to Year 1: An evaluation by HMI.* HMI 2221. London: Ofsted.

Peters, S. (2000) Multiple perspectives on continuity in early learning and the transition to school. Paper presented at EECERA Annual Conference, University of London, 29 August to 1 September.

Petriwskyj, A. (2005) Transitions to school: early years teachers' role. *Journal of Australian Research in Early Childhood Education* 12(2) pp.39–49.

Powell, R., Smith, R., Jones, G. and Reakes, A. (2006) *Transition from Primary to Secondary School: Current arrangements and good practice in Wales.* Final Report. Slough: NFER.

Robinson, M. and Martin, K. (2008) *Approaches to Working with Children, Young People and Families for Traveller, Irish Traveller, Gypsy, Roma and Show People Communities: A literature review.* Leeds: CWDC.

Sanders, D., White, G., Burge, B., Sharp, C., Eames, A., McCune, R. and Grayson, H. (2005) *A Study of the Transition from the Foundation Stage to Key Stage 1.* Nottingham: DfES.

Sharp, C. (2009) International research and policy on season of birth. Westminster Education Forum on the Future of the Primary Curriculum, 22 June.

Sharp, C. and White, G. (2005) How children make sense of the transition to Year 1. Paper presented at EECERA Annual Conference, Dublin, 31 August–3 September.

Smith, N. (2003) Transition from nursery to school playground: an intervention programme to promote emotional and social development. Paper presented at EECERA Annual Conference, Glasgow, 3–6 September (http:extranet.edfac.unimelb.edu.au/LED/tec/).

Turnball, A. (2006) *Children's Transitions: A literature review.* Cambridge: Cambridgeshire's Children's Fund.

7. Children's voice
David Morris

- reflect systematically on the effectiveness of lessons and approaches to teaching
- contribute to the design and provision of an engaging curriculum.

5. **Adapt teaching to respond to the strengths and needs of all pupils**
- have a secure understanding of how a range of factors can inhibit pupils' ability to learn, and how best to overcome these
- demonstrate an awareness of the physical, social and intellectual development of children, and know how to adapt teaching to support pupils' education at different stages of development.

7. **Manage behaviour effectively to ensure a good and safe learning environment**
- manage classes effectively, using approaches which are appropriate to pupils' needs in order to involve and motivate them
- maintain good relationships with pupils, exercise appropriate authority, and act decisively when necessary.

A note on terminology

In this chapter the terms 'children's voice', 'student voice', 'pupil voice' and 'pupil participation' can be considered to be interchangeable, although the term chosen in any given context may vary. For example, discussion about School Council may invite the term student voice more readily, whereas examples of listening to children and children being heard in the classroom may better be described as children's voice.

The United Nations Convention on the Rights of the Child

The evolution of children's voice has moved on a long way since the Victorian adage that 'children should be seen and not heard', an expression that we know today but the origins of which actually date back to the fifteenth century. You can read in Chapter 1 about how the Education Reform Act (1944) did a great deal to shape the model of the education system we have in the UK today, but perhaps the most recent development of significance in terms of children being heard appears in the form of the United Nations Convention on the Rights of the Child (UNCRC) (UNICEF, 1989). As a teacher, this is an important piece of global legislation that you will need to become familiar with, if you are not already. A copy of the full charter can be found at http://www.unicef.org.uk/Documents/Publication-pdfs/UNCRC_PRESS200910web.pdf and there is a child-friendly version available at http://www.unicef.org/rightsite/files/uncrcchilldfriendlylanguage.pdf.

In summary – and in plain English – the main articles in the UNCRC which relate to this chapter on children's voice are:

- **Article 3:** The right for adults to act in the best interests of children when making decisions which affect them.

- **Article 12:** The right for children's voices to be heard, listened to and taken seriously.

- **Article 13:** The right for children to voice their opinions and share what they think with others.

Activity: Reflecting on the UN Convention

Study and read carefully the articles in the UN Convention – in doing so you may wish to read both versions of the Convention above in tandem. Considering the school and class where you are teaching, carry out an initial audit of how the Convention impacts on your day-to-day teaching. Consider in particular:

- the age of the children you are working with – and how the Convention can be made relevant to them – and how they may need to engage with it;
- the curriculum and daily routines already established in your classroom;
- the implications of the Convention in relation to the wider policies and practices in your workplace;
- being able to provide concrete examples of how you see the Convention being observed and adhered to in your setting.

This information gathering process and analysis may involve discussions with other members of staff in school.

Research Focus: A pedagogical overview of student voice

Forty years ago, and well over a decade before the UN Convention was launched, Lawrence Stenhouse – a prominent British educationalist of the last century – claimed that pupils would do better at school if they were treated 'with respect as learners … and (their) ideas listened to and taken seriously' (Stenhouse, 1975, p.32). Rudduck and Fielding (2006), in their account of the antecedents of the student voice movement, refer to the fact that in the 1970s, while researchers were interested in students' perspectives, there was little commitment on the part of the schools they were working in to actually promote student voice. Henry Giroux – also an eminent critical pedagogue of our time – has considered student voice to play a particularly important role in schools. Not just in terms of the process of student voice being emancipatory for children, but more as a means for them to question, challenge and become involved with decision-making processes in schools.

→

An important final, if not obvious point to consider here, is that 'students make up around 95 per cent of a school's population ... [and] are often bright vibrant people who have much to offer' (Roberts and Nash, 2009, p.174), which supports Soo Hoo's (1993) pertinent notion that through our children and their voices, we need to value and recognise the treasure that they bring to our own back yard.

Defining voice

Student voice can appear in many different forms in schools, but broadly speaking it can be defined as any process of consulting with children and inviting them to enter a dialogue with each other, their teachers or other school staff. This dialogue may concern teaching or learning or wider school issues within the context of policy and practice. Such dialogues may result in situations where pupils are consulted about making changes or improvements in school, for example as being part of School Council. However, it is important to recognise that student voice is more than this, and among other things it should be about facilitating children to take ownership of their environment and become leaders themselves.

How student voice operates in schools

The ways in which student voice initiatives may manifest themselves in schools is almost entirely down to the ways in which the head teacher and senior management team or school leadership team give weight to their importance. This may be determined by the many factors that concern the school's population, the socio-economic demographics and any other idiosyncrasies which could include:

- the breadth, number and dominance of community languages spoken;
- the percentage of children in Key Stage 2 eligible for free school dinners;
- the percentage of children with special educational needs or disabilities (SEND);
- the ergonomics of the school site including access and resources;
- any wider social, environmental or demographic issues unique to the setting.

You may well find that in the schools where you work or undertake training there are existing systems, policies or practices in place. These may depend upon the age of the children and may vary between different key stages. For example, the ways in which children's voices are heard, valued or recognised in a nursery setting may well manifest themselves differently in a Year 6 classroom. Having said this, if your practice spans more than one key stage, you may well be able to establish some common patterns or trends. For example:

- inviting children to assess how well they felt they have learned something in a lesson;
- situations where children assess each other's work;

- situations where children give class presentations or perform assemblies to the whole school;

- how they feel about themselves within the context of their formal learning, social setting or their interaction with their peers;

- what they think about their school and the provision, education or facilities it provides.

Most schools operate a School Council which includes pupil members, and you may find some schools have a student voice or student participant policy. These determine the systems and procedures for allowing children to be heard in school and will be looked at in turn later in this chapter.

Activity: Listening to children's voices in the classroom

Observe the different ways in which children are given opportunities to talk or express themselves in the classroom:

- individually;
- with a partner;
- within a group.

Note in particular how this may vary depending upon the subject or situation. Consider how these opportunities may benefit pupils' learning, understanding or emotional wellbeing.

The different types of voice

Dialogic teaching

The concept of 'dialogic teaching' was developed by Professor Robin Alexander (a widely published and respected educationalist) at the beginning of this century. His principal belief is the importance of pupil dialogue or classroom talk being crucial to developing and extending pupils' understanding and learning. He believes that it also enables and affords teachers assessment opportunities whereby they can be more precise and diagnostic about identifying children's learning needs and therefore assist in monitoring and tracking their progress.

You will note how you and other teachers engage the pupils in being asked and answering questions as well as informal dialogues taking place between children and their teacher. This may involve closed questions, which require 'yes' and 'no' type responses, or open questions which invite opinion or justification; but dialogic teaching amounts to much more than this. The framework Alexander (2014) proposes requires:

- **interactions** which encourage students to think, and to think in different ways;

- **questions** which invite much more than simple recall;

- **answers** which are justified, followed up and built upon rather than merely received;
- **feedback** which informs and leads thinking forward as well as encourages;
- **contributions** which are extended rather than fragmented;
- **exchanges** which chain together into coherent and deepening lines of enquiry;
- **discussion and argumentation** which probe and challenge rather than unquestioningly accept;
- **professional engagement with subject matter** which liberates classroom discourse from the safe and conventional;
- **classroom organisation, climate and relationships** which make all this possible.

To sum up the process of dialogic teaching, it is a collective and reciprocal process whereby the children and teacher share ideas with each other and entertain a range of viewpoints. It is also a cumulative process of building upon ideas as well as promoting a supportive environment where ideas are expressed freely without fear of providing a 'wrong' answer. Finally, dialogic teaching needs to be purposeful whereby the teacher considers the desired educational goals and outcomes and then plans and steers classroom talk to achieve these.

Everyday voice in the classroom

There are many different ways in which you will see examples of children's voice taking place in the classroom. The principal or most obvious example you may notice will be children responding to questions posed by yourself or the teacher. Although it is tempting to choose the child who you know will know the answer, you need to be mindful of equality of opportunity in ensuring that all children's voices are heard. This can be challenging when you are working with the whole class to know who has had a chance to speak and who hasn't. Some teachers use a system of lollipop sticks as a way of monitoring this. Each stick has a child's name on it and all the sticks are kept in a pot or container. When directing questions the teacher takes a stick from the pot and invites that child to respond. Removing a stick in this way each time ensures every member of the class gets the opportunity to speak. It also focuses the children as they won't know whether it will be them who will be chosen. Another way of achieving this is by planning who you will invite to respond in advance. This can be achieved by using a class list not just to monitor who has or hasn't spoken but also to help you direct different questions to different children.

Talk partners

During whole class activities such as introductions to lessons, teachers generally do the majority of talking. One way of overcoming this imbalance is by employing 'talk partners'. This is a system where the teacher considers the dynamics in the classroom and uses this to inform the pairing of the children. However, there are no hard and fast rules about pairing and this can be random. When they are on the carpet they sit next to their partner. The teacher then presents the children with a question or topic for discussion. For example, this might be talk about what they already know about a topic, a concept or process in maths, characters or events in stories, or how they feel or think about something. The teacher usually gives the children a time reminder of how long they have to talk to each other and then they are invited to share their responses with the rest of the class.

Talk partners is beneficial in several ways:

- It allows them to think through talking.
- All children get the chance to talk.
- It provides a supportive climate for them to develop ideas.
- It provides opportunities for them to learn from one another.
- It allows less confident children the chance to talk in a safe environment.
- It helps them develop and process their thoughts before presenting their ideas to the class.

Finally, another benefit of talk partners is that pairings can be changed, which allows children to talk to other children they might not usually get the chance to work with and in this sense can help build better class dynamics as well as enriching learning.

ICT and voice

Another useful vehicle for promoting children's voices in the classroom is the use of information and communications technology (ICT). One of the most beneficial aspects is that ICT is multi-sensory and can engage pupils in different ways (see Chapter 4 for more on learning styles) including tactile experiences. It is also a motivational tool which most children enjoy using. If children work collaboratively in small groups it also allows them to develop talk based around learning. Below are some examples of how this may look in the classroom:

- Children could work together to program a Bee-Bot or other floor robot to follow a particular route or carry out a task.
- Children could work together to create a podcast. This can take many forms. It could be a news bulletin, a report, a story or play, an interview, a radio station or an informative account about what they have learned in a particular subject area.
- Children could alternatively create a video for some of the above or could work collaboratively to create a narrated movie using stop-go animation.
- Children could use a voice recorder to carry out interviews or record a poem or other piece of work they have written or express their views on a particular topic.

ICT can also be used in other ways for children to express their 'voice' but without them physically having to speak. This could be useful for children who find it challenging to express themselves orally.

For example, they could share their opinions or thoughts through a blog, through writing a story using an online story builder such as Story Bird, or express themselves through writing music using software such as 2Simple's Music Toolkit (2Simple, no date) or GarageBand (Apple Inc., 2005).

Activity: Using ICT as a vehicle to promote children's voices

Depending upon the resource setting in your school, use one of the ideas above, or one of your own, to plan a lesson or sequence of lessons linked to the scheme of work you are using in your school. Focusing on a small group of children in the class produce a reflective piece of writing that focuses on:

- how the use of ICT generated talk related to learning;
- how the ICT generated social talk related to communicating and working as a team.

Also consider:

- whether any quieter or less confident children benefited from the activities and if so in what ways;
- whether any children dominated the talk and if so the strategies you used to ensure parity of dialogue and involvement;
- whether there were any opportunities as a result of the activity for the children to present their work to a wider audience.

Circle time

Circle time is a concept that was developed by educational consultant Jenny Mosley back in the late 1990s. It involves the whole class sitting in a circle, including the teacher. An object is passed round the circle and the rule is that only the person who holds the object can speak. If a member of the circle does not want say anything, there is no pressure for them to contribute and the object can be passed on.

The main purpose of circle time is to:

- provide a supportive environment for children to build confidence and self-esteem;
- build positive relationships and develop social skills;
- assist in developing speaking and listening skills.

Although Personal, Social, Health and Economic education is not a statutory subject in the 2014 National Curriculum, circle time can be a useful strategy for you to develop teaching and learning in this area, for example, in building class dynamics or dealing with sensitive areas such as bullying. It can also be used to develop curriculum knowledge, for example, in learning times tables in mathematics or developing speaking and listening skills in the Early Years Foundation Stage (EYFS). Above all, circle time can provide valuable situations where some children wouldn't otherwise choose to speak out.

Voice within the wider school context

It is important to briefly consider how children's voices are heard in the wider community. This can take the form of school newsletters for parents which celebrate children's achievements. It could also involve local press covering events in school or pupils talking on local radio about fundraising events they are involved in at school. In this digital age there is plenty of opportunity for children's voices to be heard on the internet. A good way to achieve this is through the school's website, where pupils' podcasts and blogs, for example, can be accessed; all of this, however, needs to be in line with school policy.

School Council, school policy and voice

You may find that your school has a School Council which includes staff members, school governors and a group of pupils to represent the views of all the children in the school. Usually the aim and purpose of the School Council is to improve the school in some way. School Councils meet regularly to discuss any problems identified and then work towards finding solutions. Sometimes this may have financial implications so pupils may be involved in helping with fundraising activities. A common way to prioritise and decide which issues to tackle can be through the use of communal suggestion boxes where children can leave a message anonymously or alternatively through the use of pupil surveys.

School Councils usually have two peer-elected representatives (one boy, one girl) from each class in the school. At meetings a member of staff and possibly a school governor will be there to chair them. These meetings usually follow standard procedure – a record of those present or absent as well as minutes from the previous meeting. Minutes are taken, actions are noted and then this is fed back to staff and the student body.

Although, in principle, School Councils aim to work for the best interests of the children and the school, there are some contentious aspects to consider concerning the ways in which they operate in schools, and this will be returned to later, in 'The politics of voice' section in this chapter.

It is generally more common to find student voice policies in secondary schools rather than in the primary sector, although they do exist. A typical policy will have a rationale that includes a commitment to listening to the views of the pupils and involving them in decision-making processes. In doing so, schools believe that this makes a positive contribution to the environment and ethos of the school. The policy will usually outline the ways in which children's voices are promoted; for example, the role of the School Council and other initiatives such as:

- fundraising projects;
- playground buddies (for example, supporting new arrivals to the school);

- consultation on school practice (for example, helping with redrafting the behaviour policy);
- involvement with helping design school-wide pupil surveys in order to canvas opinion and bring about change.

In many cases there may well be mention of how student voice is embedded in the curriculum, for example where teachers ask the pupils to formulate the success criteria for lessons or where after-school clubs have been provided in response to pupils' requests.

Although the summary above outlines what may take place on a routine basis, there are some schools where policy and practice are much wider and more ambitious in scope, as illustrated by the two case studies below.

Case study: Pupil leadership with ICT

As part of their school-based placement tasks, trainees were asked by one of their university tutors to find out about student voice initiatives in their school and write a short report. Here is Marco's report:

This is my second placement school and I am in a Year 3 class. It's on the fringe of a large city and has a two-form intake. The school population is diverse and there are more than 10 languages spoken here. The school is very well resourced, particularly concerning ICT. The school has won various awards for its use of technology and how these are used to support teaching and learning, and in terms of my student voice report, I have chosen to focus on that. They have a pupil leadership scheme here called Digital Leaders. This involves children from each class in Key Stage 2 being part of a team that supports digital learning in school. Their main role is to help the ICT coordinator evaluate resources, so before the school buys any hardware or software the Digital Leaders have time to try out and evaluate the equipment and with the teachers they suggest and decide which things they think the children in the school will benefit from and enjoy, so they get to make decisions regarding purchasing and resourcing. I interviewed the ICT coordinator and found out that the feedback from the Digital Leaders is important because this then informs how the teachers in the school plan the schemes of work. The Digital Leaders also become involved in planning the curriculum and help decide on activities using the various technologies and how they can support learning in different subject areas. They can also be called upon to troubleshoot in lessons when teachers experience problems with equipment. Another unique thing is that apart from helping with developing the school's curriculum and use of ICT, the Digital Leaders become involved in the school's training days. The school has a partnership with a local university who send trainees here on a training day and the trainees get to interview the Digital Leaders about their role in school. It's a unique school which really empowers and encourages pupils to become leaders. This is the kind of school where I would like to work because it really values what the children have to offer.

Case Study: Student voice policy in action

As part of a research project concerning student voice initiatives, Ruksana was interviewed by an educational researcher to talk about how student voice policy operates in her school.

Ruksana is a member of the Senior Leadership Team in a large inner-city primary school. Ninety-seven per cent of pupils have English as a second language, 20 per cent are refugees and before recent government legislation over 35 per cent received free school meals. The school has a student voice policy and a School Council. Ruksana explained to the researcher that despite the challenges, they see their role as developing leaders and creating opportunities for leadership both in the classroom and in school. The school has a student leadership working group which includes teachers and support staff. The group met together to come up with a mission statement and determine what they wanted in terms of school improvement. Following this they drew up a student voice policy. Ruksana explained that she believes the pupils in her school have a lot to offer and this led to some children becoming Student Ambassadors. Ruksana explained how this relates to their capabilities: some work in reception answering the phone and greeting visitors and then taking them on a tour and providing them with information about the school. Other Ambassadors carry out a different role and are involved in co-planning with teachers. This involves a process whereby pupils observe teachers teaching lessons and they then give the teachers feedback on how they could make the lesson more engaging – as Ruksana explained to the researcher, this role typically belongs to upper Key Stage 2 pupils. Following lesson observations, these pupils then assist and advise with short and medium term planning. There are also Student Ambassadors who sit in on interview panels when recruiting new staff, with their opinion of candidates being considered as valid as those of the staff.

As you can see, student voice can operate in many different ways. In the studies above you will also note how the children's roles are tailored to their abilities and strengths. Two things that they share in common, however, is the way pupils are empowered to lead and how these initiatives actively encourage pupils and teachers to work together.

Activity: Investigating how student voice operates in schools

In your school, undertake a similar study to mirror the ones outlined above. Find out if there is a student voice policy and/or a School Council and then investigate the following:

School Council:

- How many pupil representatives are there and to what extent does this reflect the school population?
- What processes are in place to decide how these pupils are chosen?
- How frequently do they meet and are how are staff and governors involved?

- What current or recent initiatives have been put into place and what was the rationale?
- What systems are in place for reporting back to the School Council?

Select a small number of pupils (four to six) who represent the age range in your school and talk informally with them about their role. Note down their feelings about being on School Council and how they feel they have benefited, what skills they have acquired and how they feel the school has improved through the work they do.

Student voice policy:

> *Locate the policy, if there is one, although it may come under another banner, for example, Student Participation or Student Leadership. Annotate and highlight any key aims or initiatives and then find evidence to support that the policy is being put into practice. This may arise from talking to staff or children, observing what goes on in school, and sitting in on School Council meetings if this is possible.*

> *Find out who coordinates student voice in your school and have an informal chat with them. Note down what they perceive to be the benefits of operating student voice initiatives in school and whether they consider there to be any drawbacks. It may be useful – and provide you with greater insight – to repeat this exercise in another placement school to determine the different ways in which student voice operates in different schools.*

Research Focus: Distributed leadership

The case studies above provide examples of how some schools are willing to encourage and engage pupils in carrying out leadership activities and the models of practice described here represent what is widely referred to as 'distributed leadership'. Distributed leadership is 'a term that is used to describe approaches to school leadership' which are considered to be 'conducive to school improvement' in a climate where the nature of the context in which schools operate has become increasingly 'complex' (Ritchie and Woods, 2007, p.363). Defining distributed leadership is problematic in the sense that there is a lack of clarity as to 'what distributed leadership actually means' (Leithwood et al., 2007, p.38). The manner in which leadership is distributed in schools varies widely and so having one definition is difficult because it 'means different things to different people' (Timperley, 2005, p.396). Any situation where leadership is handed over to someone else involves trust and the word 'trust' crops up in the literature with a high level of frequency. The literature on distributed leadership makes scant reference to children as leaders and almost exclusively considers it in the context of head teachers and their staff. The same principles that are applied to adults, however, apply to any stakeholder in the institution – in this case the children. The National College for Student Leadership (NCSL) consider trust to be 'a crucial element' in forming professional relationships (2010, p.12), although for head teachers 'trust presents the most acute of dilemmas' because 'trusting others to deliver implies a risk'; as ultimately they hold responsibility for others' actions (MacBeath, 2005, p.353). A pertinent moment which Ruksana shared with the educational researcher and which is reflected here, is how the leadership team presented the Ambassadors with a contract about what it was the staff and students were agreeing to do together. The Ambassadors did not want the contract because they felt that it undermined the genuine feeling of trust that they considered to be already there.

The silent voice

It is all very well to plan for and create opportunities for children's voices to be heard, but what happens when you come across barriers where some children either do not want to be or are unable to be heard? These may take shape in many forms and you may see examples for yourself in the classroom and in the schools where you are on placement. Some pupils may be reluctant to speak out, and returning to the earlier notion of trust, they may feel that what they have to say may 'not be liked or welcomed' (Gunter and Thomson, 2007, p.184). They may not enjoy school or may resent authority, and feelings of anger or frustration may mean that they are unwilling to voice their opinion. You also need to be aware that a silent voice may be a 'vulnerable' voice, particularly for those children who come from low-income or disadvantaged backgrounds; for them speaking out may be compromised by feelings of low self-esteem, unworthiness (Batchelor, 2006) or lack of an academic ability to articulate what they want to say (Bragg, 2007).

Through reading this chapter you will have developed an awareness of the need to be mindful in monitoring those children who find it hard to express themselves. Conversely, pupils with English as an Additional Language (EAL) or SEND may want to get their voice across but may experience difficulty with it being heard. The use of flash cards and word/picture banks may help them articulate what they think or how they are feeling. Consider providing all of these 'harder to reach' groups of children with strategies to get their ideas across, for example through circle time, allocating another adult to support them, choosing a supportive talk partner or considering the use of available technologies to assist in ensuring that their voice is heard.

Building capacity for leadership

Rather than asking the School Council about what should or shouldn't be in a packed lunch box or bewailing the state of the school's toilets, student voice amounts to much more than this. It is more to do with not only harnessing children's capabilities and knowledge as experts in their environment, but empowering them to find solutions for themselves. Students as researchers or consultants are both common themes in the literature on student voice. Jean Rudduck and Michael Fielding, in particular, champion this approach, where pupils are trained how to become researchers, how to identify the data they need, how to design instruments to collect it, how to interpret their findings, and how to then make recommendations for change within their school. The process of nurturing these skills is very much about building capacity for children to become leaders – and perhaps facilitates the most powerful way their voices can be heard. It is also about equipping them with the skills and the ability to gather evidence, and therefore the autonomy in making decisions. Ultimately, it needs to be the children and not the adults in school who lead and drive student voice initiatives in order to bring about change.

Dana Mitra (2006, p.7) exemplifies this process by constructing a pyramid of student voice (see Figure 7.1).

Figure 7.1 The pyramid of student voice (after Mitra, 2006)

The bottom of the pyramid pertains to the more common or generic examples of voice which may include children identifying factors or conditions in school that affect their welfare. The second tier acknowledges the unique knowledge and perspectives that children have and may entail them being involved in data collection and research in order to bring about change in their school. The top of the pyramid is about enabling children to lead and take ownership of student voice initiatives, as well as becoming fully involved in school-wide decision-making processes (Mitra and Gross, 2009).

In your setting, you will need to identify where, how and, indeed, if this is actually happening. Are teachers actively seeking to help train pupils with the skills they need in order to carry out these kinds of projects? Are pupils actively being encouraged to take ownership and leadership where they are given the licence to research, investigate and bring about change for themselves, or are teachers or parents speaking too readily or too presumptuously on their behalf (Fielding, 2001)?

A word of caution

As mentioned earlier, there are some political and ethical issues that you will need to consider when thinking about the scope and nature of children's voices in schools. It may be one thing to ensure all children have their right to their voice being heard in your classroom but, as outlined below, school-wide student voice initiatives may present a different set of challenges altogether.

Research Focus: The politics of voice

It is important to consider the motives behind school-led student voice initiatives and to ask yourself certain questions. Where have these initiatives have come from, and why? Do they seek to serve the political interests of those people who have chosen to implement them, or is there a genuine intention to capitalise on learning from the student body who are considered to be our 'expert witnesses' (Flutter and Rudduck, 2004, p.105)?

Any shift in policy or practice that attempts to 'acculturate' stakeholders into 'distributed leadership' remains, however, 'a politically driven intervention' (Wallace et al., 2011, p.261). Furthermore, interventions such as implementing a student voice policy can be seen as a public relations exercise in promoting the school's image as well as determining not just what stakeholders can do 'but also the things they can and cannot say' (Cremin et al., 2011, p.592). This raises the question as to whether student voice initiatives are tools of manipulation and put into place for the sake of Ofsted and parents as opposed to a genuine commitment to teachers' and children's 'demographic agency' and their ability to bring about change in their own setting (Fielding, 2001, p.123).

Finally, there is the question of the extent to which children's voice and pupil participation in schools can be truly democratic. Although democracy implies that all stakeholders, including pupils, are involved in decision-making processes (Mullis, 2011; Woods, 2004), this model of democracy is flawed because responsibility is delegated by those in power to the chosen few and does not always ensure that everyone has the right to exercise their democratic agency (Hatcher, 2005).

Learning Outcomes Review

Thinking about the school in which you are currently placed, or in which you most recently undertook a placement, respond to the questions or prompts which follow each of the intended learning outcomes as a means of identifying your knowledge and understanding of the issues covered in the chapter.

- **Be familiar with the main principles of the United Nations Convention on the Rights of the Child and how these inform school policy:**

    - In what ways does this translate itself into classroom practice and how does it vary between different schools?

> - **Understand some of the theories on student voice and their implications for teaching and learning:**
>   - Revisit the research focus boxes and for each theorist (a) summarise their principal theory or belief in one sentence, and (b) suggest how these may transform themselves into classroom practice.
>
> - **Recognise not just how the importance of children's voice operates in the classroom on a daily basis through routine activity, but also how it is expressed through wider school policy and initiatives:**
>   - In what ways do children benefit from classroom-based as well as school-wide student voice initiatives? Provide examples from your own practice if possible.
>
> - **Understand the benefits of student voice initiatives for both pupils and staff, but also recognise some of the pitfalls, limitations and inequalities of implementing student voice in schools:**
>   - What are the pros and cons of student voice in schools? You may draw upon your own experiences from more than one of your placement schools.

Note

The author would like to thank Dana Mitra for her kind permission to reproduce Figure 7.1.

Further Reading

Czerniawski, G. and Kidd, W. (eds) (2011) *The Student Voice Handbook*. Bingley: Emerald.

Rudduck, J. and McIntyre, D. (2007) *Improving Learning through Consulting Pupils*. Abingdon: Routledge.

References

2Simple (no date) Music Toolkit (computer program). Available from www.2simple.com/product/music-toolkit accessed 26/11/14.

Alexander, R. (2014) *Dialogic Teaching*. Available from http://www.robinalexander.org.uk/dialogic-teaching/ accessed 25/11/14.

Apple Inc. (2005) GarageBand (computer program). Available from https://www.apple.com/uk/mac/garageband/ accessed 26/11/14.

Batchelor, D.C. (2006) Vulnerable voices: an examination of the concept of vulnerability in relation to student voice. *Educational Philosophy and Theory* 38(6) pp.787–800.

Bragg, S. (2007) 'Student voice' and governmentality: the production of enterprising subjects? *Studies in the Cultural Politics of Education* 28(3) pp.343–58.

Cremin, H., Mason, C. and Busher, H. (2011) Problematising pupil voice using visual methods: findings from a study of engaged and disaffected pupils in an urban secondary school. *British Educational Research Journal* 37(4) pp.585–603.

Fielding, M. (2001) Students as radical agents of change. *Journal of Educational Change* 2, pp.123-41.

Flutter, J. and Rudduck, J. (2004) *Consulting Pupils: What's in it for Schools?* London: Routledge.

Gunter, H.M. and Thomson, P. (2007) Learning about student voice. *Support for Learning* 22(4) pp.181–8.

Hatcher, R. (2005) The distribution of leadership and power in schools. *British Journal of Sociology of Education* 26(2) pp.253–67.

Leithwood, K., Mascall, B., Strauss, T., Sacks, R., Memon, N. and Yashkina, A. (2007) Distributing leadership to make schools smarter: taking the ego out of the system. *Leadership and Policy in Schools* 6(1) pp.37–67.

MacBeath, J. (2005) Leadership as distributed: a matter of practice. *School Leadership and Management* 25(4) pp.349–66.

Mitra, D.L. (2006) Increasing student voice and moving toward youth leadership. *The Prevention Researcher* 13(1) pp.7–10.

Mitra, D.L. and Gross, S.J. (2009) Increasing student voice in high school reform: building partnerships, improving outcomes. *Educational Management Administration and Leadership* 37(4) pp.522–43.

Mullis, G. (2011) Student voice: changing practice and developing partnerships. In Czerniawski, G. and Kidd, W. (eds) *The Student Voice Handbook: Bridging the Academic/ Practitioner Divide*. Bingley: Emerald, pp. 209–24.

National College for School Leadership (NCSL) (2010) *Distributed Leadership.* Nottingham: NCSL.

Ritchie, R. and Woods, P. (2007) Degrees of distribution: towards an understanding of variations in the nature of distributed leadership in schools. *School Leadership and Management* 27(4) pp.363–81.

Roberts, A. and Nash, J. (2009) Enabling students to participate in school improvement through a Students as Researchers programme. *Improving Schools* 12(2) pp.174–87.

Rudduck, J. and Fielding, M. (2006) Student voice and the peril of popularity. *Educational Review* 58(2) pp.219–31.

Soo Hoo, S. (1993) Students as partners in research and restructuring schools. *The Educational Forum* 57, pp.386–93.

Stenhouse, L.A. (1975) *An Introduction to Curriculum Research and Development*. London: HMSO.

Timperley, S. (2005) Distributed leadership: developing theory from practice. *Journal of Curriculum Studies* 37(4) pp.395–420.

United Nations International Children's Emergency Fund (UNICEF) (1989) *United Nations Convention on the Rights of the Child*. Available from http://www.unicef.org.uk/Documents/Publication-pdfs/UNCRC_PRESS200910web.pdf accessed 25/11/14.

Wallace, M., Tomlinson, M. and O'Reilly, D. (2011) The mediation of acculturation: orchestrating school leadership development in England. *Educational Management Administration and Leadership* 39(3) pp.261–82.

Woods, P. (2004) Democratic leadership: drawing distinctions with distributed leadership. *International Journal of Leadership in Education* 7(1) pp.3–26.

SECTION 3
THE DEVELOPING TEACHER

8. Teaching as a profession
Tony Ewens

Learning Outcomes

By the end of this chapter you should have developed and clarified:

- an understanding of the concept of a profession and what makes teaching a profession;
- knowledge of professional and legal frameworks within which teachers operate;
- an appreciation of ethical principles underpinning teachers' practice;
- an awareness of the professional knowledge, understanding, skills and attitudes which teachers must display;
- your knowledge of the mechanisms by which teachers' accountability to pupils, parents/carers, employers, fellow-professionals and the public is monitored.

TEACHERS' STANDARDS

A teacher must:

8. Fulfil wider professional responsibilities

- make a positive contribution to the wider life and ethos of the school
- develop effective professional relationships with colleagues, knowing how and when to draw on advice and specialist support
- deploy support staff effectively
- take responsibility for improving teaching through appropriate professional development, responding to advice and feedback from colleagues.

PART 2: PERSONAL AND PROFESSIONAL CONDUCT

- **Teachers uphold public trust in the profession and maintain high standards of ethics and behaviour within and outside school, by:**
  - treating pupils with dignity, building relationships rooted in mutual respect, and at all times observing proper boundaries appropriate to a teacher's professional position
  - having regard for the need to safeguard pupils' well-being, in accordance with statutory provisions
  - showing tolerance of and respect for the rights of others
  - not undermining fundamental British values, including democracy, the rule of law, individual liberty and mutual respect, and tolerance of those with different faiths and beliefs
  - ensuring that personal beliefs are not expressed in ways which exploit pupils' vulnerability or might lead them to break the law

- Teachers must have proper and professional regard for the ethos, policies and practices within the school in which they teach, and maintain high standards in their own attendance and punctuality
- Teachers must have an understanding of, and always act within, the statutory frameworks which set out their professional duties and responsibilities.

What makes teaching a profession?

Before beginning teacher training, you probably made yourself familiar with some of the repertoire of skills that teachers deploy, and became aware of the type of education and training associated with becoming a teacher.

Activity

Reflect on why you think teaching is a 'profession'. Do you agree with this description? What characteristics do you think entitle an occupation to be called a profession, rather than a trade, a vocation or simply a job? Who do you think monitors teachers' work, to ensure that their practice is professional? What should happen if teachers fail to display professional conduct?

The following research focus asks you to check your initial thoughts about teaching as a profession in the light of general principles associated with professionalism.

Research Focus

Jacques and Hyland (2007, p.202) write about the implications of describing teaching as a profession. They describe professions as characterised by:

- possession of specialised knowledge and skills;

- successful completion of intellectual and practical education and training;

- conformity to ethical standards when dealing with clients;

- commitment to the competence and integrity of the profession as a whole;

- membership of an organised body involved in testing competence and regulating competence and conduct.

Professional bodies

Politically, education is a devolved responsibility within the four countries of the United Kingdom, and the last 20 years have seen increasing divergence in policy and practice. From 1998 to 2012 the professional body for teachers in England was the General Teaching Council for England (GTCE), established by Act of Parliament to 'contribute to improving standards of teaching and the quality of learning, and to maintain and improve standards of professional conduct among teachers' (DfEE, 1998). This was controversially abolished by the government in 2012 amid claims that it had done little to raise standards or improve professionalism. Responsibility for registering and regulating teachers in England now lies with the National College for Teaching and Leadership (NCTL), an executive agency of the Department for Education. The NCTL took on the key functions previously undertaken by the Training and Development Agency for Schools (TDA), General Teaching Council for England (GTCE), Children's Workforce Development Council (CWDC) and the Qualifications and Curriculum Development Agency (QCDA).

The abolition of the GTCE raises a question about the ability of the teaching profession in England to act as 'an organised body involved in testing competence and regulating competence and conduct', a feature of professions identified by Jacques and Hyland. Evans' (2011) analysis of the concept of professionalism leads her to claim that when professionalism is imposed by government intervention, it leads to a lop-sided view of teaching by overemphasising teachers' behaviours, to the exclusion of their attitudes and intellectual capacities. However, the concept of qualifying to enter and continue in the profession remains significant.

Scotland, Wales and Northern Ireland continue to have General Teaching Councils independent of government control, with responsibility for maintaining registers of qualified teachers and for regulating the profession. This is significant if you move around the United Kingdom. If you qualify in England, then wish to work in another UK country, you must register with that country's GTC. If you took a full-time PGCE or a four-year degree with QTS this should be straightforward. However, if you took a three-year degree with QTS, an employment-based route or a part-time PGCE, check that your award is recognised for registration in the country to which you are moving. If you are leaving the UK, find out whether your qualifications are accepted in your new location, and whether additional qualifications or experience are needed for recognition as a teacher there.

The Teachers' Standards illustrate how teaching matches Jacques and Hyland's description of professions. Achieving the standards is only the first stage of your career. You are expected to maintain and enhance your competence. For example, during your career you 'will be expected to extend the depth and breadth of knowledge, skill and understanding that [you] demonstrate in meeting the standards, as is judged to be appropriate to the role [you] are fulfilling and the context in which [you] are working' (DfE, 2012, p.4).

Working with others

Teaching is not a solitary profession, as it requires various types of teamwork. Two main examples of this involve curriculum leadership and working with teaching assistants.

Since the 1970s primary schools have been encouraged to deploy teachers' specialist subject knowledge for the benefit of their colleagues, without fundamentally challenging the notion of the generalist class teacher. Ewens (2014, pp.138–42) offers a survey of the development of the role of subject leaders and identifies numerous activities that they typically undertake. Trainee teachers can often benefit from the expertise of curriculum specialists, and you should not hesitate to ask them for guidance.

Alexander (2010) challenges a reliance on class teaching as the main strategy in primary schools, arguing that subject expertise is crucial to educational quality and that the demands upon teachers' knowledge, especially at Key Stage 2, point to a much greater use of subject specialist teaching in junior classes (Alexander, 2010, p.37). However, in many schools the number of staff, or the balance of teachers' specialisms, would not readily support that approach. Only very large schools might have enough teachers in Key Stage 2 to support a significant amount of specialist teaching. In others, some of the teachers with specialist knowledge would be class teachers in Key Stage 1 or EYFS classes. Moving them from their own classes to teach their specialist subject in Key Stage 2 could well have negative consequences for their own classes. You could usefully investigate how teachers' specialist knowledge is deployed in the school in which you are working and discuss the issue with your mentor and other colleagues.

For lessons in which you are taking the lead, you will frequently be required to plan the work of teaching assistants (TAs) assigned to your class. An extensive research project (Blatchford et al., 2012) showed that despite a large increase in the number of TAs in English classrooms, their overall impact on pupil performance was often negative. The finding contradicted the positive perceptions about TAs' impact expressed by teachers, and is all the more concerning since local authorities often saw TA provision as the best way to support pupils with special educational needs (SEN). Among the report's key messages are:

- the importance of focusing on educational achievement rather than task completion;
- a need for teachers to ensure that TAs have the requisite subject and pedagogical subject knowledge;
- finding ways in which teachers can share their planning and intended learning outcomes with TAs other than simply by means of a copy of the lesson plan.

Urgent work was undertaken to identify best practice in the training and deployment of TAs. The outcomes, published by Russell et al. (2013), identify:

- the importance of teachers learning how better to manage the work of TAs and other adults in the classroom;
- the need for improved training in subject and pedagogical knowledge for TAs;

- allocation of Planning and Preparation (PPA) time together;
- a focus on the nature and quality of TAs' interactions with pupils.

The implication of an analysis of teamwork among a school's staff is that all teachers have responsibility for managing the work of other adults, whether as curriculum leaders throughout the school or as classroom teachers responsible for children's learning in one class. Managing, and being managed, are both integral to professional practice.

As well as being responsible to fellow teachers for upholding high standards of professional practice, you must work effectively with colleagues from other professions.

When working with children with special educational needs and disabilities (SEND), you will collaborate with other professionals, for example educational psychologists and the school's special educational needs and disabilities coordinator (SENDCO).

Another example of inter-professional work is in child protection, covered in Chapter 10, when cooperation with professionals in social work, health and police can play a crucial role in safeguarding children. This is set out in in Part B of the Standards: 'have regard for the need to safeguard pupils' wellbeing, in accordance with statutory provisions'.

Developing your professional competence

The responsibility for maintaining and enhancing your professional competence is yours. Others, such as your mentor or tutor, will meet you to review your progress, and later in your career you will experience regular appraisals with senior colleagues. However, you are expected to take the initiative, by monitoring your own performance, knowing your strengths and weaknesses and identifying where you need training or guidance from more experienced colleagues. Placements provide an excellent opportunity to practise this, as the following example illustrates. Notice how the trainee initiates discussion and seeks her mentor's advice in this case study.

Case Study: Shainaz's placement progress review meeting

Three weeks into her placement, Shainaz meets her mentor to review her progress. She has identified assessment as an area for improvement and has worked on the skills described in Standard 6: 'Make accurate and productive use of assessment.' Shainaz has used various assessment strategies and demonstrates consistency in assessing pupils' work accurately. Reflecting on her performance, Shainaz asks, 'How do I know whether a child's achievement represents real progress? I'm not sure whether I set tasks at the right level of difficulty.' Commending her incisive insight, the mentor suggests addressing Standard 2: 'Promote good progress and outcomes by pupils.' After discussion, Shainaz decides to seek evidence of pupils' previous attainment, by looking through exercise books, consulting earlier test results and using questioning to identify their levels of understanding. The mentor agrees that this should help her to set appropriately challenging expectations for groups and individuals.

This case study is an example of the notion of reflective practice, notably described by Schön (1983) and Eraut (1994). For these authors, using techniques of analysing your own practice, then deducing ways of improving it, is fundamental to professionalism.

Research Focus

Although Schön and Eraut wrote some time ago, both volumes remain invaluable for understanding professionalism. Schön studied a variety of ways in which a range of professionals reflected on their practice, and outlined sophisticated variations, for instance the ability to build reflection into ongoing professional tasks. Eraut further extended an understanding of how professionals develop their knowledge and skills, with examples of reflection in action. For example, his explanation of 'routinisation' (Eraut, 1994) may help to explain how and why teachers seem to function as if on 'autopilot', when particular aspects of practice become integrated into their regular routines and are repeated automatically.

Teachers, professionalism and the law

Many of a teacher's professional responsibilities are linked with legal requirements, so you should know something about the legal framework within which you work. Ignorance of the law is not accepted by courts as an excuse.

Some laws affecting teachers are part of general legislation applicable to everyone, especially employees. For example, the Health and Safety at Work Act 1974 requires you to protect the safety of others in the workplace. When applying for jobs you are protected by laws prohibiting discrimination, such as the Race Relations Act 1976, Sex Discrimination Act 1975, Disability Discrimination Act 1995 and Employment Equality Regulations regarding sexual orientation (2003), religion or belief (2003) and age (2006). In return, you must be open and honest in job applications. It is, for example, an offence to misrepresent your qualifications or to attempt to conceal a conviction.

Other laws relate specifically to teachers. The Secretary of State can bar people from teaching, for example, on certain medical grounds or following serious misconduct. Some criminal convictions, for instance offences against children, and being on the Sex Offenders' Register, are also reasons for being barred from teaching. An 'enhanced' DBS check is required before you are employed, and teachers cannot have previous convictions treated as 'spent', as described in the Rehabilitation of Offenders Act 1974.

You should join one of the teaching unions, which can advise you about your professional responsibilities under the law, and provide support and representation should you encounter any legal difficulty.

Your contract of employment

In maintained schools in England and Wales teachers' contracts are based on *The School Teachers' Pay and Conditions Document*, known as the Blue Book. Local authorities and schools are obliged to implement these regulations, which prescribe what you are required to do as a teacher and what you will be paid. The obligations and pay scales are updated annually. Your point on the pay scale is determined by the school's governing body, within the national framework. Other, non-statutory conditions of service, agreed between the teaching unions and the local government employers, cover entitlement to sick leave, maternity and paternity leave, periods of notice and entitlement to belong to a union. They are in *The Conditions of Service for Schoolteachers in England and Wales*, the Burgundy Book, which is revised regularly. Local authorities accept these conditions as binding.

Maintained schools include Community Schools (formerly County Schools), Voluntary Controlled Schools (mostly Church Schools, where the local authority is the employer but the governors may make conditions related to the school's religious character), Voluntary Aided Schools (mostly of a religious character, where the governing body as the employer may make conditions including reference to candidates' religious commitment), and Foundation Schools, where the governing body is the employer.

The conditions of employment in the Blue Book include a requirement to be available for 195 days annually, and to teach on 190, the remainder being 'teacher days' for staff training and development. 1,265 hours is treated as 'directed time', when you are required to attend at specific times and places, for example for parents' evenings or staff meetings in addition to teaching. The 1,265 hours include the 10 per cent allowance for planning and preparation (PPA time), but not the entire time needed for preparation, marking and associated tasks. You must do these in your own time. After-school activities are not usually counted within the 1,265 hours. Teachers' duties, according to the Blue Book (2010, para. 61), include:

- planning and teaching;
- assessing, recording and writing reports;
- participating in staff meetings;
- collaborating with colleagues in planning;
- covering for absent colleagues (up to 38 hours per year);
- directing and supervising support staff;
- contributing to the professional development of other staff;
- contributing to your own and others' appraisal;
- participating in further professional development;
- communicating with parents and carers.

Note that non-maintained schools (including independent and private schools, academies and other categories of school inaugurated following changes in public policy) are not bound by the Blue and Burgundy Books, although many choose to use them. They may have different pay scales, require different hours of work and expect additional duties. Check carefully before signing a contract, and ask your union for advice. Ask whether work in a non-maintained school will count towards the induction period (normally, one year's satisfactory full-time work or its part-time equivalent) required before final accreditation as a fully qualified teacher.

Teachers and pupils

Several areas of legislation and regulations deal with relations between teachers and pupils, for example regarding discipline. Each school will have its own policies and procedures, and these must conform to statutory requirements. When on placement you should read the school's policies and procedures covering your interactions with children, and ensure that you operate within them. Schools have public liability insurance, which would cover you against claims arising from an incident while on school business. However, if you have acted outside the school's policies you could be summoned to a disciplinary meeting, and if your actions have been wilfully reckless you could at worst face legal action for which you are only insured through your union membership. This situation is worth avoiding!

Discipline and sanctions

Behaviour and Discipline in Schools: Advice for head teachers and school staff (DfE, 2014) describes what teachers may and must do to promote and ensure discipline. Paragraph 4 expresses the purposes of a behaviour policy:

> *The head teacher must set out measures in the behaviour policy which aim to:*
>
> - *promote good behaviour, self discipline and respect;*
>
> - *prevent bullying;*
>
> - *ensure that pupils complete assigned work; and which*
>
> - *regulate the conduct of pupils.*
>
> *(DfE, 2014, para. 1)*

Schools must also have an anti-bullying policy, covering physical, verbal and emotional bullying and incorporating active measures against racist or homophobic behaviour.

You must be clear about the sanctions that you may use. Corporal punishment in maintained schools has been illegal since 1986, but in certain circumstances teachers may use physical force to restrain a child. The DfE guidance makes it clear that teachers:

have the power to use reasonable force to prevent pupils committing an offence, injuring themselves or others, or damaging property, and to maintain good order and discipline in the classroom.

(DfE, 2014, para. 38)

Further guidance explains that physical restraint should be a last resort, and that teachers should avoid anything likely to cause injury or be regarded as indecent. Written records must be made of any incidents when force is used, explaining what happened, why it was considered necessary to use force and what the consequences were. You would obviously report this immediately to the head teacher.

In the recent past some schools' policies implied that teachers should never touch a child, other than when physical restraint was justified. Guidance issued in 2013 (DfE, 2013, p.8) clarified this issue, offering the following advice:

Examples of where touching a pupil might be proper or necessary:

- *Holding the hand of the child at the front/back of the line when going to assembly or when walking together around the school;*

- *When comforting a distressed pupil;*

- *When a pupil is being congratulated or praised;*

- *To demonstrate how to use a musical instrument;*

- *To demonstrate exercises or techniques during PE lessons or sports coaching; and*

- *To give first aid.*

Remember to consult the behaviour policy when planning lessons that present particular hazards, such as some PE and technology sessions, and when designing opportunities for out-of-school learning.

Safeguarding and protecting children

Working Together to Safeguard Children (HMG, 2013) lists schools' duties in safeguarding children, and provides a framework for protecting them from abuse. Schools are required to work closely with other professions to protect children from harm and report instances where staff members are concerned about individuals. Schools must have a child protection policy and a designated person (usually the head teacher) to liaise with statutory agencies. You should read the policy and its associated procedures, so that you are alert to signs of possible abuse and know what steps to take. To read in more detail about your responsibilities regarding child protection, see Chapter 10.

It is worth remembering that teachers can help children to develop resilience. The work you do in building children's self-esteem and increasing their communication skills can strengthen their confidence to speak out if they are being ill-treated.

Most teachers never fall foul of the law. Awareness of your duties and responsibilities, and a determination to act in good faith, is the key to ensuring that your career runs smoothly.

Activity

When on placement, find in the staff handbook the policies about behaviour, bullying, rewards and sanctions, child protection and health and safety. Check them against the legislation and regulations outlined in this chapter, to enhance your understanding of the way in which head teachers and governors apply the law to the day-to-day running of schools.

Teachers' professional ethics

Jacques points out that professionalism involves behaving in a principled way towards clients. Your 'clients' include not only children and parents, but society at large. You also have ethical responsibilities to the teaching profession. Among professional attributes, Jacques identifies three incorporating overt ethical duties (Jacques and Hyland, 2007 p.202):

- maintain detachment and integrity in exercising personal judgement on behalf of a client;
- establish direct personal relations with clients based on confidence, faith and trust;
- collectively have a particular sense of responsibility for maintaining the competence and integrity of the profession as a whole.

These principles may seem abstract. However, when translated into situations that are typical occurrences for teachers, they can clarify some of the ethical dilemmas which you will meet in your work. Consider the questions posed in the following task, and identify their relationship to the bulleted points above.

Activity

1. You find some children very amiable, and others more difficult to like. How do you ensure that your personal preferences for particular character traits do not lead you to treat certain children more favourably than others?
2. During a parents' evening, Louise's mother says, 'How is Louise doing compared with her friend Anna?' How can you politely explain to Louise's mother that it would be ethically wrong to disclose to her information about another child?

3. During a placement you observe a low ability group continuing with a literacy task while the rest of the class enjoys an art lesson. You are told that this is in line with the school's policy, which targets competence in English as a major objective. You think that the group is being deprived of a broad and balanced curriculum and that the children may feel negatively towards literacy, sensing that they are being punished for making slow progress. What would you say or do?

The questions encapsulate various ethical issues facing teachers. Question 1 reflects the concept of 'teacher's pet'. Children quickly sense teachers' approval or disapproval and dislike it if teachers act unfairly towards individuals or groups. It is only human to have preferences about people that we like or dislike. It would be understandable if teachers liked children who applied themselves to their work, showed interest and asked intelligent questions. However, it is important to recognise your preferences then take steps to ensure that you communicate positively with **all** your pupils. This is implicit in Standard 5: 'Adapt teaching to respond to the strengths and needs of all pupils.'

As Jacques and Hyland point out (2007, pp.151ff.), equality of opportunity is a statutory right of all pupils. Standard 5 illuminates the difference between equality of opportunity and equality of outcome. Children's educational potentials differ, so their attainments will differ. Your responsibility is to know enough about each child's prior knowledge, interests and capacities to enable you to set appropriate expectations for the next stage of learning. Consequently you will have varying levels of expectation for different individuals. The ethical imperative is to ensure that your expectations are based on detached, objective judgements, unclouded by personal prejudice or preference.

Question 2 asks you to maintain confidentiality meticulously, while preserving good relations with a client. This example shows that professional ethics often have to be accompanied by personal tact. You must not disclose details of a pupil's performance to another child's parent, but you also have a responsibility to maintain positive relations with that parent.

In some circumstances you would be right not to maintain confidentiality. One is if you believe a child to be at risk of abuse. Another is if you learn of what appears to be a serious breach of professional conduct, or an illegal activity, by someone in the school community. Schools have 'whistleblowing' policies, guaranteeing that those reporting these things will not suffer adverse consequences unless acting maliciously.

Question 3 is about professional judgement in matching the curriculum to the pupils' needs. You are entitled to hold a personal view about professional issues. As a trainee teacher, you are a guest in the school and at most you might discuss the matter privately with your mentor, to develop an understanding of the school's thinking. If you are employed at the school, you could ask for a discussion at a staff meeting, then present a reasoned argument for changing the policy. It would be unprofessional to disregard the school's policy and substitute your own approach. Open discord among the staff of a school jeopardizes the integrity of the profession in the eyes of pupils and parents.

In some aspects of your work you may have reservations about what you are required to do, whether by the head teacher or by legislation. Upholding practices with which you disagree is often unpalatable but, unless the circumstances are so extreme as to threaten children's welfare, the ethical approach is to apply the policy while arguing for a different course of action in the privacy of the head's office or staffroom.

A different aspect of professional ethics concerns a teacher's duty to promote children's moral development (Ewens, 2014, pp.119ff.). You may think that this is not your job, especially since there are sincere differences of opinion in society about moral codes. But a moment's thought will convince you that you are imposing moral codes on your class regularly: be quiet, don't interrupt, wait your turn, and so on. Some of this may be conscious implementation of the school's behaviour policy; at other times you are conveying your own values, consciously or subconsciously. Sometimes you help children to work through their own understanding of right and wrong, perhaps using drama or fiction to promote moral decision-making. It is vital to remain aware of your own moral principles and how these may differ from the beliefs of others. Children will benefit neither from teachers who apply ultra-rigid codes to them, nor from those who allow them to do whatever they wish. Pupils prefer teachers who are authoritative, firm but fair, treating children with respect and regard. Your professional conduct in the classroom will teach children as much about morality as your moral education lessons.

Teachers' knowledge, understanding, skills and attitudes

The standards outline areas of professional competence that you must display before gaining QTS. You can usefully consider them under the headings subject knowledge, knowing how learners learn, pedagogy, and the school and wider contexts.

Subject knowledge

Your need for a command of the subject matter that you want your pupils to learn is underpinned by Standard 3: 'Demonstrate good subject and curriculum knowledge'. This requirement is more complex than it first appears. At one level, each subject can be viewed as a collection of pieces of information that the teacher conveys to the class, to be memorised and recalled when required. Beneath this superficial, though important, level lie other features of subject knowledge. Each subject has its set of skills; examples are estimating in mathematics, hypothesising in science and jumping in PE. At a still deeper level are the key concepts, the big 'ideas' on which the subject is founded. Examples include fair tests in science, timbre in music and worship in religion.

Classroom tasks related to any concept can be simple or advanced. For instance, reception classes can discuss how to make a sampling task a fair test, while a medical research team, addressing the same concept at an advanced level, will ensure that plans for testing new drugs incorporate blind trialling with control groups. The concept – a fair test – applies at both levels.

The three types of knowledge – information, skills and concepts – are distinct from one another but complementary, and you can add a fourth aspect, attitudes. For example, environmental studies can be a means of encouraging an attitude of responsibility towards our planet.

You need to develop an appreciation of the information, skills, concepts and attitudes associated with each subject. A shallow education, restricted to transmission of factual information, may produce a class of quiz champions. A rich educational diet, incorporating all four elements, equips learners to apply and extend their knowledge and gradually grow into independent, lifelong learners.

Knowing how learners learn

Standard 2 focuses specifically on this topic: 'Promote good progress and outcomes by pupils (demonstrate knowledge and understanding of how pupils learn and how this impacts on teaching)'.

Educational psychology has illuminated how children's minds develop in a sequenced way and this has sometimes resulted in an 'ages and stages' approach to curriculum planning. Be careful not to fall into the trap of 'waiting until the children are ready' before introducing more complex ideas that you judge to be theoretically beyond their capacities. Bruner (1960) and Vygotsky (1978) showed that learners can pass more rapidly through stages of learning when teachers provide scaffolding to support their development.

Appreciating psychology's contribution to your understanding of children's development as learners is an important professional attribute. Another is knowledge of how children's home and community backgrounds influence their educational chances and progress. Attitudes towards learning expressed at home, various medical conditions, whether the internet is available at home, whether adults can spend time helping with homework, whether English is spoken at home: these, and many other factors, impact upon a learner's development. In being aware of these issues, you must ensure that you do not create self-fulfilling prophecies, for example by expecting lower achievement from children from a particular background. Remember that the Teachers' Standards require you to have high expectations of **all** children, so that they can achieve their full educational potential.

Pedagogy

The word 'pedagogy' refers to the science (or is it an art?) of teaching.

Pedagogy links the two previous sections, 'subject knowledge' and 'knowing how learners learn'. Children are not empty vessels that teachers fill with knowledge. They bring ideas, impressions, abilities and information from outside school. Naturally inquisitive, they explore, ask questions and make discoveries for themselves. Your task involves capitalising on these characteristics through your understanding of how learners learn, then exposing your pupils to a well-selected range of knowledge, understanding and skills drawn from across the curriculum. An influential report explained the central thrust of pedagogy in this way:

> *While it is self-evident that every individual, to an extent, constructs his/her meanings, education is an encounter between these personal understandings and the public knowledge embodied in our cultural traditions. The teacher's key responsibility is to mediate such encounters so that the child's understanding is enriched.*

> *(Alexander et al., 1992, para. 64)*

This point is well illustrated in the following case study:

Case Study: Warren's placement progress review meeting

At his mid-placement review, Warren agrees that the major priority should be to ensure a better match between the subject matter in his weekly plans and the learning styles that the children use. He agrees with his mentor that he spends too much time transmitting factual information to the class, and has planned insufficient variety in the tasks that he sets for children. Consequently, many pupils have failed to apply the new knowledge that Warren has introduced, and have not fully understood the work. The class also becomes restless if Warren speaks for too long. Warren identifies the following targets:

- Teach the children some skills that they can use to find something out for themselves.

- Select knowledge that children need to acquire, then design tasks so that they access the desired knowledge, using the skills they learned.

- Prepare questions and exercises to assess how well they have understood the material.

- Study the children's answers to diagnose misconceptions, then prepare explanations and re-teach as necessary.

The mentor is planning to stretch Warren's skills by pressing him to carry out the assessment, diagnosis and re-teaching during plenaries, since prompt feedback is particularly valuable.

Notice how Warren's plans involve thinking about pupils' roles in the lessons, rather than his role. Inevitably, early in your training you will focus on what you will do during lessons. With experience, you can move forward rapidly, by planning what the children will do. By planning activities appropriate to the learners' needs, you turn the spotlight away from yourself and concentrate on supporting children's learning. Twiselton (2006) describes how trainee teachers progress from seeing themselves as managers of tasks to being deliverers of the curriculum and finally to a stage where they enable children to build concepts and skills. Warren's mentor has this progression in mind when advising Warren about his targets.

The school and wider contexts

Part of your professional expertise involves working as a team member, understanding that learning progresses through the combined efforts of the school staff and the children's parents and carers. Standard 8 is especially relevant: 'Fulfil wider professional responsibilities (make a positive contribution to the wider life and ethos of the school)'.

Superficially, a classroom may appear to be directed by the class teacher, and independent from the rest of the school. You quickly appreciate that the truth is more complex.

First, within the classroom you notice the teacher working regularly with teaching assistants or volunteers, operating as a team leader. Analyse how the teacher shares the lesson plans with other adults. Assistants obviously need clear instructions about the task for which they are responsible, but they must also appreciate why the teacher has set the task, so notice how the teacher explains the intended learning outcomes as well as describing the task.

Next, observe liaison between school and home. Reading books often go home, accompanied by a notebook in which teachers and parents exchange messages about all sorts of things, not just reading. Some parents like to chat with staff when dropping off or collecting children, and more formal arrangements, such as parents' evenings and annual written reports, allow teachers and parents to communicate. Teachers need an ability to get on the right wavelength with each parent, so think carefully about the language you use. Too much educational jargon may mystify a parent; on the other hand, if you 'unpack' the technical vocabulary too much you may appear patronising. In this aspect of your work there is no substitute for experience, so seek opportunities for contact with parents during placements.

Finally, since classrooms do not exist in isolation, you need to be conscious of the range of expertise among the staff of the school.

Initially, you will probably work with your class teacher on curriculum and lesson planning. Other staff may be involved, especially in a large school with more than one class for each age group. Later, you may want further advice about specific areas. Your mentor can point you to appropriate colleagues. The breadth and depth of the primary curriculum places great demands on teachers' subject knowledge. Asking for help from a subject leader is not a sign of weakness, but provides evidence towards Standard 8: 'Fulfil wider professional responsibilities (develop effective professional relationships with colleagues, knowing how and when to draw on advice and specialist support)', since it shows you understand the purpose of teamwork. Similarly, you will probably consult the school's SENDCO to discuss the work of pupils with SEN or disabilities in your class.

The picture of a primary teacher in this section points to the need for a wide range of knowledge and skills. Much of this develops gradually through classroom experience, but it is helpful to use the Teachers' Standards as a checklist, to address both the breadth and depth of your professional obligations.

Teachers' accountability

Jacques and Hyland (2007, p.202) identify 'membership of an organised body involved in testing competence and regulating competence and conduct' as one mark of professionalism. Achieving the standards and passing your training course form the first steps to being recommended for QTS. After that, judgements made by senior colleagues each year will check that you continue to meet the Teachers' Standards. Failure to do so results initially in a programme of support and development, and possibly the withholding by the school's governors of an incremental point on the salary scale. Continued underperformance could lead to disciplinary action including, ultimately, dismissal. These arrangements are how you demonstrate your accountability as fit to work as a teacher.

When appointed to a school you are accountable to the governing body for performing your professional duties. A mentor will support you, and monitor and review your work against the relevant standards. You are expected to be active in undertaking continuing professional development activities, in line with Standard 8: 'Fulfil wider professional responsibilities (take responsibility for improving teaching through appropriate professional development, responding to advice and feedback from colleagues)'.

Apart from your general accountability as an employee, there are other ways in which you are answerable for the quality of your work. Your contribution to the school is reflected in inspection reports and in results published in performance tables. You have to provide written reports at least annually to parents and carers, and attend parents' evenings to discuss children's work. You are accountable to your fellow professionals, for example by participating actively in teamwork for planning, assessing and recording.

Importantly, you are answerable to the children for the quality of your planning, teaching, assessment and feedback, for the care and guidance that you provide and for ensuring that they experience equality of opportunity and the chance to fulfil their educational potential.

Finally, you are accountable to yourself. If you believe that teaching is a vocation as well as a profession, you may find that it takes you over, to the detriment of your home life and leisure activities. Finding an appropriate work/life balance is vital. Teachers should be rounded people with a range of interests and life experience who bring something into school from the outside world, and model to children the possibilities that lie ahead for them. While satisfying your conscience that you have done sufficient work to do a good job, make sure that you also have a fulfilling life outside school.

Learning Outcomes Review

Thinking about the school in which you are working or have recently worked, respond to the prompts after each intended learning outcome, to identify your knowledge and understanding of the issues covered in the chapter.

- **An understanding of the concept of a profession and what makes teaching a profession:**

   Identify from the staff handbook instances of teachers' duties or responsibilities that exemplify Jacques and Hyland's description of professional characteristics.

- **Knowledge of professional and legal frameworks within which teachers operate:**

   - What policies and procedures have been adopted by your placement school to ensure that teachers deal with pupils' behaviour lawfully?
   - What information tells you what to do should you become seriously concerned about a pupil's safety and welfare?
   - Identify two occasions when you collaborated with other staff members (not counting your mentor or class teacher) to make effective provision for the children.

- **An appreciation of ethical principles underpinning teachers' practice:**

   - How have you avoided showing favouritism to particular children or groups in your class?
   - Supposing you had reservations about the actions of a fellow staff member, do you think that remaining silent would be more or less unprofessional than gossiping about it with a colleague?

- **An awareness of the professional knowledge, understanding, skills and attitudes which teachers must display:**

   - Identify one non-core subject that you find hard to teach. Make a list of key concepts associated with this subject, then select examples of skills and information that you could teach to help children understand these concepts.
   - Identify an example of when you changed teaching and learning methods in your planning because of a lesson evaluation.
   - Which member(s) of staff would you turn to for advice about teaching the subject(s) that you find hard to teach? How clear are you about the system of subject leadership operating in your school?

- **Your knowledge of the mechanisms by which teachers' accountability to pupils, parents/carers, employers, fellow professionals and the public is monitored:**
  - Think of an occasion when your performance as a trainee teacher was reviewed. Identify how the quality of your work was measured, and what part you played in assessing your own achievements.
  - Think about how you might prepare for a parents' evening in your first job. What could you usefully find out during your placement to help you be ready for this?
  - Identify ways of saying 'no', politely but firmly, to requests to do additional tasks that you really do not wish to undertake.

Further Reading

The book by Browne and Haylock provides a comprehensive overview of the professional status of teachers and its practical implications, while the Bristol Guide (which is regularly updated) gives full coverage of the laws, statutes and regulations applicable to the work of all professionals and volunteers in schools.

Browne, A. and Haylock, D. (eds) (2004) *Professional Issues for Primary Teachers.* London: Paul Chapman Publishing. See especially the chapter by Manning entitled 'Teaching as a Profession'.

University of Bristol (2014) *Handbook for Education Professionals: The Bristol Guide.* Bristol: Graduate School of Education.

References

Alexander, R. (2010) *Children, Their World, Their Education: Final report and recommendations of the Cambridge Primary Review.* Abingdon: Routledge.

Alexander, R., Rose, J. and Woodhead, C. (1992) *Curriculum Organisation and Classroom Practice in Primary Schools: A discussion paper.* London: DES.

Blatchford, P., Russell, A. and Webster, R. (2012) *Reassessing the Impact of Teaching Assistants.* Abingdon: Routledge.

Bruner, J. (1960) *The Process of Education.* Cambridge, MA: Harvard University Press.

DfE (2012) *Teachers' Standards.* London: DfE. Available from www.education.gov.uk/publications

DfE (2013) *Use of Reasonable Force: Advice for head teachers, staff and governing bodies.* London: DfE.

DfE (2014) *Behaviour and Discipline in Schools: Advice for head teachers and school staff.* London: DfE.

DfEE (1998) *Teaching and Higher Education Act 1998. {c30}.* London: DfEE.

Eraut, M. (1994) *Developing Professional Knowledge and Competence.* London: Routledge Falmer.

Evans, L. (2011) The 'shape' of teacher professionalism in England. *British Educational Research Journal* 37(5) pp. 851–70.

Ewens, T. (2014) *Reflective Primary Teaching*. Northwich: Critical Publishing.

HMG (2013) *Working Together to Safeguard Children*. London: The Stationery Office.

Jacques, K. and Hyland, R. (2007) *Professional Studies: Primary and Early Years* (3rd edition). Exeter: Learning Matters.

Russell, A., Webster, R. and Blatchford, P. (2013) *Maximising the Impact of Teaching Assistants*. Abingdon: Routledge.

Schön, D. (1983) *The Reflective Practitioner: How professionals think in action*. London: Temple Smith.

Twiselton, S. (2006) The problem with English: the exploration and development of student teachers' English subject knowledge in primary classrooms. *Literacy* 40(2) pp. 88–96.

Vygotsky, L. (1978) *Mind in Society: The development of higher psychological processes*. Cambridge, MA: Harvard University Press.

Pay and conditions of service

The Blue Book: *The School Teachers' Pay and Conditions Document*. London: DfE, updated annually, can be viewed at: www.publications.education.gov.uk/default.aspx

The Burgundy Book: *The Conditions of Service for Schoolteachers in England and Wales*. London: Local Government Employers, can be viewed at: www.lge.gov.uk/lge/core/page.do?pageId=119369

Websites of national professional bodies, professional unions and associations

The General Teaching Council for Northern Ireland: www.gtcni.org.uk

The General Teaching Council for Scotland: www.gtcs.org.uk

The General Teaching Council for Wales: www.gtcw.org.uk

The National College for Teaching and Leadership: www.nationalcollege.org.uk

ATL Association of Teachers and Lecturers: www.atl.org.uk

NASUWT National Association of Schoolmasters Union of Women Teachers: www.nasuwt.org.uk

NUT National Union of Teachers: www.nut.org.uk

Voice (formerly Professional Association of Teachers): www.voice.org.uk

9. Establishing your own teacher identity

Denis Hayes

Learning Outcomes

By the end of this chapter you will:

- understand how motivation for teaching influences your actions and decisions;
- have a clearer view of the kind of teacher you want to become;
- understand the meaning and significance of teacher identity;
- have learned how to develop as a reflective practitioner;
- understand the significance and impact of different teaching approaches;
- have gained an overview of professional responsibilities and development;
- have learned about appropriate conduct and behaviour on school placement.

TEACHERS' STANDARDS

A teacher must:

1. **Set high expectations which inspire, motivate and challenge pupils**
   - demonstrate consistently the positive attitudes, values and behaviour which are expected of pupils.

2. **Promote good progress and outcomes by pupils**
   - demonstrate knowledge and understanding of how pupils learn and how this impacts on teaching
   - encourage pupils to take a responsible and conscientious attitude to their own work and study.

8. **Fulfil wider professional responsibilities**
   - make a positive contribution to the wider life and ethos of the school
   - develop effective professional relationships with colleagues, knowing how and when to draw on advice and specialist support
   - take responsibility for improving teaching through appropriate professional development, responding to advice and feedback from colleagues.

Motivation for teaching

What kind of teacher do you want to be is a question frequently posed by tutors and lecturers to their trainees. Answers invariably include reference to attributes such as being kind, fair and caring; to skills such as being a good listener; and to general aims such as helping children to learn and reach their potential. These aspirations provide a core set of beliefs for teachers and yet, in practice, some teachers are more successful than others, which raises a number of issues, not least whether everyone has the potential to be a teacher – or only those who have natural talent.

Every study shows that people become primary teachers because they love to work with children; as such, they are almost invariably very fond of the children in their care and, like a responsible parent, want to do everything possible to ensure each child's welfare. Primary teaching has traditionally been a female-orientated profession and teachers historically see themselves as substitute parents with moral responsibility for children. More recently, there has been an increase in the number of men working with primary age children and, to a lesser extent, the early years' sector (children 3 to 5 years of age).

The fact that primary teachers care deeply about children is indicated by the frequent reference they make to 'my' children. Such affection is not confined to the working day but taken home every evening, occupying minds and actions to such an extent that over time the emotional demands, coupled with the physical exertion and long working days, can lead to mental and physical fatigue. Although teaching primary age children is fun and challenging, you must learn to pace yourself and build your expertise and effectiveness gradually, aided by tutors, colleagues, your own studies and constantly thinking about ways to improve.

Teacher self-identity

In addition to the centrality of altruistic (wanting to help others) motives on their desire to teach, primary teachers tend to judge their own worth as persons in terms of their success at work. As a result, failings in school – whether real or imagined – affect every aspect of their lives. While teachers are always interested in finding ways to boost the self-esteem of children, it is also important that they pay attention to enhancing their own confidence and *self-identity*.

A number of factors influence self-identity: competence and skill level; affirmation by others; practical support from more experienced colleagues; and last but not least, moral conviction, including religious faith, driven by a deep-seated conviction that your teaching makes a positive difference to children's lives. It is often stated that 'schools exist for kids'; while that statement is obviously true, it is also the case that schools are places where large numbers of adults work, each of whom deserves to be nurtured and valued.

Mullen (2007) suggests that the construction of teacher identity is largely affective (the power to move the emotions) and that an investigation of the emotional components of the job helps in an understanding of the teacher's self-identity. Your emotions control the extent to which you will resist or embrace advice and change affects your professional growth; as such, the way you handle your feelings strongly influences your development as a teacher.

Activity

Use the following list as a basis for considering what kind of teacher you want to become.

1. Well-informed about the subjects I teach.
2. Kind and compassionate towards children and colleagues.
3. Approachable, pleasant and responsive.
4. Good listener and communicator.
5. Keen sense of humour.
6. Clear in explaining things to children.
7. Patient but decisive.
8. Make fair judgements.
9. Make sensible decisions.
10. Careful time manager.
11. Clear about what I want children to learn.
12. Willing to respond positively children's genuine interests and questions.
13. Team player and cooperative.
14. Offer positive comments and suggestions.
15. Take account of criticism from others and act appropriately.
16. Take every opportunity to encourage my colleagues.
17. Now make a list of the characteristics you want to avoid.

Values and teaching

It is helpful to think of education as being grounded in five fundamental values: spiritual, cultural, environmental, aesthetic and political. Each of these values is expressed in terms of your *personal* values with regard to self; your *moral* values with regard to others; and your *social* values with regard to the community in which you are placed. For instance, one of your personal values might be to treat others as you wish to be treated; a moral value might be to listen carefully and respond compassionately to colleagues' concerns; a social value might be to volunteer for an after-school club in a desire to contribute expertise for the benefit of others.

Eaude (2006) argues that 'the person' as a teacher cannot be separated from the person you are at all other times. As a result, the values that you bring to the classroom, through your personality, enthusiasm, emotions and priorities, combine to influence children and affect their feelings of self-worth and desire to learn. The relationship (bond) between you and the children is therefore an essential factor in determining your success as a teacher. Children respond well to adults who relate to them naturally and are always approachable. No amount of posturing and forcefulness on your part will compensate for establishing and maintaining caring relations with the children for whom you have responsibility. See also Chapter 4 in this book.

Teacher identity and integrity

Studies about teachers' professional identity indicate that we must pay careful attention to: (a) the relationship between concepts of 'self' and 'identity'; (b) the importance of what counts as 'professional' in professional identity; (c) the impact of the educational setting in shaping identity; and (d) the place of emotions, temperament and personality. In 1997, P.J. Palmer wrote an influential article in which he defines identity and integrity (Palmer, 1997a). Thus, identity is described as:

> *An evolving nexus {set of connections} where all the forces that constitute my life converge in the mystery of self: my genetic makeup, the nature of the man and woman who gave me life, the culture in which I was raised, people who have sustained me and people who have done me harm, the good and ill I have done to others, and to myself, the experience of love and suffering ...*

In similar vein he explores the related characteristic of integrity:

> *Integrity requires that I discern what is integral to my selfhood, what fits and what does not – and that I choose life-giving ways of relating to the forces that converge within me. Do I welcome them or fear them, embrace them or reject them, move with them or against them?*

Palmer goes on to say that by choosing integrity, you become more whole, but that wholeness does not mean that you never make mistakes. He identifies the relationship between the two qualities of identity and integrity such that identity lies in the diverse forces that make up a life, whereas integrity consists of forces that bring the person wholeness and life rather than fragmentation and deadness. (See also Palmer, 1997b.)

Activity
Think of three teachers you have known well and evaluate their identity and integrity as outlined by Palmer (1997a). List the sorts of key decisions you need to make and priorities you need to establish as you seek to develop your own identity and integrity as a teacher.

Adopting a reflective approach

As the prime satisfaction for most primary teachers is the pleasure of interacting with children and positively affecting their lives – rather than a desire for monetary rewards or status – a teacher's value position is rooted in a need to cherish, serve, empower and benefit the children in their care. As a result, primary teachers constantly need to evaluate their work regarding the fundamental purpose of what they are doing as educators and the daily task of translating those beliefs into practical teaching. A key ambition in your professional life should be to become a 'reflective practitioner', both during lessons (reflecting 'in' teaching) and following teaching sessions (reflecting 'on' teaching).

Activity

If you haven't done so already, begin the reflective process by keeping a record of your classroom experiences (for example, assessing how clearly you communicate ideas and instructions to children) under four main headings.

1. What I did: e.g. *I explained how children should set out their work.*
2. Why I did it: e.g. *I wanted to improve the appearance of their written work.*
3. What was good about it: e.g. *I spoke slowly and carefully and answered their queries using child-friendly language. My pedagogical knowledge was good.*
4. What could have been improved: e.g. *I need to ensure that every child is paying attention before I speak.*

Your personal values and ideas about priorities in education and life more widely have a strong impact on shaping classroom practice, as you encourage children to respect other viewpoints, speak plainly but courteously, collaborate, weigh up situations, summarise key points, evaluate options and communicate ideas carefully in a supportive (non-judgemental) way.

Research Focus: Teachers as reflective practitioners

Larrivee (2008) reviewed the research on creating a learning climate conducive to facilitating the development of teachers as reflective practitioners and concluded that the process involves a willingness to be an active participant in professional growth. The author argues that the aim of reflective practice is to think critically about one's teaching choices and actions. Consequently, reflective practice involves teachers questioning the goals, values and assumptions that guide their work and entails interrogating the way things are done, the purpose of education and the contexts in which learning takes place. See also Ghaye and Ghaye (1998).

Motivating the children

Your enthusiasm for a subject is important but is not of itself a sufficiently strong factor to ensure that children are motivated to learn. You also need empathy, compassion, commitment, patience, spontaneity and an ability to make sound judgements to produce what is sometimes described as 'loving relations' in the classroom. O'Quinn and Garrison (2004) argue that by nurturing loving recognition and by being brave enough to take risks in learning to allow for children's own shortcomings and vulnerabilities, you can help to develop a tolerant, harmonious and caring learning climate. Children are not only impressed by your knowledge and teaching skills but also by human qualities such as your patience, kindness and encouraging manner.

Values education

A good education is founded on developing the human personality in all its dimensions – intellectual, physical, social, ethical and moral (Sridhar, 2001). Thornberg (2008) argues that *values education* does not depend on following a planned programme of work but is often unplanned and should be embedded in everyday school life. In common with Palmer (see earlier), Thornburg argues that values reflect the personal concerns and preferences that help to frame relationships between children and adults. In other words, your effectiveness as a teacher has as much to do with the heart (emotions) as with the mind (intellect). In practice, teachers use this spontaneity in conjunction with the curriculum to enhance the social and emotional aspects of learning, usually referred to as SEAL.

The values that you bring to the classroom should be the result of careful and informed thinking, as you seek to dovetail your personal morality (inner beliefs) with impartial justice (fair to all). The reason for taking such care is well expressed by Richards when he refers to the teacher as a 'frighteningly significant person whose teaching helps to shape attitudes to learning at a most sensitive period in children's development' (2009, p.20). While most children grow up to develop competent moral skills, a small number of them fail to do so and cultivate a highly sophisticated form of deviance (Rossano, 2008). In the light of this trend, the author recommends the promotion of deliberate moral practice, suggesting that religious participation provides the basic elements to facilitate it.

You must decide how best to inculcate children into behaving appropriately, while resisting the temptation to give the impression that your way is the *only* way – their parents may have different ideas. For example, you might impress on the children that bullying is wrong, while some parents might be telling them to 'stand up for themselves', even at the expense of others' suffering. Whatever you discuss or declare, it pays to be aware that children often repeat at home things they hear you say in school, so be clear with them about what is right and wrong but be cautious about imposing your own morality on them in a way that might invite criticism.

Developing your teaching approach

Factors influencing your teaching

A teaching approach consists of the methods and strategies that teachers employ to help children learn effectively and reflect the beliefs that practitioners hold about the nature of learning and education in general. Thus, one teacher might believe that children learn best when they are motivated by opportunities to explore ideas as a group, while another teacher may be convinced that they learn best when working individually. Again, one teacher may employ a considerable amount of direct teaching, utilising question-and-answer supported by repetition of facts, while another teacher prefers a problem-solving method in which children are encouraged to raise their own questions and seek their own solutions. One teacher's style may be informal and strongly interactive, using humour and good-natured banter, while another teacher might adopt a more detached and serious manner. Many teachers vary their approach depending on the subject area; thus, an investigative science session might involve a large percentage of group work whereas a phonics lesson will probably be geared towards a more systematic, teacher-led approach.

As a trainee teacher, you will gradually develop your own style of teaching, influenced by five factors: (a) your evolving beliefs about effective teaching and learning; (b) the approach that works best for you; (c) the influence of more experienced teachers; (d) the approach that children seem to enjoy best; (e) the approach the regular teacher uses with the children. The final point is important – if you are on school placement and attempt to use a significantly different approach from the usual teacher, the children might struggle to understand your intentions and what is expected of them. It is better to observe the regular teacher's methods and closely follow them for a time before gradually introducing small changes of your own.

Whatever teaching approach you adopt, teaching primary age children relies heavily on the creation and maintenance of a bond of trust and mutual respect between adult and child. You need to have insight into the things that children find significant if you want to create effective communication networks that will enhance learning and maintain good relations. Children appreciate adults who are fair, interested in them as individuals, transparent in their dealings, clear about their intentions, helpful in their explanations, non-judgemental in their attitude yet unflinching in confronting unsatisfactory situations. They benefit from teachers who are prepared to listen carefully to what children say to them, which enhances self-esteem, motivation and academic success. Your positive attitude, enthusiasm and high expectations can make a considerable difference in the way that children view learning, their behaviour and the extent to which they are willing to persevere.

Research Focus: Views of teaching

An interesting insight into primary teachers' views of teaching was exposed by Taylor (2002) who found that out of a group of 55 experienced teachers, over 80 per cent of them opted for an approach that can be broadly defined as 'child-centred' (Doddington and Hilton, 2007, p.34), defined as follows.

$\longrightarrow$

- Learning comes naturally to children.

- Children/students learn because they want to learn and not because they are told to do so.

- Play and work are indistinguishable.

- Learning is a communal activity rather than individual.

- The main aim of teaching is to develop the whole person (academic, social, spiritual).

- The curriculum should be related to the child's or student's needs.

- The teacher should encourage children to develop their own mode of learning.

Child-centred philosophy

Taylor (2002) – see Research Focus above – notes that the results of his research are almost identical to those carried out among primary teachers some 25 years earlier (Ashton et al., 1975). Only about one-fifth of the teachers in Taylor's sample group aligned themselves with a view encapsulated in the ideology promoted in recent years, notably that:

1. Real learning cannot possibly be easy.

2. Children must be made to work rather than do so out of interest.

3. Play is not work unless it is highly structured and controlled by adults.

4. Learning is an individual matter.

5. The main aim of teaching is to develop the intellect, not the emotions.

6. The curriculum should relate to the needs of society.

7. The teacher's job is to motivate and direct learning rather than involve children.

Instead, Taylor's findings that the majority of teachers preferred a child-centred approach reflected research carried out among aspiring teachers in England by Hayes (2004) and in Australia (Manuel and Hughes, 2006). Manuel and Hughes concluded that many prospective teachers enter teaching 'with a sense of mission to transform the lives of young people and open opportunities for growth through learning and connecting' (p.21).

Activity
To what extent do each of the seven principles based on the work of Taylor (2002) reflect your own view of teaching and learning? Take each principle in turn and for each one select from: agree strongly/agree/tend to disagree/disagree strongly. Discuss your conclusions with others.

Continuous professional development

Teachers are required to undergo continuous professional development (CPD) from the moment they enter a course of training until they retire from the job. CPD is defined as the systematic maintenance, improvement and broadening of knowledge and skills, together with the development of personal qualities, all of which are necessary for the execution of professional and practical responsibilities throughout a working life. See Chapter 12 for further discussion on CPD. Qualified teachers commonly refer to CPD as *in-service training* or INSET as they are developing expertise 'on the job'. Over time, you are expected to expand your subject knowledge; improve your organisation and management of teaching; learn new skills (e.g. specific uses of information technology) and increasingly contribute to the school's academic performance and attractiveness – especially to parents. Great teachers are forged from a combination of inspiration and perspiration; you need a substantial amount of *both* qualities.

Newly qualified primary teachers tend to use the teaching approach that they developed during training or modelled on a teacher whom they admire. As they progress, teachers gradually extend the reaches of their experience, focus their energies more efficiently and become more upbeat about school life, though a few older members of staff grow bitter and cynical. As a new teacher, you are advised to avoid being drawn into negative conversations with pessimistic colleagues. Instead, smile, nod and quickly find something else to do.

Reflecting in and on action

As noted earlier, you need to improve your competence through a process of self-evaluation in two ways: (a) at the end of a lesson or series of lessons (reflection *on* action), and (b) during the lesson (reflection *in* action). In other words, you must not only take time to 'stand back' at the end of the session but be mentally active throughout the session(s) in evaluating your role and assessing how well the children responded to what you said to them and concentrated on their allocated work.

It is helpful to reflect *on* action by asking two key questions: (1) How well did I undertake and exercise my responsibilities as teacher? (2) How well did the children learn? The second question is more difficult to answer than the first because learning is never smooth and uninterrupted; most children learn a little, forget a little, become confused for a time then understand better, grapple with imponderables and gradually digest knowledge as they think and talk about ideas and reinforce their tentative understanding by asking questions, practising skills and exploring problems.

The model of teaching and learning that advocates a linear progression – *Teach ... learn ... evaluate learning and modify the next lesson ... teach ... learn* and so on – fails to take account of the complexity of the learning process and the need for constant reinforcement. Assessing and evaluating a small portion of work, followed by allocating grades or giving marks to represent attainment, is deceptively appealing. You *do* need to evaluate children's progress – and giving a grade or mark can be useful, providing they understand its significance – but you also need to recognise that learning is complex and cannot be reduced to a simple formula. See Chapter 4 in this book for further details.

Reflection *in* action presents its own challenges, not least the fact that it takes place during the lesson at a time when you have so much else to consider. Nevertheless, you will need to discipline yourself to think on your feet, evaluate your teaching spontaneously and make decisions about a range of issues, including:

- the length of time you spend on each part of the lesson (lesson phase);
- the length of time you spend assisting each child or group of children;
- the way that you respond to children's questions;
- the way that you handle instances of indiscipline;
- the standard of work that you accept from children;
- the opportunities you offer for children to explore ideas, investigate and discover new knowledge for themselves.

It is normal for inexperienced teachers to spend more time reflecting *on* action than *in* action. However, over time and with perseverance, you will find it easier to keep a 'mental running commentary', as you rapidly evaluate your actions and the children's responses and make rapid adjustments to what you say and do. It pays to concentrate on one or two aspects of your classroom practice at a time. For example, during one lesson you might make a conscious effort to differentiate the questions you use to ensure that less capable children can respond to simpler ones and more capable children have to think hard about tough ones; in a second lesson, you might pay particular attention to the nature of pupil feedback and your use of praise.

Professional advancement

The need for teachers to provide evidence that children have benefited directly from their teaching has been integral to career advancement, so teachers have to be able to point to measurable and verifiable aspects of pupil learning. Most teachers take advantage of internal promotion opportunities in the school but only a very small number become head teachers. See Neil and Morgan (2003) and Bubb (2004) for an overview of issues attached to professional progression across a career. The National College for School Leadership in England established in 2000 – now known as the National College for Teaching and Leadership – prepared and trained aspiring subject leaders, deputy head teachers and head teachers. This signalled that professional advancement was increasingly dependent on external forms of verification. See Chapter 12 for more about professional advancement. Now, the focus of the NCTL, an executive agency sponsored by the DfE, aims to improve the quality of the education and early years workforce and encourage schools to help each other improve. NCTL works with schools to develop an education system supported locally by partnerships and led by the best head teachers (https://www.gov.uk/government/organisations/national-college-for-teaching-and-leadership/about).

Professional responsibilities

In recent years, a lot of legislation has been passed specific to the role of teachers that has had an impact on the way that they relate to children in school. A teacher's responsibility for pupil welfare has grown beyond the original standard of *in loco parentis* (standing in the place of the parent). Depending on the age of the children, the person or persons with a primary duty of care must ensure that all reasonable precautions have been taken to protect and safeguard their welfare (Nixon, 2007).

There has been a substantial increase in the amount of litigation in society generally and this trend has influenced the work of adults in school. Consequently, all teachers are obliged to keep abreast of the way in which laws and codes of practice impact upon their behaviour. Teachers must also conform to their professional duties as required by the head teacher, in line with their contracts of employment. A refusal to do so can be interpreted as a breach of contract and invite disciplinary procedures. All new teachers receive a letter of appointment from the school governors/school board specifying matters such as salary, duties and tenure.

Teachers' professional values and practice includes having high expectations of every pupil, respecting a child's social, cultural, linguistic, religious and ethnic backgrounds, and showing wholehearted concern for their academic and social development. The establishment of standards for qualified teacher status and what amounts to a national scheme for teacher training is intended to maintain overall competence.

The need for an acceptable standard of teacher behaviour is discussed in detail in Chapter 8. It is important because primary teachers act as models or examples to their children and local communities. General Teaching Councils (GTCs) in Wales, Scotland and Northern Ireland exist to promote a sense of collegiality and consistency across the teaching profession. However, the GTC (England) was disbanded in 2010. Teachers are bound by formal and implicit codes of ethics that specify how they are to fulfil their duties and obligations with respect to the education they provide. Teachers can be reprimanded for misdemeanours as diverse as repeatedly failing to hand in planning and assessment files to the head teacher for monitoring; demonstrating overt insensitivity to children; or using inappropriate language in front of children and colleagues.

To avoid problems, make every effort to be positive about life in general, avoid complaining and listen respectfully to the things that children and colleagues say. At all cost, avoid any trace of arrogance or giving the impression to staff that you can manage perfectly well on your own and don't need their advice. You can enhance your reputation by arriving in good time for school, staying behind to complete tasks, being courteous and pleasant to colleagues, using your time productively during the day and persevering to improve your teaching skills.

School placement issues

A significant part of a teacher training course is time spent on school placement. To make the best use of these periods you need to do a lot of thinking and preparation before and during the placement. Before you begin, you will be given plenty of advice by tutors and allocated tasks that you must undertake during the time in school. There is nearly always a lot of paperwork to complete, so grit your teeth and get on with it! In the case of extended placements, it is normal to make a preliminary visit to the school or educational setting to meet staff and children and become familiar with the set up. Don't forget to be friendly, smile a lot and reassure the host teacher by your positive but mature attitude that you will be an asset and not a liability.

During the placement, it takes time to adjust to a new situation, so don't be discouraged if you struggle and feel a bit overwhelmed, especially during the first few days. Hayes (2009) suggests that however hard you work and however sincere is your level of commitment, the time you spend on placement in school is always going to be challenging as well as rewarding. The placement provides opportunities for you to hone your teaching skills and learn about the various teacher roles, supported by a tutor and the school staff. One of the most important things to do is to learn the children's names. Another is to clarify with the teacher/tutor/mentor precisely what is expected of you, when you will be taking responsibility and what you need to prepare. A third is to show a willingness to 'get stuck in'. Don't try to endear yourself to the children by being overfamiliar; you can be friendly without compromising your teacher status.

As the placement begins and you do more teaching, you will discover that a variety of practical factors over which you have no control interfere with your carefully laid plans; for example, the school may have a special event that requires time-consuming rehearsals or a special visitor might arrive causing a session to be curtailed at short notice. Occasionally, the regular teacher is ill or absent for other reasons and you have to negotiate with one or more substitute teachers, which tends to delay or accelerate your rise to stardom. Your reaction to unexpected twists and turns reveals a lot about your suitability for teaching, so try to be flexible and view such difficulties as opportunities rather than annoying hindrances. Save your complaining for when you meet your friends in the evening.

Research Focus: Issues facing new teachers

Research carried out by Jacklin et al. (2006) about the issues faced by new primary teachers indicated that one of the greatest challenges was taking full responsibility for the whole class, including establishing and enforcing boundaries of behaviour, pupil safety, registration, liaising with parents, and so on. Trainee teachers are partially protected from this all-encompassing role but still need to recognise that there is more to being a teacher than teaching lessons. The authors go on to say that differentiated teaching, supporting and extending the least and most able children, and above all, setting high expectations and standards for all, irrespective of gender, ethnicity, race, disability or social background, are all part of the day-to-day role of a primary teacher.

The majority of placements are satisfactory or better; occasionally a placement is disappointing, either because you receive inadequate support, guidance and help from the host teacher/mentor or for some unaccountable reason you don't get on with the children. In such cases it is important to do your best to stay positive, refuse to countenance failure and make constructive use of your tutor and mentor. The reality is that although occasional setbacks are inevitable, they can be used as an incentive to do better and do not spell the end of your teaching career. Use the Activity on p. 184 as a guide for evaluating your progress.

Case Study

Two trainee teachers, who had spent time in separate schools as part of their teaching placement, reflected on ways in which their professional development had been affected by widely differing experiences. In the first example, Chris explains how she persevered with an unpromising situation. In the second example, Emma describes her 'dream placement' in a school where pupil behaviour was good and she felt welcomed by the host teachers. The case studies are in the trainees' own words.

Chris (working with Year 5 children)

> The placement didn't get off to a very good start because in my first meeting with the teacher/tutor, she confessed that she had not really wanted another trainee, so I felt like an intruder. I worked with a group of children whose classroom and learning behaviour was very challenging. They were hard to motivate and showed little interest in the work they were given to do. Many of them seemed to have switched off from school altogether. Several children had serious learning difficulties that were not recognised or being addressed by the teacher or catered for in lessons. A small group of unsettled and uncooperative children dominated much of teacher's attention throughout the

→

school day with the result that other children's needs were not being well met. The classroom environment was poor and uncared for; for instance, there was minimal work on display and children's work was often left unmarked, just lying around gathering dust. Unfortunately, my college tutor was off sick during much of the placement and the school was a long way from the university, so I felt very isolated. There was so much that I wanted to learn, see and do, but owing to the challenging conditions much remains unseen and undone. So, overall this placement was not what I had hoped for at all but in a way I learned more than in my previous school where the children were lovely, the teachers were highly supportive and I was made very welcome. The most important lesson I learned was that I have inner reserves of strength that I didn't know I possessed. I made up my mind to be the very best teacher I could possibly be in the circumstances and refused to become negative or cynical, though there were times of intense frustration. I also became aware of the sort of teacher I definitely did not want to become. Mind you, I still hope my final school placement is easier than the one I've just finished. It would have been easy to imagine that everything was my fault when in fact I think I coped well and made good progress despite the situation. Even so, I envy those some of my friends who didn't have to endure the inner turmoil, strains and stresses that I experienced. Emotions play such a powerful role in teaching, so being unsettled in school has an adverse effect on every other part of your life, too.

Emma (working with Reception children)

I was really fortunate with my placement in that I was quickly able to fit in really well with staff at the school and soon became regarded and treated like a fellow teacher and colleague. The class teacher and the two teaching assistants I worked with were highly skilled, supportive and cheerful. They gave me loads of ideas, resources and assistance with my small-scale research I had to do as part of the placement about ways that children learn through play. I felt myself grow in confidence and become a member of the team rather than a trainee teacher sitting in the corner of the room! Having such positive support and encouragement meant that the class felt like my own and as a result the children responded well to me.

Support from my class teacher really helped me when I was uncertain or struggling with an issue, as she offered advice in a constructive and pleasant way. I was never afraid to approach her even when I mucked things up, as she always tried to be positive instead of moaning. One unexpected bonus from being accepted as a teacher was the fact that parents increasingly came to me and asked about their children's progress. I was thrilled when some of the parents told me how excited their children were about what I was teaching them in school. My school mentor was very experienced and I felt 100 per cent confident about his guidance (unlike my previous school experiences). He was kind, supportive and caring, which made it my favourite placement of the year. I intend to make sure that I'm as supportive to the trainees that come into my classroom when I'm qualified.

The above instances show that both trainees developed their expertise and sense of self in different ways. In the first case, the trainee had to draw on her inner strength and belief and learn to be self-reliant in an unpromising situation. In the second case, the trainee had the luxury of a supportive environment and well-behaved children.

Activity

1. What were the different professional challenges facing Chris and Emma?
2. In what ways might Chris have made more progress as a teacher than Emma?
3. What sort of factors combined to create the 'inner turmoil' described by Chris?

All teachers can be persuaded that you are an asset if they see that you respond to their advice, strive to do your best and do not threaten their way of working (Hayes, 2003). Despite any reservations you may hold, try to view the teacher as your ally and strive to keep channels of communication open. Stay positive, focus on the children's learning, listen to advice, do your best to implement it and keep paperwork up to date. Thankfully, the large majority of trainee teachers enjoy their placements, though moments of uncertainty and self-doubt are inevitable. Be encouraged that the vast majority of trainees are successful and complete the time in school feeling much more like Emma than like Chris.

Activity

Evaluate your professional progress using the following coding: (1) Progressing well, (2) Progressing satisfactorily, (3) Requiring attention, (4) Requiring urgent attention.

a) I am being positive about my situation and avoid moaning.
b) I am maintaining open communication with colleagues, especially the class teacher.
c) I am listening carefully to advice.
d) I am thoughtfully acting upon advice.
e) I am being friendly, courteous and warm towards others.
f) I am acting in a considerate and caring manner.
g) I am preparing and evaluating lessons thoroughly.
h) I am maintaining necessary paperwork, including assessment of pupil progress.
i) I am reflecting on my teaching during lessons and after the session.
j) I am interacting with parents and keeping them informed.
k) I am becoming familiar with school policies for safeguarding children.
l) I am taking opportunities for leisure and recreation to 'recharge my batteries'.

Learning Outcomes Review

Thinking about the school in which you are working or recently worked, respond to the prompts after each intended learning outcome, to identify your knowledge and understanding of the issues covered in the chapter.

- **To understand how motivation for teaching influences your actions and decisions:**
  - What sort of a teacher do you want to be and why?

- **To have a clearer view of the kind of teacher you want to become:**
  - What values and personal qualities are essential for teaching?

- **To understand the meaning and significance of teacher identity:**
  - How will you go about motivating and encouraging children?

- **To learn how to develop as a reflective practitioner:**
  - What strategies will you use to safeguard your own wellbeing and identity as a person?

- **To understand the significance and impact of different teaching approaches:**
  - What forms of evidence will you use to show that you are improving as a teacher?

- **To gain an overview of professional responsibilities and development:**
  - What factors will guide your decisions about a suitable teaching approach?

- **To learn about appropriate conduct and behaviour on school placement:**
  - What impression do you want to give while you are on school placement to (a) the regular teacher (b) the children (c) the parents?

References

Arthur, J., Davison, J. and Lewis, M. (2005) *Professional Values and Practice: Achieving the standards for QTS.* London: Routledge.

Ashton, P., Kneen, P. and Davies, F. (1975) *Aims into Practice in the Primary School.* London: Hodder and Stoughton.

Bubb, S. (2004) *The Insider's Guide to Early Professional Development.* London: Routledge.

DfE (2011) *Teachers' Standards.* Available from www.education.gov.uk/publications

Doddington, C. and Hilton, M. (2007) *Child-Centred Education.* London: Sage.

Eaude, T. (2006) *Children's Spiritual, Moral, Social and Cultural Development.* Exeter: Learning Matters.

Ghaye, A. and Ghaye, K. (1998) *Teaching and Learning through Critical Reflective Practice.* London: David Fulton.

Hayes, D. (2003) *A Student Teacher's Guide to Primary School Placement.* London: Routledge.

Hayes, D. (2004) Recruitment and retention: insights into the motivation of primary trainee teachers in England. *Research in Education* 71, pp.37–49.

Hayes, D. (2009) *Primary Teaching Today.* London: Routledge.

Jacklin, A., Griffiths, V. and Robinson, C. (2006) *Beginning Primary Teaching.* Maidenhead: Open University.

Jeffreys, M. (1971) *Education: Its nature and purpose.* London: Allen and Unwin.

Larrivee, B. (2008) Meeting the challenge of preparing reflective practitioners. *The New Educator* 4(2) pp.87–106.

Manuel, J. and Hughes, J. (2006) It has always been my dream: exploring pre-service teachers' motivations for choosing to teach. *Teacher Development* 10(1) pp.5–24.

Mullen, C. (2007) *Curriculum Leadership Development.* London: Routledge.

Neil, P. and Morgan, C. (2003) *Continuing Professional Development for Teachers.* London: Kogan Page.

Nixon, J. (2007) Teachers' legal liabilities and responsibilities. In Cole, M. (ed.) *Professional Attributes and Practice.* London: David Fulton.

O'Quinn, E. and Garrison, J. (2004) Creating loving relations in the classroom. In Liston, D. and Garrison, J. (eds) *Teaching, Learning and Loving.* London: Routledge.

Palmer, P.J. (1997a) The heart of a teacher: identity and integrity in teaching. Available from www.newhorizons.org/strategies/character/ palmer.htm

Palmer, P.J. (1997b) *The Courage to Teach: Exploring the inner landscape of a teacher's life.* San Francisco: Jossey-Bass.

Richards, C. (2009) Primary teaching: a personal perspective. In Arthur, J., Grainger, T. and Wray, D. (eds) *Learning to Teach in the Primary School.* London: Routledge.

Rossano, M.J. (2008) The moral faculty: does religion promote moral expertise? *International Journal for the Psychology of Religion* 18(3) pp.169–94.

Sridhar, Y.N. (2001) Value development. National Council for Teacher Education (NCTE). Value Orientation in Teacher Education conference, New Delhi.

Taylor, P.H. (2002) Primary teachers' views of what helps and hinders teaching. *Education 3–13* 31(2) pp.34–9.

Thornberg, R. (2008) The lack of professional knowledge in values education. *Teaching and Teacher Education* 24(7) pp.1791–8.

10. Safeguarding children
Pat Macpherson

Learning Outcomes

By the end of this chapter you will have had the opportunity to:

- think about a range of safeguarding and child protection issues, both generally and with specific reference to children in the primary age phase;
- consider implications for your professional practice with regard to safeguarding and child protection in meeting national standards for gaining qualified teacher status and maintaining your licence to teach;
- know about the roles of key school and other agencies' personnel related to safeguarding and child protection;
- become familiar with key statutory and non statutory documents related to safeguarding and child protection.

TEACHERS' STANDARDS

A teacher must:

1. **Set high expectations which inspire, motivate and challenge pupils**
- establish a safe and stimulating environment for pupils, rooted in mutual respect.

2. **Promote good progress and outcomes by pupils**
- be accountable for pupils' attainment, progress and outcomes.

5. **Adapt teaching to respond to the strengths and needs of all pupils**
- have a secure understanding of how a range of factors can inhibit pupils' ability to learn, and how best to overcome these
- demonstrate an awareness of the physical, social and intellectual development of children, and know how to adapt teaching to support pupils' education at different stages of development.

8. **Fulfil wider professional responsibilities**
- develop effective professional relationships with colleagues, knowing how and when to draw on advice and specialist support.

PART 2: PERSONAL AND PROFESSIONAL CONDUCT

- **Teachers uphold public trust in the profession and maintain high standards of ethics and behaviour within and outside school, by:**
  - having regard for the need to safeguard pupils' wellbeing, in accordance with statutory provisions
- **Teachers must have an understanding of, and always act within, the statutory frameworks which set out their professional duties and responsibilities.**

Introduction

As a trainee teacher you will 'be' the teacher for much of your time on placement. Even in the early days of your education and training to become a teacher you will be in role as a teacher when you are in school. Through your theoretical learning and your practical experience in school you will develop over time your knowledge and understanding of children together with your skills and competences in managing an appropriate learning environment for them. Safeguarding and child protection are essential parts of your work as a trainee teacher and so have to be central to all of your practice and interactions with children and colleagues. You will explore this further within this chapter but please remember that links can be made with other chapters in this book.

The notion of safeguarding is about an approach that ensures that children grow up in circumstances consistent with the provision of safe and effective care, so that they have the best chances in life. Child protection is a particular instance of safeguarding undertaken to protect specific children who are suffering, or at risk of suffering, significant harm (HMG, 2013, p.85).

Safeguarding

Safeguarding is first and foremost about promoting children's welfare. One way of doing this is to build their resilience, since by developing their confidence and knowledge teachers can reduce children's vulnerability to some possible risks. This does not mean systematically removing all risks from the classroom, because learning to deal with risks within a secure setting is a helpful way of building pupils' resilience. Creating a positive relationship between you and your class is a central factor.

Safeguarding and child protection derive from many aspects of your practice – classroom climate, a good grounding in child development (including emotional development and how children develop feelings of security and resilience) and your knowledge and understanding of different patterns of family life and the position of children in families and communities. Establishing an appropriate emotional climate in your classroom (as well as an appropriate learning environment) requires a genuine commitment from you to children's wellbeing. Get it right and you will be the sort of teacher that children can trust; someone they can turn to or talk to about problems and issues. Teaching allows you to establish close and, hopefully, productive relationships with children, and social and emotional interactions that occur each and every day in the classroom lie at the heart of those relationships. If you get the relationships right then children will feel welcomed and valued in your classroom, and if they feel welcomed and valued by you as their 'teacher' then they are more likely to tell you if something is going wrong in their life.

In addition to creating an appropriate emotional climate in your classroom, you can also use the curriculum as a means of building children's resilience. Teaching about the safe use of the internet and online communications, how to eat healthily and keep fit, and how to use equipment and apparatus safely are obvious examples, all of which are made more effective if put into practice as well as spoken about. Choosing specific learning approaches can also contribute. For example, structured work in small groups can enable some children to voice their opinions and concerns, whereas they might not readily speak in front of the whole class.

In general, safeguarding is associated with the thoughtful implementation of good professional practices.

Promoting children's wellbeing includes measures such as ensuring that your classroom contains no obvious physical hazards, monitoring procedures for moving safely around the school and giving clear directions for the use of apparatus in, for instance, technology and PE. Particular care is needed when planning to take children away from the school premises. Schools have policies and protocols for educational visits, designed to enable teachers to anticipate and avoid problems, and these are directed by an educational visits coordinator (EVC). You will need to liaise with this colleague before planning such activities. Your duty of care extends to these situations but ultimate responsibility lies with the head teacher and governing body. For some trips outside the classroom you will need to gain formal permission from the governors to undertake the visit as well as completing a risk assessment; for others it will be enough to complete a risk assessment only. The EVC will be able to provide information on this. Other sources of support in the area of out-of-school activities are the teaching unions and you will find they provide useful guidance and information. Basically, though, it is essential that you follow all elements of the school's policy and procedures in organising and conducting out-of-school activities and trips. These can vary in detail from school to school but all will require that the following checklist has been completed satisfactorily:

- full, detailed planning of all aspects of the trip – travel, transitions, access to meals and drinks, toilet break, spending money (if this is permitted), educational opportunities from the visit;
- supervision ratios and arrangements;
- a completed risk assessment;
- contact details for children's parents and/or carers.

As you read the case study below, think about the responses you would make, both before and after the trip if you were Simon's friend.

Case Study: A school trip

Simon's class teacher intends to provide an out-of-school activity for the children. He is asked to read the school's policy on out-of-school trips prior to meeting with her to go through the planned activity. Simon tells his friend that he has read the policy but that he does not see the point of it. 'Common sense is all that is needed,' he says.

$\longrightarrow$

After the visit, Simon reflects on his experience. He shares with his friend that he now understands how important it is to follow the school's policy and procedure. For example, he explains the reasoning behind one teacher driving her own car to the venue instead of all staff and adults travelling on the coach with the children. He understands that in this case, one teacher drove her own car to provide immediate access to transport should an emergency arise. She had checked that her own personal car insurance covered her for work-based travel.

As well as adopting good practices you need actively to avoid poor practice, not least because it might give rise to suspicions or allegations against you. Some issues are clear cut; for example, sanctions involving physical punishment are prohibited. Other areas are greyer. Some people suggest that teachers should avoid touching children, while others maintain that offering comfort to a distressed child or restraining an aggressive one are integral to a teacher's professional duty. As a teacher, you have easy access to children, you are present when they are changing clothes or undressing, for swimming, for example, and you can sometimes be alone with a child. Your personal conduct at these times must be beyond reproach.

Child protection

Every child should be safe. Sadly, not every child is. Shockingly, some children are at risk of harm from the very people they should be able to rely on for love and care. We all have a responsibility to do everything possible to protect those vulnerable children.

(DfES, 2009)

This quotation is taken from the government's response to Lord Laming's report (2009) into progress in child protection practice following the case of Victoria Climbié, who died at the hands of the adults who were supposed to be looking after her. It exemplifies the principles and commitments that underpin legislation and policy in child protection. Protecting children is everybody's responsibility but this is particularly the case for professionals – including teachers – who work with children. The statement also helps us recognise and understand the enormous responsibilities teachers have in ensuring that they play their part in helping to keep children safe and protected – at school and, as part of a wider, multi-disciplinary team, at home and in the community. The constituent parts of that responsibility are introduced and explored below. No hierarchy is intended in the order in which these are presented; rather they reflect my approach to considering child protection for intending teachers.

There are three elements that help inform your understanding of how a (shared) responsibility for child protection in primary schools and other educational settings can be demonstrated in and through your practice. These elements are the emotional, legal and professional dimensions.

The emotional dimension

Thinking about how you respond to a child for whom there is a child protection concern can be very upsetting. You may feel anger and resentment towards abusers, frustration that not all children are indeed protected fully from abuse or fear that you will not be able to fulfil your professional obligations and duties.

Activity

Write down two or three feelings which come to mind when thinking about child abuse and child protection.

Consider and reflect on the range of feelings that you have identified.

What feelings emerged? You may have listed any or all of the following: anger, frustration, confusion, panic, self-doubt, disgust, despair, feeling overwhelmed, disbelief, fear, protectiveness. You may have mentioned other feelings and emotions and you may have experiences in your past which inform those feelings. Whatever your starting point in thinking through feelings and emotions that emerge when you think about child protection, it is important to recognise that child abuse does raise strong emotions for many people and that it is a subject influenced by our personal value systems and experiences. You also need to remember that you are not alone in dealing with such cases because there will be other professionals (both in and out of the school setting) who will work with you and support you.

Research Focus

Baginsky and Macpherson (2005) carried out research which led into the development of a training pack for trainee teachers published by the NSPCC. They set out to identify the extent to which trainee teachers:

- learned about child protection on their courses;

- were supported on their placement in developing their understanding of child protection;

- felt confident about responding to child protection issues.

The concerns that trainee teachers reported to the researchers included:

- the sensitivity of the subject matter;

- the belief that the reality would be much harder to cope with than they had been led to believe by the course;

→

- the importance of the approach taken by the school and the support offered;

- a recognition that time constraints in their ITE course and other factors meant that the coverage had been superficial and was not adequate preparation;

- the failure to deal with the subject in an integrated way throughout the initial teacher training course;

- a fear of dealing inappropriately with a disclosure.

In light of these concerns, review how your own course (including placements) helps assuage similar concerns that you may have.

Another important aspect of understanding our emotional responses to issues of child protection is acknowledging why children need protecting and from what. Children are largely disempowered and that lack of power makes them potentially vulnerable. Teachers, along with other professionals, are a central part of the multi-professional team helping to counter-balance that lack of power and safeguard them.

Activity

When you are on placement, obtain a copy of the school's policy on safeguarding and child protection; find out who the designated teacher for safeguarding (sometimes called the safeguarding or child protection officer) is, what you should do if on placement a child discloses to you that they are being abused, or you have suspicions from the way a child behaves that they may be being abused. Annotate the policy with aspects that impress you and points you want to find out more about. Rehearse in your mind the sequence of steps that you would follow if you have reason to believe that a child is being abused.

The legal dimension

There is a range of legislation and statutory guidance that underpins your work as a trainee teacher. This relates to a wide range of activities undertaken in a primary school: compulsory schooling, the National Curriculum, statutory assessment and reporting, accountability and Ofsted inspections, teachers requiring a licence to teach, health and safety in the workplace (school) and, of particular relevance in this chapter, safeguarding and child protection. Your school(s) will be expected to comply with all legislation concerned with health and safety at work and you, as a visitor and/or employee in the school, are required to comply with the school's guidance on this. You need, therefore, to check the school's policy and procedures on this matter also.

In relation to safeguarding and child protection you need to be aware especially of the statutory guidance on keeping children safe in education, including safer recruitment practices (DfE, 2014a, 2014b and 2014c), statutory guidance on multi-professional working in safeguarding (HMG, 2013) and schools' duties in working with social workers to provide help and protection to children (DfE, 2014d).

Research Focus

Previous official guidance about safeguarding and child protection has been collected together in recent years. The key documents from the Department of Education are as follows:

Working Together to Safeguard Children (HMG, 2013), which outlines procedures for multi-disciplinary working among education, medical, police and social services staff.

Use of Reasonable Force: Advice for head teachers, staff and governing bodies (DfE, 2013), which gives guidance on when and how physical restraint might properly be used.

Keeping Children Safe in Education (DfE, 2014a) a comprehensive set of guidance on schools' responsibilities, including safe recruitment practices. It includes the requirements for Disclosure and Barring Service (DBS) checks (formerly known as CRB checks) to ensure that people with convictions for certain offences are debarred from working with children.

Keeping Children Safe in Education: Information for all school and college staff (DfE, 2014b), a shorter version of the above providing key guidance to school staff on day-to-day practice. This is a key document, with which you should be thoroughly familiar.

Keeping Children Safe in Education: Childcare disqualification requirements – supplementary advice (DfE, 2014c). This extends the scope of DBS checks, so that those working with young children must disclose offences committed by other people who live or work in their households. This is a response to cases in which people working with children have been coerced by other household members to commit offences against children in their care.

Schools: Statutory Guidance: Supporting social workers to provide help and protection to children (DfE, 2014d), explaining in detail how schools and social workers should collaborate.

There is also wider legislation that makes an important contribution to understanding safeguarding and the teacher's role in this, especially human rights legislation that accords children a range of universal rights. Children, then, have a number of legal entitlements or rights. Your role as a trainee teacher brings with it responsibilities to help ensure that children's rights are met. Children are protected in law through having rights. Children should be protected by schools, through you (and your colleagues) exercising and carrying out your professional obligations (see Chapter 8 about your professional responsibilities). That is, keeping children safe goes with the job of teaching and we owe a professional and legal obligation to all of the children we teach.

What this means in practice is that you as a trainee teacher have a duty of care towards children and that this duty of care in the safeguarding and child protection process requires you to do three things.

- *Notice* that something might be wrong (from your observations, from what a child says or writes, from what someone else tells you, from what can best be termed as a listening ear to your professional warning bells).

- *Record* – write down what you have seen, heard, read etc. Date your notes and sign them.

- *Report* on to the class teacher or your school's designated teacher for safeguarding. This person may have a different title such as the child protection officer but the role will be the same.

This sequence of actions is important because teachers make such a crucial contribution to helping identify children who are being harmed or who are in possible danger of being harmed. As a trainee teacher you are required in law and professionally to play your part. At its simplest this means that you have to notice that something may not be right, record it and pass it on to the class or designated teacher (as determined in the school's safeguarding policy). Senior personnel in the school (in particular the designated teacher, the head teacher and the school governor with responsibility for safeguarding) have a higher duty of care and, therefore, greater responsibility. This is support for you also. You will not be working alone to help safeguard children. You need also to be aware that you can never promise to keep secret information you find out (from whatever source) that relates to safeguarding. You must pass the information on. Once you have done so, your responsibility has been discharged.

One of the more worrying aspects of a trainee teacher's role relates to physical contact with children. The law is very clear on some aspects of this.

First, there must be no sexual contact or sexual relationship of any kind with children. This would be considered a very serious abuse of trust as well as being against the law. It might seem obvious that any form of sexual contact with a child is wrong but teaching (and other professions associated with children) involves close, trusting relationships and contact with children, a genuine trust of you by a child. Sometimes such trust is broken. Because of this teaching is a profession that adheres to employment practices which deter the unsuitable. Statutory guidance on safe recruitment to teaching makes it clear that schools (*inter alia*) must 'help to deter, reject or identify people who might abuse children, or are otherwise unsuited to work with them' (DfES, 2014a).

Second, it is illegal for teachers to use physical punishment or chastisement when disciplining children. This includes all forms of corporal punishment – striking, hitting, pushing, using implements, etc. Chapter 15 on behaviour management will help you know and understand a range of behaviour management strategies that bring about orderly classrooms and appropriate learning environments.

Other aspects of physical contact with children are not as clear, though. For example, consider whether, as a trainee teacher, you can touch children at all. There is no law that says you cannot touch children in a non-sexual way. Indeed, statutory guidance makes it clear that this is not the case.

Research Focus

The Department for Education (DfE, 2013, p.8), in guidance principally designed to give advice about the use of reasonable force, has clarified its position on when it is proper and/or necessary to touch a pupil other than for purposes of restraint:

Examples of where touching a pupil might be proper or necessary:

- *Holding the hand of the child at the front/back of the line when going to assembly or when walking together around the school;*

- *When comforting a distressed pupil;*

- *When a pupil is being congratulated or praised;*

- *To demonstrate how to use a musical instrument;*

- *To demonstrate exercises or techniques during PE lessons or sports coaching; and*

- *To give first aid.*

Read this short circular and consider how it might affect your professional practice.

This guidance should dispel the fears that some schools have had that any contact of any kind could be considered inappropriate and the teachers' motives questioned. Clarity and a professional freedom to respond appropriately to children are to be welcomed. However, such professional freedoms require good practice to underpin them. In determining whether or not any physical contact is appropriate, you need to consider who initiates contact, where physical contact takes place (location), where the child is touched (parts of the body), whether other people are there or whether you are alone with a child.

The final strand of the legal dimension is defining child abuse and responding to its occurrence or suspicion. There are a number of types of abuse which fall into the following broad categories – sexual abuse, emotional abuse, physical abuse and neglect. More recently other types of abuse have been recognised. These include financial abuse, bullying, children affected by gang activity, fabricated or induced illness, forced marriage, honour-based violence and female genital mutilation. The foundation of this lies in the Children Act 1989 which introduced the concept of significant harm – actual or suspected – as a justification for compulsory intervention in family life. However, as the document makes clear, there are no absolute criteria on which to rely when judging what constitutes significant harm. Further detail and explanations of abuse and neglect can be found in the statutory guidance *Working Together to Safeguard Children* (HMG, 2013).

Physical abuse

Physical abuse may involve hitting, shaking, throwing, poisoning, burning or scalding, drowning, suffocating, or otherwise causing physical harm to a child. Physical harm may also be caused when a parent or carer feigns the symptoms of, or deliberately causes, ill heath to a child whom they are looking after. This situation is commonly described using terms such as factitious illness by proxy or Munchausen syndrome by proxy.

Sexual abuse

Sexual abuse involves forcing or enticing a child or young person to take part in sexual activities, whether or not the child is aware of what is happening. The activities may involve physical contact, including penetrative (e.g. rape or buggery) or non-penetrative acts. They may include non-contact activities, such as involving children in looking at, or in the production of, pornographic material or watching sexual activities, or encouraging children to behave in sexually inappropriate ways.

Emotional abuse

Emotional abuse is the persistent emotional ill treatment of a child that may cause severe and persistent adverse effects on the child's emotional development. It may involve conveying to children that they are worthless or unloved, inadequate, or valued only in so far as they meet the needs of another person. It may feature age or developmentally inappropriate expectations being imposed on children. It may involve causing children frequently to feel frightened or in danger, or the exploitation or corruption of children. Some level of emotional abuse is involved in all types of ill treatment of a child, though it may occur alone.

Neglect

Neglect is the persistent failure to meet the child's basic physical and/or psychological needs, likely to result in the serious impairment of the child's health or development. It may involve a parent or carer failing to provide adequate food, shelter and clothing, failing to protect a child from physical harm or danger, or the failure to ensure access to appropriate medical care or treatment. It may also include neglect of, or unresponsiveness to, a child's basic emotional needs.

Policy into practice

There are a number of broader issues associated with safeguarding and child protection that you may wish to explore further. These include cultural understandings and interpretations of safeguarding, the debate on whether parents should be banned in law from smacking their children, domestic abuse and the sexualisation of children in the media.

This research focus concerns the impact of domestic abuse on children's development.

Research Focus

Ward et al. (2010) produced a government-commissioned report into the impact of domestic violence on young children. They sampled a number of very young children who were identified as suffering, or likely to suffer, significant harm before their first birthdays and were then followed until they were three. Although the report was designed to inform governmental policy, it has significant implications for your practice.

The potential impact on children included delayed speech and language development and aggressive behaviour. There were also high levels of frustration in responding to a range of situations reported. The authors of the study indicated that these behaviours are likely to impact on children's chances of making progress at school.

The research above was welcomed by a number of agencies and associations. The spokesperson for the Women's Aid Federation of England said that it was essential that domestic violence was discussed openly in schools because children 'have a right to know about their own safety' (Maddern and Dorrell, 2010). Given this, consider the implications for schools and teachers in responding to the issue of domestic violence.

If you teach a child for whom there is any safeguarding or child protection concern – suspected or known – then you may be involved in the investigation of that concern. Investigations are undertaken under Section 47 of The Children Act 1989. The investigation will be led by an experienced social worker. Your input to the investigation may be through direct involvement (you attend and participate) or indirect involvement (your school's designated teacher represents the school), but your contribution will be an essential source of information about the child and their needs and how they are being met. Teachers – including trainee teachers also – can and do provide information that arises from a disclosure (directly from a child or from something they have said) or indicators of a potentially abused child (unexplained bruising or injuries, sexually explicit language or actions, or a change in behaviour observed over time). The aim is that all professionals involved in legally safeguarding children do so in a coordinated way which focuses on a child's needs. You can further information on this in *What to Do if You Are Worried a Child is Being Abused* (DfES, 2006).

The professional dimension

As a trainee teacher you are required to act professionally at all times. Determining what counts as professional behaviour (as opposed to unprofessional behaviour) is, therefore, critical if you are to be successful and if your practice is not to be called into question. In working towards and achieving qualified teacher status you will be assessed against all of the standards related to your practice as a trainee teacher. This will cover all elements of practice as outlined in the standards: relationships with children, frameworks, communication with others, subject knowledge and children's learning. The Teachers' Standards listed at the beginning of this chapter show just how many standards relate to safeguarding and child protection. For example, the standards concerned with subject knowledge, teaching and learning are obviously directed at discrete subjects but they also relate to personal, social and health education; the being safe strand of Every Child Matters, health and wellbeing, and the notion of a protective curriculum in the primary school; achievement and diversity; the learning environment; team work and collaboration.

Your work as a trainee teacher (and later, once you are qualified) is underpinned not only by legislative and statutory frameworks but also by professional frameworks for working with children. A key principle of any professional framework will relate to safeguarding and child protection and will be written in a way that makes it clear and explicit that you need to put the wellbeing and development of children first.

Case Study: Professional dialogue

Jessica is on placement in a class that is shared by two teachers, one working in the first half of the week and the other working in the second half of the week. The two teachers meet every Wednesday to review planning and the children's achievements. Jessica notices over the first three weeks of her placement that one particular child in the class exhibits different behaviours on Mondays and Fridays and she mentions it during the following Wednesday meeting. The class teachers are very grateful for Jessica's observations, realising that their focus in meetings has tended to be about children's attainment and progress and less about non-academic matters. As a result they set up a way of being able to monitor the particular child's behaviour over each week.

In order to put the wellbeing and development of children first you need to demonstrate commitment to their learning and development – personal, social, emotional as well as academic. You need also to demonstrate good practice in how you meet that commitment so that your practice is considered appropriate and so that no one questions your motives for working with children in the primary age range. This applies to all aspects of your work as a trainee teacher: when teaching and managing the curriculum for children, in how you establish relationships with children and with which children; what classroom routines and procedures you make use of and how they are applied; in interactions with children and their parents/carers and with colleagues. You need to ensure that you treat all children as equally as you can, with no obvious favourites among the children. This is not always as easy or straightforward as it might seem. At times you may teach children you find either very easy or very hard to like, for a variety of reasons. Remember that you must keep the relationship professional. All children in your class deserve to be in an environment where they feel, and where they are, welcomed and valued. You, as the professional, have to create the right sort of climate for this to happen. Children are more likely to tell you when something is wrong in their life or circumstances if you have the right sort of relationship with them. So, you need to make sure that you do not ignore or put down a child who you find it hard to like; you need to make sure that you do not have favourites and that you do not single out favoured children for special treatment.

Case Study: The impact of school context and policy

Jagdeep has undertaken three placements in different schools. He notices that each school has a different policy towards children changing for physical education sessions. For example, he sees that the policy for each school has been influenced by the school context, including:

- the gender of the teacher;
- the age of the children;
- the changing facilities available.

He talks about his observations with his mentor. She explains that each school formulates an understanding of what constitutes good practice and that this varies from school to school. She reminds Jagdeep that all schools have a safeguarding policy and that he should always check how this impacts on other elements of his professional role. She goes on to say that she previously worked in a school that had only one policy covering all elements of relationships in the school. It was called 'the personal and social policy' but it comprised safeguarding, bullying, health education and extra-curricular activities as well as personal and social education.

Remember that the full range of the school's policies may impact on judgements made about your practice and behaviour. For example, the school may have procedures and/or a policy about other aspects of school life that relate to safeguarding and the notion of good practice for trainee teachers as well as qualified teachers. For example, what is the school's policy and procedure for breaktimes/playtimes and children staying in to finish work? Is it considered appropriate to leave a child in a classroom; does the teacher have to remain in the classroom with the child; are teachers expected to take children who are staying in to a central area where supervision and care of them is shared and more public?

The final aspect of professional good practice considered in this chapter is that of *vigilance*. First, vigilance of the children through what they do, say, write, draw. What will you do about the child who is often hungry, dirty, smelly, loud, anxious, bruised, sleepy, poorly dressed?

LEEDS TRINITY UNIVERSITY

Second, vigilance of other trainees, teachers and adults in the school – is their practice good; do you see things that worry you or that cause you to question an adult's motives for working with a child or group of children?

Third, vigilance of yourself and your own practices so that you undertake a regular review of your classroom routines and procedures, of your interactions with individual children and the class, of the type of classroom climate you establish and promote. Do you create a climate that encourages children to feel safe and to talk to you if they have any safeguarding or child protection issues? How confident are you that you are the right sort of teacher? Do you treat all children well? How do you respond to children who are dirty, smelly, loud, unhappy, anxious, etc.? Good practice means operating in an atmosphere of transparency so that no one questions your motives or actions.

Drawing the three principles together

The three principles that have been presented above underpin the trainee teacher's role in safeguarding and protecting children: recognising and understanding that complex emotions are involved; complying fully with all legal and professional duties; demonstrating good professional practice and vigilance.

- Be aware of your own emotional responses and needs as well as those of the children. Remember that you are part of a team – both within the school and in the wider multi-professional network.

- Be absolutely clear that you have a duty to safeguard children and that this is both a legal and a professional obligation.

- Make sure that you demonstrate good practice at all times. If you touch a child, make sure you do so in an open, public area and in an appropriate way ensuring there is no touching of a child's more intimate areas; use appropriate language when talking to children; dress appropriately; do not swap mobile telephone numbers or personal email addresses with children; do not add children as a 'friend' on social networking sites; maintain a good professional distance – not too distant, though, or else there is a danger that you will not establish a protective relationship with the child; ensure you know and understand what is required when in the role of a teacher so that you know who key personnel for safeguarding and child protection in the school are and what safeguarding/good practice means in each school. This list is not finite and new recommendations will emerge in time. For example, a few years ago the notions of cyber-bullying and inappropriate internet use were not well known. New forms of technology and communication will come online in the future and so good practice in this area will vary and change depending on those developments.

- Be vigilant – of the children, of all other adults in school, of what you see/hear, of yourself. As a professional you need to be transparent in your practice and your actions need to be open to scrutiny.

Finally, remember and take heart from the fact that it is not laws and/or statutory guidance or a school's policies or professional registration requirements per se that keep children safe and protected from harm; rather, it is teachers themselves – trainees included – who do this through being informed, understanding legal requirements and undertaking their professional role with a view to the best possible practice in all of their dealings in school and with children.

Learning Outcomes Review

From your reading and from thinking about the school in which you are currently placed, or in which you most recently undertook a placement, respond to the questions which follow each of the intended learning outcomes, as a means of identifying your knowledge and understanding of the issues covered in the chapter.

- **A range of safeguarding and child protection issues, both generally and with specific reference to children in the primary age phase:**

  - Give examples of the range of emotions and feelings raised by the issue of safeguarding children and child protection.
  - What issues are raised in trying to recognise children who may be or are in need of protection?
  - Which of these are relevant to classroom practice and which are relevant to wider family contexts that involve other professionals?

- **Implications for your professional practice with regard to safeguarding and child protection in meeting national standards for gaining qualified teacher status and maintaining your licence to teach:**

  - What is good practice when working with children in the primary school?
  - What boundaries should you be aware of at all times when working in a school?
  - In what ways do you try to create and sustain an appropriate classroom climate so that children feel able to trust you? How do you do this, and how effective is it?
  - List the ways in which your professionalism is judged through your behaviours and actions in both university and the school and classroom.
  - Identify examples from your placement(s) when you demonstrated appropriate professional practice and conduct in your relationships with children.
  - In what ways can you help ensure that you do not face allegations of poor practice or child abuse when working in the primary school?

- **Know about the roles of key school and other agencies' personnel related to safeguarding and child protection:**

  - What agencies are involved in safeguarding and protecting children?
  - What should you do if you have a concern about a child and this concern relates to a possible safeguarding and child protection issue?
  - What is your role as a trainee teacher in the safeguarding process?

- **Become aware of key statutory and non-statutory documents related to safeguarding and child protection:**

  - Which governmental Acts of Parliament and statutory and non-statutory documents guidance underpin and influence your work with children?
  - Give examples from your placement school(s) of how you have made provision to address the aim that children should feel safe and be safe.

Further Reading

Blyth, M. and Solomon, E. (eds) (2012) *Effective Safeguarding for Children and Young People: What next after Munro?* Bristol: Policy Press.

This book offers a survey of child protection in the wake of the Munro Report of 2011, commissioned by the government to investigate all aspects of child protection, and to make recommendations for improvements in policy and practice. Its key message is the importance of putting the child at the centre in all instances.

DfES (2006) *What to Do if You Are Worried a Child is Being Abused.* London: TSO.

This remains a useful source of guidance intended for anyone working with children. Its aim is to assist practitioners to work together to safeguard and promote children's welfare.

Lindon, J. (2012) *Safeguarding and Child Protection: 0–8 Years* (4th edition). Abingdon: Hodder Education.

This book provides a comprehensive overview of legal and professional aspects. It includes a valuable section on equality practice and safeguarding, which surveys cultural traditions and practices, some of which are in tension with public policy tenets.

Walker, S. and Thurston, C. (2006) *Safeguarding Children and Young People.* Lyme Regis: Russell House Publishing.

The central theme of this book is the need for professionals (including teachers) to develop more effective, holistic and integrated practice. The chapter on children and young people at risk provides a good overview of the types and causes of abuse; signs, symptoms and effects of abuse; and risk and resilience factors in children and young people.

References

Baginsky M. and Macpherson P. (2005) Training Teachers to Safeguard Children: Developing a Consistent Approach. *Child Abuse Review* 14, pp.317–30.

Department for Education (2011) *Teachers' Standards.* Available from www.education.gov.uk/ publications

Department for Education (2013) *Use of Reasonable Force: Advice for head teachers, staff and governing bodies.* London: DfE.

Department for Education (2014a) *Keeping Children Safe in Education.* London: DfE.

Department for Education (2014b) *Keeping Children Safe in Education: Information for all school and college staff.* London: DfE.

Department for Education (2014c) *Keeping Children Safe in Education: Childcare disqualification requirements – supplementary advice.* London: DfE.

Department for Education (2014d) *Schools: Statutory Guidance. Supporting social workers to provide help and protection to children.* London: DfE.

DfES (2006) *What to Do if You Are Worried a Child is Being Abused.* London: TSO.

DfES (2009) *The Protection of Children in England: Action plan – the government's response to Lord Laming.* London: TSO.

Her Majesty's Government (2013) *Working Together to Safeguard Children.* London: TSO.

Laming, H. (2009) *The Protection of Children in England: A progress report.* HC 330. London: TSO.

Maddern, K. and Dorrell, E. (2010) Children 'have a right' to learn about domestic violence 'taboo'. *TES*, 5 September. Available from www.tes.co.uk/article.aspx?storycode=6062352 accessed 13/05/15.

Ward, H., Brown, R., Westlake, D. and Munro, M.R. (2010) *Infants Suffering, or Likely to Suffer, Significant Harm: A prospective longitudinal study.* DfE Research Brief DFE-RB053. London: DfE.

11. The school community: being part of a wider professional environment
Tony Ewens

Learning Outcomes

By the end of this chapter you should have developed and clarified:

- an understanding of the concept of community, and its application to the school as a community;
- an appreciation of the notion of fundamental British values and how teachers might promote them;
- an awareness of the importance of understanding pupils' social and cultural contexts when planning their learning;
- your knowledge of the ways in which the local and wider community can offer a rich setting within which learning can take place, and how community members can enhance classroom activities;
- an understanding of key factors in planning safe, effective and stimulating opportunities for pupils to learn outside the classroom and at home.

TEACHERS' STANDARDS
A teacher must:

1. Set high expectations which inspire, motivate and challenge pupils
- establish a safe and stimulating environment for pupils, rooted in mutual respect
- set goals that stretch and challenge pupils of all backgrounds, abilities and dispositions
- demonstrate consistently the positive attitudes, values and behaviour which are expected of pupils.

2. Promote good progress and outcomes by pupils
- plan teaching to build on pupils' capabilities and prior knowledge
- demonstrate knowledge and understanding of how pupils learn and how this impacts on teaching.

5. Adapt teaching to respond to the strengths and needs of all pupils
- demonstrate an awareness of the physical, social and intellectual development of children, and know how to adapt teaching to support pupils' education at different stages of development

- have a clear understanding of the needs of all pupils, including those with special educational needs; those of high ability; those with English as an additional language; those with disabilities; and be able to use and evaluate distinctive teaching approaches to engage and support them.

8. **Fulfil wider professional responsibilities**
- make a positive contribution to the wider life and ethos of the school
- develop effective professional relationships with colleagues, knowing how and when to draw on advice and specialist support
- deploy support staff effectively
- communicate effectively with parents with regard to pupils' achievements and wellbeing.

What counts as a community?

We use the term 'community' in a number of ways.

Research Focus

Kerridge and Sayers (2006, p.23) summarise a sociological analysis of the term under three headings:

- physical proximity, as in neighbourhood;

- civic identity, as in populace;

- collective identity, as in unity, co-operation and shared interest.

An example of the first of these might be the people who live in a particular village, or a district within a town or city. Simply by living in that place, a person counts as a member of that community. The second category can be exemplified in terms of language or ethnicity, as in the Chinese, traveller or black community. The third category, collective identity, refers to groups based on interests, sporting or cultural for instance. Examples would include the biking, painting or athletics community. By definition, members of these communities are active participants in their chosen activity. The three categories are not mutually exclusive but overlap and intersect. A group such as a religious community could be described in each of the three ways. The Christian community could refer to locality (for instance, those who attend the village church), to civic identity (members of the population who accept the label 'Christian') or to collective identity (people anywhere in the world who participate in Christian practices such as worship and social activities).

Most people belong to a number of different types of community.

What makes a school a community?

The threefold analysis outlined above can help us to understand various ways in which the school is a community. Consider a school in which you have undertaken a placement. It may be the only primary school serving a village or suburb. If so, it may be a subset of the community in its geographical location. However, this situation has become increasingly rare, because the policy of parental preference in choice of schools results in many children travelling from one area to another to attend school. Pupils and staff may have little connection with the immediate hinterland of the school so, despite many schools being named 'Community Primary School', the relationship between local community and local school may be tenuous.

Activity

Discuss with staff at your placement school the nature of the pupil and staff community. How many live locally, and how many travel some distance? Do some local children go out of the area to attend more distant schools? What reasons might parents have for their choices of school? You might also like to discuss with staff members the benefits and drawbacks of working at a school close to where you live.

Your placement school might, however, have a close relationship with one or more particular communities within its town or city, as well as being the most convenient choice for parents living close by. Groups who are spread across quite a wide geographical area may try to enrol their children in a school where they will learn alongside others who share their cultural identity or philosophical outlook. The school can seek to build on such a feature, for example by offering additional services for children and families, both during and outside school hours. Read the following case study, and consider the ways in which St Agatha's School serves and contributes to the various communities with which it interacts. What does the information provided tell you about the kind of community that the school seeks to be?

Case Study: St Agatha's RC Primary School

Jane is beginning a placement at a Roman Catholic primary school in a large town. During her pre-placement visits she begins to develop an insight into the characteristics of the school population. A proportion of the children are from practising Roman Catholic families, some travelling across the town, or from neighbouring villages, to attend. The parish priest leads worship once a week and the parish also provides Catholic instruction for children preparing for confirmation. However, the school also has a strikingly open admissions policy, and Jane notices that a substantial

→

number of children of Asian heritage are on the register. She discovers that they are from an Indian community, Hindu in faith, and that some also travel lengthy distances to the school. The school offers adult education classes in English as an additional language, and there is a good uptake for these. Additionally, many children attend the school because it is the closest to their homes. Jane observes that some of these arrive at school very early, because of parents' work patterns. She finds out that the school provides a well-used breakfast club, and that an after-school club is also fully subscribed. Some children are at school from 8 am to 6 pm. The school's facilities are also used by a local sports club, some of whose members assist with activities for children attending the after-school club.

You can readily see the complexity involved in describing St Agatha's RC School as a community. To some extent it serves the geographical neighbourhood in which it is situated. More widely, it serves two distinct communities characterised by a shared faith or a cultural and linguistic identity. Finally, it plays a small part in supporting the area's sporting community because it allows its facilities to be used by members of the general public outside school hours. Jane's findings reveal that St Agatha's supports various communities, for example spiritually and culturally as well as practically.

However, none of this is enough to make St Agatha's a community in its own right. Much will depend on the way in which those who run the school ensure that those who attend it gain a positive experience of belonging to a community. The climate of values, codes of conduct and quality of relationships (sometimes summed up in the term 'school ethos') can make the vital difference to whether children know themselves to be valued persons enjoying cordial and productive relationships with adults and children, as they experience life in an organisation driven by clear goals and civilised values.

Activity

Re-read the Teachers' Standards at the beginning of this chapter. What do these standards suggest about the type of community that any school should aspire to become?

The role of the school's governing body

As a trainee teacher undertaking a placement at a school, your understanding of the school community and the communities which it serves will derive from your conversations with your class teacher, mentor and other staff, from your interactions with pupils and from reading school documentation. Even at this early stage in your career, however, it is valuable to appreciate the role of the school's governing body as a key link between school and community.

The governors are responsible for the overall strategic direction of the school, and the head teacher exercises day-to-day leadership and management within the framework of policies adopted by the governing body. Staff and parent representatives are elected to serve as governors, the local authority appoints some governors and the head teacher is automatically a governor. In community and foundation schools, these governors appoint a number of other members to act as community governors. Typically, these include representatives of significant cultural groups in the school's locality, employers, members of voluntary organisations and people who bring specific experience or skills, such as finance, construction or human resource management. In Voluntary Aided or Controlled schools, the sponsoring body (normally a church or other religious foundation) appoints governors to sit alongside staff, parent and local authority representatives. You can readily see how a carefully selected governing body can create and sustain good links with the complex array of communities to which the school may relate.

St Agatha's School, which features in the case study above, includes among its governors the secretary of the Hindu Community Centre, a tutor from the local FE college and a councillor who sits on the sports and cultural affairs committee, as well as the parish priest and other church representatives. These individuals have been of great help in forming links with different community groups, and you will notice how several of the school's activities link with the experience that they bring with them. Jane, the trainee teacher placed at St Agatha's, learned a great deal about the backgrounds of her Asian heritage pupils from the governor who worked at the Hindu Community Centre, because he came into her class as a volunteer for two sessions each week. Through talking with him, Jane was able to develop her knowledge of the social, religious, ethnic, cultural and linguistic influences on this group of pupils, thus collecting valuable evidence in relation to Standards 1, 5 and 8.

Research Focus

Gardner (2007) explores and illustrates the social categories that influence the development of each child's identity. Warning against a simplistic view of this process, he demonstrates by means of a Venn diagram (p.21) ways in which dominant and subordinate cultural groups in society intersect. Gardner describes ways in which children attending a school whose roll is drawn from a mixture of social, ethnic and linguistic groups may be introduced to perspectives other than those with which they have grown up, while other children may attend schools in monocultural communities with little or no exposure to the range of cultures represented in the country as a whole.

It follows from Gardner's analysis that each school needs to consider its unique circumstances when planning its work in relation to social cohesion. As a trainee teacher on placement you therefore need an understanding of the concepts of social cohesion and fundamental

British values, and the ways in which you might contribute to their promotion, and also an appreciation of the particular setting of your school and its children.

The requirement to promote fundamental British values

A cursory overview of education legislation since the mid twentieth century reveals two main trends. The teaching and assessment of an academic curriculum is one; the other is a concern with building a harmonious, healthy society on a basis of shared values. In England and Wales, the Education Act of 1944 required local education authorities 'to promote the spiritual, moral, mental and physical development of the community' (DES, 1944, preamble), and regarded the education service as contributing part of the 'glue' that held society together. Detailed attention in those days was also paid to ensuring access to good nutrition and medical services at a time when these were major concerns because of scarcities during a world war. Nowadays social priorities are different, reflected, for example, in a concern to ensure harmony in a society comprising people from a wide range of ethnic, religious, cultural and linguistic backgrounds, but the underlying principle – that the education service should contribute significantly towards holding society together – remains a key element of public policy. Current statutory guidance states: 'The national curriculum provides pupils with an introduction to the essential knowledge they need to be educated citizens' (DfE, 2014a, para. 3.1.), and reasserts the overall aim of education in England as the provision of a curriculum which:

- *promotes the spiritual, moral, mental and physical development of pupils at the school and of society*

- *prepares pupils at the school for the opportunities, responsibilities and experiences of later life.*

(DfES, 2002, section 78)

In recent years, the advice given by government to schools to help them to address these aims has frequently changed. A few years ago, a requirement to promote 'community cohesion' highlighted the importance of teaching children to value diversity, while promoting shared values (DCSF, 2007), and schools' work in this area attracted close scrutiny during school inspections. Subsequently, the notion of 'community cohesion' came under challenge as an approach that focused helpfully on the needs and concerns of different ethnic and cultural groups, but failed to consider the factors that linked those groups (for example, Thomas, 2011). The most recent DfE advice sets out to identify those shared factors, which it describes as 'fundamental British values' (DfE, 2014b), and calls upon schools to promote 'values of democracy, the rule of law, individual liberty, and mutual respect and tolerance of those with different faiths and beliefs' (DfE, 2014b, p.5).

Of particular note is the DfE advice about the rule of law, which asserts, 'it is expected that pupils should understand that while different people may hold different views about what is "right" and "wrong", all people living in England are subject to its law' (DfE, 2014b, p.4). This notion has the potential for friction with some faith groups, who would reject any perception that God's law could be seen as subservient to the law of this – or any other – land. This issue is a critical debating point in the quest for a common set of values within which people of all religious and cultural traditions can coexist harmoniously, and it implies that faith traditions are likely to need to accommodate their teachings to the law of the land, in the interests of social cohesion. You should pay close attention to the advice that: 'if schools teach about religious law, particular care should be taken to explore the relationship between state and religious law. Pupils should be made aware of the difference between the law of the land and religious law' (DfE, 2014b, p.4).

Activity

Read the following extract from the DfE's guidance on promoting fundamental British values (DfE, 2014b, p.5):

Through their provision of SMSC, schools should ...

- *encourage students to accept responsibility for their behaviour, show initiative, and to understand how they can contribute positively to the lives of those living and working in the locality of the school and to society more widely;*

- *enable students to acquire a broad general knowledge of and respect for public institutions and services in England;*

- *further tolerance and harmony between different cultural traditions by enabling students to acquire an appreciation of and respect for their own and other cultures.*

Now read Standards 1 and 5, noting their connection to the duty to promote a cohesive community within the classroom, and also Part 2 of the Standards, which outlines your professional duties as a teacher in this regard. Identify some of the challenges to you as a trainee teacher on placement in designing the curriculum and sharpening your professional practice in response to these demanding objectives.

It is important to guard against thinking that, solely because a school draws its pupils from a range of cultures so that children are being taught together, this will automatically lead to a more cohesive school. After all, the children might simply form monocultural groups in the classroom and playground and remain largely unaware of, uninterested in, and even hostile to the backgrounds of their classmates. School staff members have to take active measures to ensure that the guidance outlined above leads to the desired outcomes.

Equally to be avoided is a view that children educated in a largely monocultural environment are necessarily ignorant about wider society. If schools in such areas make full use of visual media, teach a broad and balanced RE scheme, introduce pupils to diversity through literature and the arts and draw on news stories from around the world, children can develop positive attitudes and sound knowledge regarding social diversity.

It is sometimes claimed that the existence of faith schools impedes the achievement of community cohesion. While it can be the case that school admissions policies based on parental religious practice result in children being divided on faith lines among different schools, there are alternative scenarios. Some faith-based schools, like St Agatha's in the earlier case study, actively seek to recruit pupils from a range of different belief communities. Proponents of faith schools also make the point that the major religions teach about the value and worth of all people, and thus promote social cohesion through the beliefs and practices of their faith communities and schools. You will need to think carefully about your own position with regard to this topical debate.

Whatever the type and location of the school, its policies and practice with regard to curriculum design, targets for achievement and attainment, and extended services are expected to lead to positive, identifiable outcomes in terms of community cohesion.

The following case study outlines a project devised by two trainee teachers, Peter and Sarah, who had been placed in very different schools in the same county. Their work demonstrates the value of partnerships among schools and other agencies in creating sustainable opportunities to develop mutual understanding and respect.

Case Study: Peter and Sarah on final placement

For a final placement, Peter was placed in an urban school in a city with a mixed population. The majority British-English community was complemented by a substantial British-Pakistani group. At Peter's school, almost 95 per cent of the children were drawn from the latter. The school had noticed that the population near the school comprised approximately equal numbers of British-English and British-Pakistani households. However, many British-English children travelled away from the area to attend schools elsewhere in the city, and conversely some British-Pakistani children on the register actually lived a considerable distance from the school. The head teacher had concluded that decisive action was needed to broaden the pupils' experience of other cultural groups, and she was hoping that Peter's addition to the staff team for a term could help towards this.

Sarah, meanwhile, had been placed in a Church of England school in a small village 20 miles away. All the pupils were British-English and this reflected the local populace. The school had examined its work in promoting an appreciation of diversity. The head teacher was pleased

$\longrightarrow$

with the impact of changes to the curriculum, which had been made in the interests of encouraging greater awareness of diversity and promoting positive attitudes towards differences in ethnicity, religion and culture. However, he wanted the children to meet people from different groups, as well as learning about them in the classroom. Sarah offered to help with this.

Through the online discussion board linked to the university's virtual learning environment, Peter and Sarah became aware of their respective schools' plans, and decided to work together. With the support of both heads they arranged an informal 'twinning' between their two classes. Initially, letters were exchanged, and this led to a substantial ICT project enabling children and staff to share information and respond to one another's questions. The project culminated in an exchange of visits, each class experiencing a day in the life of the other school and taking it in turn to host their visitors. Several parents and governors from the two schools accompanied the visits.

Evaluation of the project revealed that, in addition to realising the key intention that the children should meet people from different ethnic, religious and cultural backgrounds, the visits had highlighted differences between urban and rural settings. Indeed, many of the children had been more surprised by the environmental context of the other school than by differences of ethnicity or culture. The schools have resolved to build upon this promising beginning.

A key point arising from the work done by Peter and Sarah is that while you must be clear about the objectives of collaborative work between schools, you must also be ready to adapt the project in the light of your findings from ongoing monitoring. Initially, Peter and Sarah thought that the opportunity to mix with children from a very different school was the main vehicle for promoting an appreciation of diversity. However, they came to appreciate that the children actually gained greater knowledge of each other when they worked in mixed groups on tasks that were only incidentally related to their personal and social education. This judgement shows clearly that you should not see your teaching of the subject-led formal curriculum as being separate from your work in helping children with the formation of their beliefs, values and attitudes. Both aspects of education are most effectively pursued when planned and taught in an integrated manner.

Activity

Read the following extract from Ofsted's school inspection handbook (Ofsted, 2014, para. 133).

The social development of pupils is shown by their:

- *use of a range of social skills in different contexts, including working and socialising with pupils from different religious, ethnic and socio-economic backgrounds*

- *willingness to participate in a variety of communities and social settings, including by volunteering, cooperating well with others and being able to resolve conflicts effectively*

- *acceptance and engagement with the fundamental British values of democracy, the rule of law, individual liberty and mutual respect and tolerance of those with different faiths and beliefs; the pupils develop and demonstrate skills and attitudes that will allow them to participate fully in and contribute positively to life in modern Britain.*

Consider the case study above of Peter and Sarah's placement. To what extent does the work they did provide evidence of the success of their respective schools in promoting pupils' social development when measured against these statements from Ofsted?

Learning about belonging to a community

'The most important single factor influencing learning is what the learner already knows. Ascertain this and teach him accordingly' (Ausubel et al., 1967, p.vi). David Ausubel's advice applies not only to children's learning of traditional subjects but also to how they can most effectively learn about their relationships to and within the communities to which they belong. You will rightly be expected to apply your knowledge of techniques in assessment for learning (AfL) to identify pupils' prior knowledge in each subject, and to use your findings as the basis for planning lessons in which the concepts and activities are appropriately matched to children's developmental needs as learners. The same processes and procedures apply to personal and social learning, by which is meant learning about how individuals relate to groups.

When you start working at a different school or with a new class you should consequently find out as much as you can about the social and cultural settings from which the children are drawn. Teachers need to know about the preconceptions and expectations that children bring with them to school, which reflect the beliefs and values of their parents and carers. Initially, you will probably be able to identify general data about ethnicity, socio-economic circumstances, language, religion and culture. Gradually, you will be able to sharpen this information as you get to know individual children's family circumstances, interests and strengths, and the process is further refined when you meet parents and carers at open evenings and informal school events. You may think that this approach appears to be inappropriately intrusive on your part, but if you take Ausubel's advice seriously you will recognise the importance of gaining a rounded view of each child. Remember, then, the crucial need to maintain strict professional confidentiality regarding sensitive personal information. You must also monitor your own reactions to the contextual information about the class that you acquire. In particular, in the light of Standard 1, it is crucial that you do not allow your high expectations of children to be affected by any personal views and prejudices that you may hold about any sector of society. To give just one example, it is a misconception to assume that pupils for whom English is not the first language are less likely to perform well; studies (e.g. Baker, 2006) have shown bilingualism to be advantageous to learning in the medium to long term.

Having built, and checked the accuracy of, a picture of the groups from which your pupils are drawn, you should then analyse your data and devise ways of extending the children's knowledge of people from other backgrounds, to enhance and enrich their experience of diversity. This will probably involve a mixture of face-to-face contact, as in the earlier case study involving Peter and Sarah, and classroom learning using a variety of media.

Case Study: Children learning about community

The following table offers brief outlines of activities undertaken by a number of teachers. Notice how they are based on reflective analysis by teachers of their observations, and also that many of the ideas are quite simple in conception and implementation. Can you identify ways in which they respond to Ausubel's advice to identify the stage that pupils have reached in their learning?

Staff at a large primary school noticed that pupils rarely interacted with children from other age groups. They experimented with mixed age groupings for drama, and observed that much of the role-play that occurred mirrored typical scenarios involving relationships among siblings. The children developed their abilities to explain how interactions between children of different ages could succeed or fail. It was decided do extend the experiment, despite timetabling difficulties, and to look for other opportunities for mixed-age learning.
At a small village school teachers noticed that most children had little regular contact with elderly people, and that very few had grandparents living nearby. The head spoke to the local pensioners' association, whose members started attending lunch at the school once a week. Mixed tables of children and pensioners were arranged. Initially, topics for conversation were suggested by the teachers, but this soon became unnecessary. The children gained much knowledge about their village from the pensioners, and their oral English, powers of concentration and table manners also benefited.
The head of an all British-English primary school wanted to extend the children's knowledge and experience of ethnic diversity. He booked a speaker from the Commonwealth Institute to give a presentation about India, its geography, culture and customs to the Key Stage 2 pupils. He invited a school from another district, some of whose pupils were British-Indian, to attend the occasion. The school meals contractor provided a selection of Indian food for lunch. The visit provided a stimulus for a substantial project about India at both schools, and the families of the British-Indian pupils were able to help with information in response to questions from pupils and staff at both schools. The Year 6 teacher at the visiting school commented that the event had led to an interesting debate in her class about the extent to which children felt themselves to be British and/or Indian.

$\longrightarrow$

At a rural church school the head discussed with the chair of governors (the parish priest) her concern that the children had almost no knowledge of religious diversity. She had been disturbed by negative comments made by one child about Muslims. It was agreed to build visits to places of worship into the school's RE scheme, including a mosque and a synagogue as well as three different Christian denominations. At each place of worship the children explored the building and formulated questions which were answered for them by members of the respective congregations. The teachers evaluated this learning approach very positively. They found that basing the content on children's queries helped to match it to their levels of understanding, whereas presentations by members of the religious communities might have been inappropriately pitched.

Staff members at a large urban school with a very mixed catchment were concerned about tensions in relationships among children from different communities. In addition to providing direct guidance about conduct during school assemblies, and arranging tighter monitoring of break times, the head decided to tackle the issue through the curriculum. As part of the school's SEAL (social and emotional aspects of learning) work, children in one year group took part in structured role-play involving encounters between people from different groups. Once children had grown accustomed to this way of working, they began to show insight into the links between the fictional situations explored and their own relationships at school. Encouraged by their initial evaluation of this approach, the staff decided to extend it to other year groups.

The examples presented here share the common characteristic that, in each case, teachers were careful to consider the developmental stage that pupils have reached in their learning. The starting point for each piece of work was thorough analysis by staff members of incidents and situations that they have noticed in their schools. They then used their knowledge of the children, their understanding of teaching methods and their skills in tailoring the curriculum to their pupils' needs in order to help the children to progress. You will frequently have encountered this model of working in connection with English, mathematics and other subjects, and you can feel confident that the same approach is effective in promoting children's learning about what it means to live in a diverse society and to belong to a community.

You will also notice from these instances the importance of teachers and other staff members working together. In each case, identification of the issues needing to be addressed came from staff discussion, and the success of the actions taken resulted to a large extent from collaborative working by teaching and support staff, with the approval of the governing body in specific cases. When you analyse what happened at the different schools, it becomes evident that staff members at each school were in agreement about the values and attitudes that they wished to foster in their pupils. This raises the issue, discussed in Chapter 9, as to whether teachers and others who work in schools are required to subscribe to specific sets of beliefs and values as representing the basis for an ideal society.

The topics under consideration here point to the fact that during your placement you will be part of the adult community at the school, not just an individual teacher working with one class. As a member (albeit temporarily) of the staff room, you can learn a great deal from your colleagues' conversations about the local area and the circumstances of the children who attend the school. You can also extend your knowledge of the children in your class by talking with other staff members who have worked with them and their families previously. The range of perspectives that you will encounter is in itself an eloquent illustration of what it means for a school to operate as a community.

Local and wider communities: their contributions to learning

A school's curriculum can be significantly enhanced if it incorporates ways of using the communities it serves, or among which it is placed, within the children's regular programme of learning. People, buildings and activities situated close to the school can provide opportunities for learning at first hand about the businesses and services that help society to function as well as about the locality's historical, religious and cultural infrastructure. An emphasis on the types of employment available in a district is a particularly helpful curriculum focus, as it can help children to appreciate how some of what they learn at school relates very closely to knowledge and skills required in different types of work. Since the early 1980s, when it was termed 'economic and industrial understanding', introducing primary age children to the world of work has been a vital aspect of the curriculum, even if it later tended to be obscured by the subject-driven National Curriculum. Its incorporation into personal, social, health and economic education (PSHE) is the most recent strategy to revitalise it (DfE, 2013), and the community around the school can be a helpful resource.

The following case study exemplifies some of the potential of working in this way. Can you identify ways in which the teachers concerned have drawn upon their local communities in order to enrich the curriculum?

Case Study: Curriculum and community

- Children at a small rural school regularly walked to the top of a hill overlooking the village. They made sketch maps of the locality; then, back at school, they produced a large-scale map of the village. They identified key buildings and also studied land use. Visits to a farm, the post office, the pub and the church enabled them to interview members of the community about people's work and its value to the community. They also studied how other services were provided for local residents (doctor, vet, police, public transport, mobile library, secondary education). A group of older residents visited the school and were questioned about ways in which the village had changed over the past 50 years.

- A Key Stage 2 teacher from a school in a market town acquired detailed statistics from the school's liaison police officer about road traffic accidents on the busy main road that passed the school. The class analysed the data, producing charts and graphs to show the frequency of different types of accident, and highlighting accident blackspots and the most hazardous times of day, days of the week and months of the year. The local police used the children's work as the basis of a road safety campaign.

- Children from a Reception class visited a sub-post office. The class teacher invited the sub-postmistress to visit the school and together they helped the children to set up a post office counter in the classroom. Subsequently the children designed, produced, wrote and sent postcards to other members of the school community, bought and sold 'stamps' at the counter and arranged a delivery system around the school.

These examples raise several points about the link between curriculum and community. First and foremost, a community cannot be divorced from its physical setting. An influential curriculum planning document on environmental education (DES, 1986) emphasised the interaction between people and places. It illustrated how the physical and built environment influences human activity and conversely how human aspirations and values help to shape what is built and how land is used. You need to consider this fundamental factor when planning units of work around the community.

Second, there is a balance to be achieved between taking children out of school to visit people and places in the community and inviting community members to come to the school to work with the children. The first of these is obviously easy to accomplish when you are dealing with the community as a particular geographical locality. However, as we saw earlier in this chapter, a community is not necessarily contained within neat physical boundaries. The Chinese community, for example, may be spread across a wide geographical area, and this might mean that visitors to school would be the best approach. Either way there are vital issues to be addressed to ensure the children's safety and welfare, whether you are planning an educational visit or inviting community representatives to school. You need to be fully aware of your placement school's policies and procedures and ensure that you comply with them.

If you plan to take children out of school you should, after discussion with your class teacher and mentor, consult the school's educational visits coordinator. This colleague will advise and support you regarding the permissions to be obtained and the risk assessments to be undertaken prior to the visit. There will also be a need to ensure that an appropriate number of adults will accompany the visit, and that they meet the school's requirements regarding vetting volunteers. It is important not to allow these daunting procedures to deter you from undertaking out-of-school learning with your class. The first-hand experiences gained during a well-planned and organised visit can stimulate interest in a topic that continues back at school long after the event itself.

If visitors are being invited to school, you will equally have to ensure that you have followed the school's procedures. You should follow school policy on asking whether visitors must hold a recent DBS clearance and check that the children are at all times being supervised by a member of the school staff. You must also brief your visitor about what you want them to do while they are with you. Remembering that not all adults are skilled at matching their input to the needs of primary age children, you may find it valuable to base the session on questions that the children have previously devised, rather than on a presentation planned and delivered by the visitor.

The value of linking the curriculum to communities is not limited to those which are close to the school. Once children have formed a set of concepts about what communities are, and what it means to belong to them, through a study of the immediate locality, they are in possession of a powerful model for understanding distant communities as well. You can therefore build on the knowledge gained from studying the school's locality by planning a topic about a distant place, using a 'compare and contrast' approach.

Finally, and with a further reference to Ausubel's thinking about the crucial importance of beginning with what the learner already knows, you may like to think about the links between the school and the community as represented by homework. Each child's closest community is the home and the close circle of family and friends. Homework tasks which are carefully thought out can provide children with an opportunity to learn from and alongside other family members, and this process can result in narrowing the gap between home and school. Ideas presented in this chapter should provide you with effective starting points for activities to be undertaken at home.

Learning Outcomes Review

Thinking about the school in which you are working or have recently worked, respond to the prompts after each intended learning outcome, to identify your knowledge and understanding of the issues covered in the chapter.

- **An understanding of the concept of community, and its application to the school as a community:**

  - What communities are represented among the children in your class?
  - Which of these are local to the school, and which more distant or dispersed?
  - What features of the school's organisation and day-to-day operation provide children with experience of what it means to belong to a community?
  - What sort of community do you try to create and sustain in your classroom? How do you do this, and how effective is it?

- **An appreciation of the notion of fundamental British values and how teachers might promote them:**

  - Identify examples of times during your placement when you contributed to the following aspects of promoting key British values:

    o Encourage students to accept responsibility for their behaviour, show initiative, and understand how they can contribute positively to the lives of others (cf. DfES 2014b, p.5).
    o Help pupils to have an interest in, and respect for, different people's faiths, feelings and values (cf. Ofsted, 2014, para. 131).
    o Enable pupils to apply their understanding of right and wrong in their own lives, recognizing the consequences of their actions for themselves and other people (cf. Ofsted, 2014, para. 132).

- **An awareness of the importance of understanding pupils' social and cultural contexts when planning their learning:**

  - Give a couple of examples of how you have adapted your planning and teaching to take account of the experiences that pupils bring with them from their lives outside school. How have you used this approach to affirm and enrich children's understanding of belonging to communities?

- **Your knowledge of the ways in which the local and wider community can offer a rich setting within which learning can take place, and how community members can enhance classroom activities:**

  - Identify one or two instances in which you have drawn upon the local environment of people and places to enhance children's learning.

- **An understanding of key factors in planning safe, effective and stimulating opportunities for pupils to learn outside the classroom and at home:**

  - In what ways did your class experience learning outside the classroom, and how did you ensure that these occasions were both stimulating and safe?
  - Identify ways in which you designed tasks to be done at home which could foster dialogue and cooperation between children and their families?

Further Reading

Clark, R. (2013) *Childhood in Society for the Early Years* (2nd edition). London: Sage.

Curtis, W. and Pettigrew, A. (2009) *Learning in Contemporary Culture (Perspectives in Education Studies series)*. Exeter: Learning Matters.

Whalley, M. (ed.) (2007) *Involving Parents in their Children's Learning.* London: Paul Chapman.

Whalley's book asserts that those working in schools need to be proactive in engaging parents and carers as partners in helping children to learn. Curtis and Pettigrew explore, from a variety of perspectives, the relationship between learning and the changing nature of culture. Clark's volume sets childhood in broader social contexts, in which educators are but one of many important agents.

References

Ausubel, D., Novak, J. and Hanesian, H. (1978) *Educational Psychology: A cognitive view* (2nd edition). New York: Holt, Rinehart & Winston.

Baker, C. (2006) *Foundations of Bilingual Education and Bilingualism* (4th edition). Clevedon: Multilingual Matters.

DCSF (2007) *Guidance on the Duty to Promote Community Cohesion.* London: DCSF.

DES (1944) *The Education Act.* London: HMSO.

DES (1986) *Environmental Education from 5 to 16: Curriculum matters series.* London: HMSO.

DfES (2002) *The Education Act, 2002.* London, DfES.

DfE (2011) *Teachers' Standards.* Available from www.education.gov.uk/publications

DfE (2013) *Personal, Social, Health and Economic Education.* London: DfE.

DfE (2014a) *National Curriculum in England: Framework for Key Stages 1 to 4.* London: DfE.

DfE (2014b) *Promoting Fundamental British Values as Part of SMSC in Schools.* London: DfE.

Gardner, P. (2007) Living and learning in different communities: cross-cultural comparisons. In Zwozdiak-Myers, P. (ed.) *Childhood and Youth Studies.* Exeter: Learning Matters.

Kerridge, V. and Sayers, R. (2006) Community education: innovation and active intervention. In Sharp, J. et al. (eds) *Education Studies: An Issues-based Approach.* Exeter: Learning Matters.

Ofsted (2014) *Inspecting Schools: Handbook for Inspectors.* London: Ofsted.

Thomas, P. (2011) *Youth, Multiculturalism and Community Cohesion.* Basingstoke: Palgrave Macmillan.

12. Personal professional development
Sandra Eady and Cathryn Hardy

Learning Outcomes

By the end of this chapter you will have considered:

- the role of personal professional development (PPD) through QTS standards to Core standards;
- what actually counts as PPD;
- how PPD works in the Induction year;
- what is meant by Master's level study;
- about the possibilities of working at Master's level as an initial teacher training (ITT) trainee teacher;
- ways to juggle being a busy teacher/NQT with further study.

TEACHERS' STANDARDS
A teacher must:

8. Fulfil wider professional responsibilities
- make a positive contribution to the wider life and ethos of the school
- develop effective professional relationships with colleagues, knowing how and when to draw on advice and specialist support
- take responsibility for improving teaching through appropriate professional development, responding to advice and feedback from colleagues.

The role of personal professional development

One of the most effective ways to support children's learning and development is by actively engaging in personal professional development (PPD) right from the beginning of your teaching career. There is a great deal of choice and support offered and the professional standards can be a useful way to think about and guide your PPD choices. They can help you review your professional practice, identify further professional development needs and ultimately inform your future career choice.

The Teachers' Standards (DfE, 2011, updated 2013) apply to the vast majority of teachers regardless of their career stage and define the minimum level of practice expected of trainees and teachers from the point of gaining QTS. When you are a trainee, your providers will assess you against the standards in a way that is consistent with what could be reasonably expected of a trainee prior to QTS. When you are a teacher, your head teacher or their nominee will undertake the assessment using their professional judgement.

Paragraph 14 of the Teachers' Standards deals directly with progression and professional development.

> *The standards have been designed to set out a basic framework within which all teachers should operate from the point of initial qualification. Appropriate self-evaluation, reflection and professional development activity is critical to improving teachers' practice at all career stages. The standards set out clearly the key areas in which a teacher should be able to assess his or her own practice, and receive feedback from colleagues. As their careers progress, teachers will be expected to extend the depth and breadth of knowledge, skill and understanding that they demonstrate in meeting the standards, as is judged to be appropriate to the role they are fulfilling and the context in which they are working.*

The Teachers' Standards can be downloaded at https://www.gov.uk/government/publications/teachers-standards.

The Teachers' Standards form part of a wider framework of standards for the whole school workforce. This includes the occupational standards for teaching/classroom assistants and professional standards for higher level teaching assistants. There are also national standards for head teachers. These standards recognise the key role head teachers play in engaging in the development and delivery of government policy and in raising and maintaining levels or attainment in schools in order to meet the needs of every child. The standards for head teachers were reviewed in 2014 and published in early 2015 (DfE, 2015).

The continuing learning journey

Most successful teachers, regardless of the stage of their career or their seniority in school, consider professional development to be essential to their continuing development as a teacher. Initial teacher training is the first step along a road of continuing professional development (CPD), but what kind of professional learner are you and what type of professional learner do you aspire to be? Is there a correlation between your personal professional development (PPD) and your potential effectiveness as a teacher? Also, how can you ensure that you gain most from professional development?

Research Focus

Coe et al. (2014) undertook an analysis of more than 200 pieces of research and concluded that there is a clear link between professional development and the quality of teaching. Professional behaviours 'exhibited by teachers such as reflecting on and developing professional practice, [and] participation in professional development', were identified as one of the six components leading to 'great teaching' (Coe et al., 2014, p.3).

What counts as personal professional development?

Personal professional development (PPD) is about engaging with new or challenging ideas about a specific aspect of your practice. It is about reflecting on this in view of what you currently do and deciding on ways to change your practice in order to adopt and embed the new ideas/ways of working. It may also be helpful to consider PPD as a two-way process. Not only does there need to be a stimulus or input from another person, event, or book, most importantly *you* also need to actively engage and be open to listening and ready to reflect on advice, the activity, or the input in question. Thus, if you are to find PPD an effective and worthwhile activity, you need to consider how you might make changes to what you are currently doing in the classroom in order to enhance children's learning. Remember, PPD is not something that is 'done *to* you' but is something that is 'done *by* you' ultimately to support children's learning and development.

Continuing professional development (CPD) has a similar definition and is often seen as meaning the same as PPD. However, while PPD focuses purely on your developmental needs in relation to the children learning, CPD tends to include a broader collective view of professional development that locates it more in a national or local policy context where CPD priorities are primarily based on the school's development priorities which may or may not be the same as yours.

The former Training and Development Agency for Schools (TDA), now part of the Teaching Agency (http://webarchive.nationalarchives.gov.uk/20120203163341/http:/www.tda.gov.uk/), identified three different ways that PPD could take place (cited in Denby et al., 2012, p.101). These are by using:

- within-school expertise (e.g. induction, coaching, mentoring, lesson observation);

- across-school networks (these could be face-to-face meetings or virtual networks organised through local authorities, higher education institutions or school networks);

- other external expertise (e.g. external courses or funded study external speakers, consultants, or further study).

A personal professional development journal

A reflective learning journal is a useful way of tracking your engagement in personal professional development activities, but also, and more importantly, it provides a means of reflecting on the influence and impact that professional development has on your thinking and practice. PPD is much more likely to have a positive influence on pupil outcomes if you record your thinking and ideas. 'Capturing professional practice in the form of a journal can support understanding thought patterns (cognitive processes) and thus aid the process of problem solving' (Emira and Wilde, 2011).

Formulating a reflective learning journal could be based on a series of simple questions designed to help you reflect on the activity and related learning in the context of the potential impact on your teaching. For example, similar questions to those listed below

(Edge Hill University, 2010, p.1) were used as a prompt for teachers in their professional learning log for the Mathematics Specialist Teacher programme.

- What was the activity/event? Date?
- What did you learn?

So what...?

- What do you plan to change as a result of your learning? When? How?
- What influence/impact do you expect this to have on your practice and on pupil outcomes?
- Who will you involve in evaluating and monitoring these changes and outcomes?

If professional development activities are to have a positive impact on pupil outcomes, you will need to conscientiously plan and change aspects of your teaching and reflect on those changes in the context of children's learning.

CPD as reflective practice

Thinking about CPD in terms of critical reflection on your classroom practice is a powerful way of evaluating how you are supporting children's learning and whether your approaches to teaching are making a difference. The TDA defines this kind of 'CPD as a reflective activity designed to improve an individual's attributes, knowledge and understanding and skills' (cited in Bubb and Earley, 2010, p.1). It supports individual needs and improves professional practice. This definition of CPD would suggest that a whole range of both formal and informal activities engaged in could be defined as CPD as long as they involve reflection on practice. Further discussion of the value of reflection on and in action can be found in Chapter 9.

Research Focus

Wiliam (2010) suggests that, as teaching is so complex, if there is to be an improved outcome for pupils, teachers need to view professional development not just as attending courses but as 'a career-long commitment to the continuous improvement practice'. He also suggests that professional development is often seen as a means of gaining more professional knowledge in the belief that greater knowledge will lead to an improvement in classroom practice. However, it is his view that the most effective professional development not only links strongly with classroom practice but also encourages teachers to change their thinking, and that this change in thinking leads to a change in classroom practice.

The case study illustrates how often informal conversations in the staff room may be just as effective in getting you to reflect and develop a deeper understanding of what you are trying to achieve than actually attending (often costly) courses run by an external provider.

Case Study: Informal conversations as PPD

Over lunchtime break Lauren was having an informal chat to a fellow teacher about some children in her Year 2 class who were constantly calling out whenever she asked a question, despite the fact that she had told them on several occasions that they should put their hands up and wait to be asked. Her colleague agreed this was also a problem she had faced until she had been introduced to a questioning strategy while studying for a Master's degree. The strategy aimed to get all children involved in answering class questions by putting each child's name on a lolly stick and then randomly selecting one of these when a question was asked. This removed the need for anyone in the class to raise their hands. Based on this informal discussion Lauren decided to use this strategy with her class. Later she also extended the lolly stick idea by using it as a way of randomly selecting 'talk partners' or mixed working groups or deciding seating arrangements.

Lauren's case study is a typical example of how a chance conversation can lead to reflection and to changes in classroom practice. However, formalised PPD also has a role in helping you develop your knowledge and expertise in supporting children's learning and this may range from observing a more experienced teacher in your school and discussing this with a mentor, to attending a local conference run by your local authority, or other provider on a specific topic.

Research Focus

A systematic review of research by Cordingley et al. (2005a, 2005b) recommended that teachers should be involved in identifying their own PPD focus, and while PPD can involve the use of external expertise, it should also involve:

- reflection, observation and feedback from peers;
- experimentation in applying new skills in classroom teaching over a sustained period of time;
- an emphasis on peer support.

In fact the PPD that has the greatest impact on classroom practice and is most likely to become embedded and sustained over time is long term and collaborative in nature. Such PPD can have a positive impact on teachers' attitudes, knowledge and skills and improve children's learning.

PPD related to career stages

Another way to think about your PPD is in relation to what is a priority to you at this point in your career. In this sense the professional standards can be a useful way to gauge your professional needs and prioritise PPD related to your career stage. For example, early on in your career, PPD might be focused on classroom behaviour or matching teaching activities to children's abilities in your class. This type of CPD may then provide a sound basis for your next career stage or role development which may be more related to middle management or leadership.

Research Focus

In a national survey of PPD, Pedder et al. (2009) found that the types of PPD activities in which teachers spent the most time varied but tended to have an emphasis on supporting the needs of different pupil groups, teaching and learning, evaluating learning and approaches to assessment and curriculum. They also found that teachers with one to two years of experience were more likely to participate in CPD with an emphasis on behaviour management and deepening their pedagogical knowledge than their colleagues with more years of experience.

The survey showed that in general PPD tended to involve the following processes:

- a clear focus on pupil learning;

- observation and feedback;

- coaching and mentoring;

- collaborative working;

- opportunities for practice, research and reflective practice;

- involving teachers in needs identification;

- modelling of preferred practice (e.g. active learning), both in classrooms and in adult learning situations.

Note that for Pedder et al. (2009) effective PPD is likely to be rooted in the professional knowledge base of teaching and learning, with a clear focus on children's learning.

Accredited versus non-accredited PPD

It is also important to understand that some forms of professional development you might undertake will be 'non-accredited', while other forms will be seen as 'accredited' PPD.

Much PPD is 'non-accredited'. This means that it is useful in itself to help improve children's learning by providing you with updates on current government initiatives, such as literacy, the teaching of reading, or using ICT to enhance children's learning. It is not benchmarked against any specific Quality Assurance criteria, and while you may have gained a better understanding of a particular aspect of your teaching, it does not necessarily provide you with any recognised or greater expertise in the area. Some teachers feel that if they are investing their time and energies in attending professional development they want some credit and recognition for doing so.

Accredited PPD courses are designed to improve your expertise and will provide you with a nationally recognised qualification in the area that might be more worthwhile, not only in the way you support children's learning but also in terms of progressing your career. Master's qualifications are usually longer-term PPD options that will involve further study, reading, reflection and often opportunities to meet with other teachers who are on the same course. However, they can be costly in terms of finance and time. Nevertheless, they are usually recognised as good value for money as they provide greater opportunities to deepen your knowledge and develop your practice in a particular aspect of teaching over time.

PPD as developing an expertise: subject centres, longer-term accredited PPD

Becoming a member of a subject association is another good way of engaging in PPD, as many subject associations hold face-to-face local meetings, produce professional magazines and run annual conferences which often host a range of workshops on specific aspects of teaching and learning for a range of age phases. Examples of subject associations include Association of Science Education (ASE), UK Literacy Association (UKLA), the Historical Association, National Association of Music Educators (NAME), Association of Teachers of Mathematics (ATM), and there are many more. Examples of these can be found at http://www.subjectassociation.org.uk/members_links.aspx. The case study below illustrates how active involvement with a subject association can enhance not only individual professional learning but also provide support for others in your school.

Case Study: Networking as CPD

Mohammed was keen to become a science coordinator, and on the advice of his head teacher became a member of the ASE and started to attend local events. He soon began to meet other science coordinators and learn how science was organised and supported in their schools. At an annual ASE conference Mohammed attended a workshop session on the use of 'concept cartoons' (Naylor and Keogh, 2000). He became excited by the potential for supporting children's conceptual understanding by getting children to set up their own investigations and test out their existing ideas. He could also see opportunities not only for promoting pupil discussion and assessing understanding but also for providing in-service training for colleagues within his school. His head teacher agreed that the school should purchase the book so that he could try out some of the ideas in his classroom with the aim of running a staff meeting for other colleagues the following term.

Research Focus

Ofsted (HMI, 2006) found CPD to be most effective in the schools where the senior managers fully understood the connections between CPD and its potential for raising standards, and gave it a central role in planning for improvement. However, they also identified a number of concerns. In the surveys of National Curriculum subjects, inspectors found that arrangements for CPD in the subject they were inspecting were inadequate in about one-third of the primary schools. This did not mean that the school's arrangements for CPD were unsatisfactory but, usually, that there had been little or no recent professional development in the subject being inspected. The lack of such professional development was due partly to the schools' drive to improve literacy and numeracy and partly to a lack of specialist subject expertise, which meant that managers were failing to pick up important subject-related issues. For example, there was often a tension between policy driven priorities and school specific priorities.

School focused CPD versus individual or personal focused PPD

While this chapter focuses on individual professional development, it is recognised that there is often an overlap between school and individual CPD needs, and sometimes there is a clear relationship between the two. Theoretically both are concerned with supporting the enhancement of children's development. However, there can also be a tension with individual needs not always fitting with school priorities. Thus, while it might seem important for you to develop behaviour management strategies with some of the children in your class, the school may have as its focus improving the standard of written work for boys. When being on placement you may experience working towards an objective on the school development plan that may be different from your own development needs.

Bolam and Weindling (2006) found that there was a fairly common perception among teachers that issues for whole-school improvement are often prioritised at the expense of PPD needs. Furthermore, Pedder et al. (2009) found that some of the reasons why schools have difficulty in achieving a balance of school and individual teacher CPD needs may be due to a school being placed in special measures, where the CPD programme is structured exclusively around school-wide targets. Primary school teachers and teachers in schools with low achievement levels had a narrower range of CPD opportunities offered to them. In primary schools these were frequently focused on improving children's mathematics and literacy skills.

Therefore, it is worthwhile thinking about the kinds of CPD you would like access to and for what purpose. Already we have mentioned that it is important for your professional development to be focused on supporting your children and their specific needs.

Activity

Bubb and Earley (2007, pp.55–7) provide a useful list of professional development activities under the headings of 'self study', 'observing other practitioners', 'extending professional experience' and 'working with pupils'. You might find this list a helpful prompt when completing the Transition Point 1 task in your career entry and development profile (CEDP). The key questions are reproduced below. Read the section and identify which ones might be appropriate for you as you move into your induction year. Set out the professional development need and outline the type of CPD that would help you achieve it. Be as specific as possible.

1. At this stage, which aspect(s) of teaching do you find most interesting and rewarding?
2. As you approach the award of QTS, what do you consider to be your main strengths and achievements as a teacher?
3. In which aspects of teaching would you value further experience in the future?
4. As you look ahead to your career in teaching, you may be thinking about your longer term professional aspirations and goals. Do you have any thoughts at this stage about how you would like to see your career develop?

As you move towards the end of your training or if you are about to start your induction year, think about PPD in terms of the specific ways you can support children's learning within the context of your classroom practice. Remember that the central reason for all CPD is to improve children's learning. The targets identified in your career entry profile are a useful starting point for the short term. Alternatively, you may also consider your PPD in terms of the broader long-term picture of how you see your career in teaching developing in terms of supporting other colleagues to develop effective and innovative ways of supporting children's learning or teaching a subject or age phase. While PPD is likely to focus on generic curriculum teaching, learning and assessment, try not to overlook the subject knowledge development and support that can be provided through subject associations.

PPD in your induction year

Induction has been a feature for all NQTs who gain qualified teacher status (QTS) since May 1999 and wish to work in maintained and non-maintained schools in England. Its purpose has been to ensure that all new teachers are prepared for the challenges they might face in the classroom and are able to reach a uniformly high standard in their teaching. As an NQT, the induction programme will enable you to build on strengths and development needs identified at the end of your initial teacher training, in order to set the pace and direction for your professional development (Totterdell et al., 2008).

Your induction year is a three-term period of assessment which helps to ensure that your teaching career is built on a firm foundation. It consists of two main elements:

- an assessment against the core professional standards for teachers;

- a personalised programme of guidance and support providing you with the tools to be a successful teacher.

Towards the end of each term you will meet with your induction tutor or head teacher for a formal assessment. After the first two meetings they will make a report to the local authority or independent schools council teacher induction panel recording your progress to meeting the core professional standards. After the assessment in the third term they will make a recommendation about whether you have met the requirements for successfully completing the induction period. This will then be confirmed to you in writing.

As an NQT in England you can expect the following support in your induction year:

- a 10 per cent reduction in your teaching timetable to give you time to develop your teaching skills away from the classroom. This is in addition to your 10 per cent planning preparation and assessment (PPA) time;

- support from an induction tutor;

- regular reviews of your progress;

- formal discussions at the end of each term with your tutor and or head teacher.

The NQT year is an excellent opportunity for you to:

- work alongside others and becoming involved in planning with your school;

- observe more experienced colleagues;

- visit schools and settings beyond your work place;

- participate in more formal training events and courses;

- meet with your induction tutor to consider your progress and development.

As previously suggested, PPD is about you actively engaging and reflecting with the issues arising out of your classroom practice in order to enhance children's learning. Thus, just doing the above will not prove beneficial unless you engage in meaningful reflection and consider the implications for your practice and how your PPD is helping you to progress against the core standards.

Your induction tutor can help support this process by setting aside time for you to reflect on specific issues relating to your classroom practice. You could also include discussion and reflection on practice you have seen when observing a colleague teach. Similarly, you might discuss a recent course or training session in terms of the implications for children's learning in your classroom.

Your induction tutor is also likely to observe you teach and provide constructive feedback on specific aspects of your lessons at least once every half term. Following each observation your induction tutor will review with you your progress against your objectives and any PPD or wider CPD you have engaged in and revise this with you. It is a good idea for you to set the agenda or suggest the focus of discussion with your induction tutor so that you can guide the discussion.

Research Focus

Research by Totterdell et al. (2004, 2008) reports that evaluations of the induction year suggest that it is highly effective in developing classroom practice and increasing retention if there is careful consideration and support given to the novice teacher and experienced mentor in terms of time for meeting and collaborative planning. This effectiveness could be further capitalised on if the induction tutor has the appropriate experience of teaching age/phase as the NQT and support is extended over the first three years of teaching.

You can also learn informally from other professional relationships in school. Consider the following points.

- Plan with another teacher who takes the same year/age group as you or from other subject leaders in school such as a mathematics specialist teacher, the SENCO, or experienced teaching assistants.

- Looking at how other classrooms are organised can help you informally learn about how to display children's work or organise workspace.

- Talking to colleagues who have just been on a specific professional development course or who have just been teaching a long time can help you evaluate your current ways of approaching teaching.

- Talking to parents could also be a learning experience and provide alternative perspectives about how a child learns or behaves.

- Using education internet sites, or subject associations and government websites, can again provide many ideas for lessons and enable you to see what recent research says about specific aspects of teaching that might be relevant to your practice.

The key thing is that you feel in control of your own PPD and are driving it in the direction you want it to go. However, when searching for and applying for teaching posts you need to consider the school's agenda for CPD.

Master's level courses

To develop learning even further, there are many opportunities available for postgraduate study. Master's programmes are often practice-based and are designed to help you deepen knowledge and skills to make a real impact in the classroom.

Research Focus

Totterdell et al. (2008) recommend that there is a need 'to start thinking about early professional development that includes the first three years of teaching (or the first five years inclusive of initial training), with certification and accreditation for registered and/or chartered status being part of this process'.

It is possible to register for a Master's degree in education or in a specific subject or aspect of education such as inclusion, early years or leadership and management. Subject associations also offer Master's degrees in education, as do most universities. Sometimes professional programmes for a Master's in education are subsidised, which makes them more affordable to schools and individuals. Master's degrees are usually part-time, to take account of teaching commitments. Study arrangements mostly involve online learning, but this can be combined with some face-to-face sessions. Often these professional Master's programmes have open content modules which provide inputs on research skills and focus on 'teacher as researcher'. Some promote action research models of learning and study, while others take a broader approach to research. It is also worthwhile considering what forms of assessment are used. Many Master's programmes require written assignments, although more are considering other forms of assessment such as portfolios, podcasts and presentations.

Through the completion of your initial teacher training, you may have already achieved some Master's level credits. Some universities and higher education institutions (HEIs) permit the transfer of these credits towards a Master's degree. The possible transfer of credits will be considered through the process of Accreditation of Prior and Experiential Learning (APEL). For further information, contact the university or HEI where you intend to study.

While it is tremendously worthwhile to study for a Master's programme, it is a complex and relatively long-term form of PPD. Therefore, you need to consider how it fits in with your specific context, workload and personal life, both immediately and looking ahead to the long term. Some NQTs are keen to engage with Master's study straight after training, believing that it will enhance the quality of their teaching and at the same time improve their career prospects. They also feel that it will be easier to manage before they take on additional responsibilities at school or have additional ties and commitments at home such as a family. Others feel that they would like to focus at least on their induction year initially and continue with or register for a Master's in their second or third year of teaching (Jackson and Eady, 2008).

Working at Master's level as a trainee teacher

Accredited PPD at Master's level is about developing the skills to critically reflect on practice in the context of what other research has found. This is achieved by skilfully using evidence from a range of sources including books, documents, and observations of others' practice, to reflect critically on the implications for your practice.

The notion of 'action research' was first made famous by Stenhouse (1975). He introduced the notion of 'teacher as researcher', arguing that it should be the teacher or practitioner doing the research in the classroom and not external researchers. Since Stenhouse, the idea of teacher as researcher researching into their own practice has gathered momentum and it is now viewed as a powerful way of improving classroom practice, in order to enhance children's learning and achievement. Consequently, this approach to PPD underpins many of the professional Master's in education programmes run by institutions of higher education. Teachers and trainee teachers have found the notion of action research a useful and powerful way to improve or develop their practice in the classroom. They use the action research cycle to reflect on their developing practice.

The case study below illustrates how a trainee teacher adopted a 'teacher as researcher' approach in order to conduct a small-scale research project while on school placement.

Case Study: Using research to develop practice

Angela was undertaking a Primary PGCE. One of the modules, 'Improving Learning and Teaching', was at Master's level and involved undertaking a small-scale research project while on a five-week assessed placement. Although Angela had carried out some research for her undergraduate dissertation, this largely involved using statistics and she found the approach to practitioner research quite different from what she was used to.

The research skills input on the module helped her to learn about practitioner research and the use of qualitative methods within an action research methodology. She applied this approach to focus in depth on improving and developing an aspect of her teaching. The module assignment required that the research was written up in a journal format requiring critical reflection on reading as well as on practice.

The module supported Angela's reflective reading of related literature by providing a critical reading record for her to log the key points from related research and implications for Angela's

$\longrightarrow$

proposed study. By carrying out reading in this way before the placement, Angela formed a sound understanding of what aspect of teaching she would be focusing her study on; she also had an idea of what other research had been done in this area as well as a basic idea of action research and appropriate methods, including how she would tackle issues such as ethics and reliability and validity.

She took advantage of the tutorial support and action learning sets at university to shape and modify her research ideas. Initially, her ideas had been too wide-ranging and would have been difficult to do as well as plan to teach. However, by the time she was ready to start her placement, she had learned to narrow the focus of her research, planning to collect data as part of her lessons. Not only did her analysis of the data involve ongoing assessment of the children, it also provided her critical reflection of her teaching as well as how children were responding to the strategies she used.

At the end of the practice Angela felt that she had a much more in-depth understanding about her issue and about how she would change and develop her practice for the final placement. Her research also provided many more questions she wished to pursue in her final placement and in her NQT year.

The key lessons from Angela's experience are:

- Use the Teachers' Standards to help you decide on an area for small-scale research.

- Read about what other research has found out in the area you want to conduct research as this will help you shape a small-scale focus.

- Take advantage of any tutorials or action learning set seminars to discuss your ideas with others.

- Narrow your focus and keep it on your developing practice rather than on others.

- Look at ways in which data can be collected from the lessons you plan and deliver.

How to juggle being a busy trainee teacher/NQT with further study

By the time you get to this stage in the chapter you may be thinking that it cannot be possible to continue with further study while embarking on your NQT year. The case study below illustrates that with careful planning and motivation there are ways to manage Master's level study alongside teaching. Your interest and motivation are key to this, as well as having a clear plan and rationale for what you want from your PPD.

Case Study: Research as a trainee teacher

Alex was in his final year of a four-year Primary QTS undergraduate programme. He decided to conduct a small-scale research project on his use of questions in science lessons on his second school placement. He collected data by asking a teaching assistant with the class to

$\longrightarrow$

note down how many questions he asked during a science lesson, indicating whether these were open or closed questions. When he analysed his data he found that he was asking more questions than he initially thought and the majority of these were closed questions, which led to the children guessing the answers or using factual recall. He decided from his evaluation he would reduce the number of questions asked and make them more open-ended.

This research into his own practice prepared him for undertaking his final placement, where he found that he was now more receptive to children's responses to his questions. He found that using just a few open questions and allowing children to discuss the answers first was becoming more productive in terms of quality responses and getting the children to think more deeply. He began to return to the open-ended questions at the end of the lesson as well. He also realised, when discussing with his school-based tutor, that allowing children to discuss with each other was also enabling him to provide opportunities for speaking and listening, something he had not considered previously.

When observed by his school-based mentor and link tutor, both were impressed with his ability to structure questions so that he moved children on in their thinking. At the end of the placement the school had a post vacant and asked Alex to apply for it. He successfully secured the post. He also took advantage of continuing his Master's study as an NQT. He could see clearly how his initial focus of developing his questioning would enable him to work towards the Teachers' Standards.

The key lessons arising from Alex's case study are:

- Focus on key aspects of learning and teaching arising from the standards.

- Choose something that is a real interest or issue for you.

- Focus on an area that is integral to your day-to-day teaching.

- Consider using your findings from your small-scale research on your final practice.

- Talk about your experience of research and findings with enthusiasm when on interview for your first job.

Activity

Look at Standard 4, outlined below.

Plan a small research project around one of the bullet points, using your lessons as a source of data collection. What specific aspects of teaching and learning would you like to develop?

(Continued)

(Continued)

4. Plan and teach well structured lessons

- impart knowledge and develop understanding through effective use of lesson time
- promote a love of learning and children's intellectual curiosity
- set homework and plan other out-of-class activities to consolidate and extend the knowledge and understanding pupils have acquired
- reflect systematically on the effectiveness of lessons and approaches to teaching
- contribute to the design and provision of an engaging curriculum within the relevant subject area(s).

The key message running through this chapter is that PPD is not something that is done to you so that by attending a professional development course somehow you become a better teacher. Instead, we have seen that active engagement in further study is an ideal way in order to structure your future learning and can be managed if it is seen as part of the everyday role of teaching and reflecting and not as an 'add-on'.

Some practical tips for your PPD

- Focus your PPD on developing learning and teaching strategies that will ultimately benefit the children you teach.

- Focus on an issue you are interested in and how it is approached in schools.

- Ensure your further study or research is closely linked to your day-to-day teaching.

- Keep your research very specific; do not let it get too wide.

- Use children's work as part of your data collection.

Finally, an important factor in your development as a teacher is that you believe in your ability to improve your practice, ultimately for the benefit of the children you teach. This is what Dweck (2008) refers to as developing a 'growth mind set' rather than accepting you have a 'fixed mind set'. Good-quality PPD which is carefully planned and then embedded in practice is an effective way to develop a growth mindset, enabling you to expand your knowledge and understanding of what it is to be a successful teacher and make a real difference to the children you teach.

Learning Outcomes Review

Thinking about the school in which you are currently placed, or in which you most recently undertook a placement, respond to the questions which follow each of the intended learning outcomes, as a means of identifying your knowledge and understanding of the issues covered in the chapter.

- **The role of PPD through the Teachers' Standards:**

  - Familiarise yourself with the different career stages outlined by the standards.
  - Look at the standards; which ones seem of higher importance to you at this stage in your career?

- **What counts as PPD:**

  - What do you understand to be the differences between PPD and CPD?
  - Give a couple of examples of the kinds of activities you would consider to be appropriate PPD.
  - Identify ways in which you would embed PPD in your day-to-day practice.
  - Can you identify a time when a chance conversation with a colleague has resulted in you adapting your practice for the better?

- **How CPD works in the induction year:**

  - What kind of support do you anticipate receiving from the induction programme?
  - How can this help you focus on children's learning?

- **What is Master's level study:**

  - What do you see as the potential benefits for linking PPD to Master's level study?

- **The possibilities of working at Master's level as an ITT trainee teacher:**

  - Consider whether you would prefer to study for a subject-based Master's or one that focuses on generic aspects of teaching and learning.

- **The ways it is possible to juggle being a busy teacher/NQT with further study:**

  - Consider what is of real interest to you in your teaching and how you can build further study around it.

Further Reading

Chapter 3 (Survival Skills), in Elton-Chalcraft, S., Hansen, A. and Twiselton, S. (eds) (2008) *Doing Classroom Research: A step by step guide for student teachers.* Maidenhead: Open University Press.

This chapter provides practical advice about getting started with classroom-based research, either during your initial teacher education or in your first year of teaching.

For further information about the nature of CPD in the induction year and beyond, see Chapter 7, (Collaboration and Enquiry: Sharing Practice), Chapter 10 (Newly Qualified Teachers and their Induction), and Chapter 12 (Early Professional Development) in Bubb, S. and Earley, P. (2007) *Leading and Managing Continuing Professional Development* (2nd edition). London: Paul Chapman.

References

Bolam, R. and Weindling, D. (2006) Synthesis of research and evaluation in projects concerned with capacity building through teachers' professional development. Final Report, General Teaching Council for England.

Bubb, S. and Earley, P. (2007) *Leading and Managing Continuing Professional Development* (2nd edition). London: Paul Chapman.

Bubb, S., and Earley, P. (2010) Why staff development matters. In *Helping Staff Develop in Schools.* London: Sage. doi: http://dx.doi.org/10.4135/9781446251751.n1

Coe, R., Aloisi, C., Higgins, S. and Major, L.E. (2014) *What Makes Great Teaching? Review of the underpinning research.* Project Report. London: Sutton Trust.

Cordingley, P., Bell, M., Thomason, S. and Firth, A. (2005a) The impact of collaborative Continuing Professional Development (CPD) on classroom teaching and learning. Review: how do collaborative and sustained CPD and sustained but not collaborative CPD affect teaching and learning? In *Research Evidence Library.* London: EPPI-Centre, Social Science Research Unit, Institute of Education, University of London.

Cordingley, P., Bell, M., Evans, D. and Firth, A. (2005b) The impact of collaborative CPD on classroom teaching and learning. Review: what do teacher impact data tell us about collaborative CPD? In *Research Evidence Library.* London: EPPI-Centre, Social Science Research Unit, Institute of Education, University of London.

Denby, N., Price, J. and Swift, H. (2012) Continuing Professional Development and learning at 'M' level. In Denby, N. (ed.) *Training to Teach: A Guide for Students.* London: Sage.

DfE (2011, updated 2013) *Teachers' Standards.* Available from https://www.gov.uk/browse/education

DfE (2015) *National Standards of Excellence for Headteachers: Departmental advice for headteachers, governing boards and aspiring headteachers.* Available from https://www.gov.uk/government/uploads/system/uploads/attachment_data/file/396247/National_Standards_of_Excellence_for_Headteachers.pdf accessed 30/04/15.

Dweck, C. (2008) *Mind Set: The Psychology of Success.* New York: Ballantine Books.

Edge Hill University (2010) *The Professional Learning Log: Specialist Primary Mathematics Practice.* MST4010. Module materials. Ormskirk: Edge Hill University.

Emira, M. and Wilde, J. (2011) How can you overcome constraints to enhance reflective practice? In McGregor, D. and Cartwright, L. (eds) *Developing Reflective Practice.* Maidenhead: Open University Press.

Her Majesty's Inspectors (HMI) (2006) *Logical Chain.* London: HMI.

Jackson, A. and Eady, S. (2008) Perceptions of Master's level PGCE. Paper presented at BERA Conference, Heriot-Watt University, 3–6 September.

Naylor, S. and Keogh, B. (2000) *Concept Cartoons.* Sandbach: Millgate House Publishers.

Pedder, D., Storey, A. and Opfer, D. (2009) *State of the Nation.* TDA.

Stenhouse, L. (1975) *An Introduction to Curriculum, Research and Development.* London: Heinemann.

Totterdell, M., Woodroffe, L., Bubb, S., Hanrahan, K. (2004) The impact of NQT induction programmes on the enhancement of teacher expertise, professional development, job satisfaction or retention rates: a systematic review of research on induction. In *Research Evidence Library.* London: EPPI-Centre, Social Science Research Unit, Institute of Education.

Totterdell, M., Woodroffe, L., Bubb, S., Daly, C., Smart, T. and Arrowsmith, J. (2008) What are the effects of the roles of mentors or inductors using induction programmes for Newly Qualified Teachers (NQT) on their professional practice, with special reference to teacher performance, professional learning and retention rates? In *Research Evidence Library.* London: EPPI-Centre, Social Science Research Unit, Institute of Education.

Wiliam, D. (2010) Teacher quality: why it matters, and how to get more out of it. Spectator Schools Revolution Conference. London (March).

SECTION 4
TEACHING SKILLS

13. Assessment

Mary Briggs

Learning Outcomes

By the end of this chapter you will have considered:

- what assessment is and its relationship with learning and teaching;
- your role in monitoring and assessing children's progress in learning across the curriculum;
- how to share assessments with children;
- how to feed back to children on their work and/or responses;
- the role of recording assessments;
- the statutory assessments;
- reporting to parents/carers and consultations.

TEACHERS' STANDARDS

A teacher must:

1. **Set high expectations which inspire, motivate and challenge pupils**
- establish a safe and stimulating environment for pupils, rooted in mutual respect
- set goals that stretch and challenge pupils of all backgrounds, abilities and dispositions
- demonstrate consistently the positive attitudes, values and behaviour which are expected of pupils.

2. **Promote good progress and outcomes by pupils**
- be accountable for pupils' attainment, progress and outcomes
- plan teaching to build on pupils' capabilities and prior knowledge
- guide pupils to reflect on the progress they have made and their emerging needs
- demonstrate knowledge and understanding of how pupils learn and how this impacts on teaching
- encourage pupils to take a responsible and conscientious attitude to their own work and study.

5. **Adapt teaching to respond to the strengths and needs of all pupils**
- know when and how to differentiate appropriately, using approaches which enable pupils to be taught effectively
- have a secure understanding of how a range of factors can inhibit pupils' ability to learn, and how best to overcome these

- demonstrate an awareness of the physical, social and intellectual development of children, and know how to adapt teaching to support pupils' education at different stages of development
- have a clear understanding of the needs of all pupils, including those with special educational needs; those of high ability; those with English as an additional language; those with disabilities; and be able to use and evaluate distinctive teaching approaches to engage and support them.

6. **Make accurate and productive use of assessment**

- know and understand how to assess the relevant subject and curriculum areas, including statutory assessment requirements
- make use of formative and summative assessment to secure pupils' progress
- use relevant data to monitor progress, set targets, and plan subsequent lessons
- give pupils regular feedback, both orally and through accurate marking, and encourage pupils to respond to the feedback.

8. **Fulfil wider professional responsibilities**

- communicate effectively with parents with regard to pupils' achievements and wellbeing.

Introduction

Assessment is often a challenging area for those training to teach. The landscape related to assessment has recently changed, with the introduction of the National Curriculum in 2014 and the removal of the attainment levels from the new curriculum. The NC shifted from process-based learning, thinking about development and a learning continuum to a greater focus on knowledge acquisition and mastery. As a consequence the assessment requirements are also shifted, from differential tests with a best fit against level descriptions to tests with pass or fail descriptors, test scores and comparative placing. This could possibly lead to a lack of connection between the formative systems in the classroom and the systems of summative assessment at the end of key stages. Another key shift in thinking about assessment was the greater emphasis on tracking of pupils' progress, with schools free to choose their own ways of working. There are some key principles that still apply to assessment and these were updated in 2013 during the Primary Assessment and Accountability consultation.

Effective assessment systems:

- give reliable information to parents about how their child and their child's school, is performing;
- allow meaningful tracking of pupils towards end of key stage expectations in the new curriculum, including regular feedback to parents/carers;

- provide information which is transferable and easily understood and covers both qualitative and quantitative assessment;
- differentiate attainment between pupils of different abilities, giving early recognition of pupils who are falling behind and those who are excelling;
- are reliable and free from bias;
- help drive improvement for pupils and teachers;
- are closely linked to improving the quality of teaching;
- ensure feedback to pupils contributes to improved learning and is focused on specific and tangible objectives;
- produce recordable measures which can demonstrate comparison against expected standards and reflect progress over time;
- make sure the school is keeping up with external best practice and innovation;
- are created in consultation with those delivering best practice locally;
- are created in consideration of, and are benchmarked against, international best practice. (DfE, 2011)

Assessment is the aspect of teaching that is used for accountability, as teachers are judged by the results of the progress their children achieve. As a learner you may still remember the importance given to external assessments made of your work while at school. There are two linked aspects of assessment that of attainment and achievement.

Attainment is:

- a 'snapshot' of how a child is doing at a specific point in time;
- linked to the school and National Curriculum programmes of study;
- shown in marks or grades in relevant national tests or examinations or school-based assessment.

Achievement is:

- an assessment of children's knowledge, understanding and skills in relation to their capability;
- reflects the progress they make in relation to children of similar capability;
- a judgement about whether children are doing as well as they can.
- There are three main concepts associated with assessment.

Assessment for learning

This is the assessment that is completed to inform the planning of future learning and teaching. This involves the teacher and child in a process of continual review of progress

Assessment as learning

This aspect of assessment has developed from the personalised learning agenda (see Chapter 5), the increased awareness of the learner's role in their own assessment and application of different learning styles to the teaching process. This aspect focuses on reflecting on evidence of learning. This is part of the cycle of assessment where learners and teachers set learning goals, share learning intentions and success criteria, and evaluate their learning through dialogue including self and peer assessment. Learners are able to build knowledge of themselves as learners, and become meta-cognitive – in other words, they become aware of how they learn. It also helps learners to take responsibility for their learning and participate more in the process of learning.

Assessment of learning

This assessment provides a summary of the assessment to date. It involves working with the range of available evidence that enables teachers, schools, local authorities and government to check on learners' progress and using this information in a number of ways. In 2015 the SATs will still report in relation to levels of achievement, but from 2016 new SATs will assess the National Curriculum and will report using a scaled score in which a score of 100 is equal to the expected standard, potentially termed 'National Expectation'.

Assessment and personalised learning

Associated with assessment is the move to develop a personalising learning agenda, which allows for individual target settings or identification of progression objectives. Several of the elements of this agenda are helpful in relation to developing your understanding of current assessment practices. This shifts the focus of assessment from an activity that is 'done to' children to one that is 'done with' children. An area of development for many teachers, both newly qualified and

Component	Features
Learning how to learn	Giving learners skills, strategies and procedures to enable them to become meta-cognitive and self-managing learners.
Assessment for learning	Developing a wide range of assessment strategies, which place the emphasis on formative rather than summative approaches by engaging the learner in the assessment process.
Teaching and learning strategies	Providing learners with a wide range of appropriate options to enable them to learn in the most effective way for them to experience the full portfolio of teaching and learning strategies.
Curriculum choice	This involves changing the curriculum experience from the 'set meal' to the 'a la carte' menu. Students are given increasing choice as to what they study and when they study it.
Mentoring and coaching	The one-to-one relationship is central to any model of personalising learning – it is the most powerful expression of a commitment to the learning of the individual. Mentoring may be used to monitor academic progress, support meta-cognition and provide focused support for aspects of the curriculum.

Table 13.1 Elements of personalising learning

more experienced, is the involvement of pupils in reflecting on their learning in order to assist progress in learning without this becoming mechanistic. Pupils may have been asked to decide at the end of a lesson if they have achieved the learning objective, with a show of thumbs up if they feel they have achieved it and thumbs down if they feel they haven't. A partial success is demonstrated by showing one thumb up and one down, or holding both thumbs horizontally. Alternatively they may be asked to write about their learning, though this can depend upon age.

Research Focus

The Assessment Reform Group (see Black et al., 2002) developed the following principles for assessment for learning to guide classroom practice. This involves all adults working with pupils in schools and early years settings. Although this research was carried out some time ago you can see how this has helped to shape the development of the current principles for assessment, outlined at the beginning of this chapter.

Assessment for learning guide to classroom practice: 10 principles

Assessment for learning should:

1. be part of effective planning of teaching and learning;

2. focus on how students learn;

3. be recognised as central to classroom practice;

4. be regarded as a key professional skill for teachers;

5. be sensitive and constructive because any assessment has an emotional impact;

6. take account of the importance of learner motivation;

7. promote commitment to learning goals and a shared understanding of the criteria by which they are assessed;

8. give learners constructive guidance about how to improve;

9. develop the learners' capacity for self-assessment so that they can become reflective and self-managing;

10. recognise the full range of achievements of all learners.

Planning for assessment

Use of observations, tasks, tests and other activities

Observation is a key skill to develop as part of your teaching skills. You may be asked by your tutors and school-based staff to be aware of what is going on all around the classroom at all times, so that you notice a child leaving the class without asking, or interactions between children becoming heated. (See Chapter 15 for more on managing behaviour for learning.) This is quite a different observational skill from that needed to make assessments of children. You will not be able to keep track of everything in detail but you will be able to note significant events that will assist all those working with children to make judgements about progress and achievement in their learning.

By observing young children in play situations you may see them use their knowledge and therefore acquire the evidence upon which to make judgements about their learning. All the adults working with children in the EYFS will contribute to these observations, which will be used to compile the profile at the end of the EYFS. There are two kinds of observations of young children. The first will be planned observations, which you may plan with the team of adults working in the class and include activities outside as well as indoors, and the second will be the spontaneous noticing of significant learning that you will wish to record.

Focused observation can be used with older learners. Although it will give you a wealth of information about their learning, it is time-consuming. However, you may find this a helpful method of assessment if looking at the use of mathematical skills, knowledge and application when teaching using a cross-curricular approach. You may find a sheet like the one in Figure 13.1 as an initial guide to your observations.

Date	Observer		Child/group	
Context				
Related objective and learning outcomes				
Unaided task	Aided task		Practical task	
Notes				
Reference to any recording by child/group				
Objective achieved	Objective partially achieved		Objective not achieved	
Notes	Notes		Notes	
Targets set as a result of observation		Review date		

Figure 13.1 Selecting children for intervention strategies/additional input

Working with a group can provide assessment information that is more difficult to capture in the whole-class context; it provides an opportunity to discuss the mathematics in more detail with individuals in the group. The focused attention given to a group helps to inform future planning and teaching. It also gives children who are not active contributors in the whole class the opportunity to participate more directly, share their ideas and extend their learning within a small group of peers.

(Williams, 2008, p.67)

Although the focus in this quotation comes from a review of primary and early years mathematics, the same issues apply across the primary subjects.

The main focus is identifying groups of children for guided group work. You can identify children for a guided group through the following strategies:

- through day-to-day assessment of children's progression in the lesson;

- following feedback from a teaching assistant;

- as a result of a **planned** assessment activity with a focus on an identified target group;

- following periodic assessment to track progress in a specific curriculum area;

- in response to school priorities about the attainment of particular groups of children, where there is evidence of underperformance (target group).

Case Study: Using effective guided group work

Going into her final block placement, Samir had a target to focus on effective guided group work in her teaching. Over the first half of the placement, she began to feel more comfortable using it as a teaching strategy. During her mid-placement review, Samir talked with her mentor about what she had learnt about guided group work.

In terms of assessment, I see how guided group work helps me to build upon the assessment I undertook previously. It really helps me to target my teaching to the appropriate expectations for each of the children in the group and I can probe and assess children's understanding far better than when I'm working with the whole class. More generally, I now get that it is pretty fluid and it must respond to the children's learning needs. So, I can't plan for it too far in advance. I'm going to work more on using practical and ICT-based resources, as well as thinking about more appropriate subject specific models to develop children's understanding.

Marking and written feedback

Marking and giving children written feedback on their work across the curriculum is an important part of the role of a classroom teacher. By marking work you gain a sense of outcomes across the whole class and the range of ability, including pupils you may not have worked with directly during a specific lesson. This enables you to feed forward into your planning for the next lesson. This is increased focus for inspectors; in schools using different systems they will need to carry out more extensive work trawls to gain the data about progress.

Research Focus

Val Brooks (2009) has specifically researched 'marking as judgement' because she believes that this area of assessment has not received the amount of attention it deserves despite its pivotal role. This work raises important issues for primary teachers who work predominantly with criterion-referenced assessment: that is, you are matching the work against criteria that are pre-established. These criteria come from the old level descriptors in the National Curriculum, or success criteria linked to the learning objectives for a specific task within a lesson. Now the criteria is linked to the schools assessment system and the programmes of study in the new NC. Brooks cites the following research when exploring the use of criteria: 'there is no common understanding of what criteria-based means or what it implies for practice . . . Additionally, the concepts of "criteria" and "standards" are often confused' (Sadler, 2005, p.175).

Brooks goes on to argue that teachers need to be familiar with the criteria before they can use these to mark effectively, but she also explores the disadvantages of this, as once teachers think they have internalised the criteria they still tend to make judgements on the basis of their memories of how children performed tasks, and seek to use the criteria to confirm judgements they have already made. The marker can also suffer from bias, as they are likely to be swayed by the neatness of the work and legibility of handwriting. In addition, there is the issue of looking at the role of affect – which includes looking for opportunities to give credit. Brooks' paper asks us to take another look at the process of marking and the judgements teachers make when completing the task. You may see why when you read up about this marking process; there have been changes to the assessment linked to the National Curriculum.

Activity

Choose a piece of work from a curriculum area and familiarise yourself with the description of the criteria for the appropriate achievement before you mark this work. Jot down what you are paying attention to as you mark and then re-read the passage about Brooks' research and try to identify what you were focusing on. Share your thoughts about this process with other trainees on your course.

Oral feedback

There are two different kinds of oral feedback; the planned and the responsive. With planned feedback you will have time to consider how you phrase the feedback for an individual, group or whole class, so it is likely to be based upon marking a class set of books or your reflection on a previous lesson, in conjunction with your school-based tutor/mentor/class teacher's feedback. This may include general feedback on strengths and areas for development against the objectives that you might give to the class at the start of the next lesson. This can help model feedback for children to use in peer or self-assessment situations.

Responsive feedback is usually in the form of comments that you will make during the lesson to individuals, groups and to the class depending, upon the specific activity that is being undertaken. You may find this very daunting as it is part of thinking on your feet while teaching. If you are not sure, it is worth saying this directly to the individual, group or class, then you may want to take away the information and think about it before you give feedback, rather than feeling uncomfortable about the position in which you find yourself. This strategy shows that you have listened and/or observed what is going on and that you are responding. You can then plan a more considered response, but you must make sure you follow through with the response and give feedback. Don't forget. It may be an issue that you wish to discuss with your school-based tutor/mentor/class teacher before talking again to the children involved, especially if you are new to the class and need guidance on how a child might respond to the feedback given. Don't forget to ensure that all children get some oral feedback, including children with additional needs. For this group you may want to plan your feedback very carefully if it is to be a public feedback. For any pupil, negative feedback in a public arena could damage their self-esteem and their attitude to learning. Read Chapter 5 for more on supporting children with additional needs.

Peer and self-assessment

Young children are more than capable of making judgements about their own and others' work as part of the process of assessment in schools. Many schools have introduced an approach called 'two/three stars and a wish' and some even produce sheets/templates to put onto children's work.

The idea behind this approach is to get the learners to look carefully at their work and reflect on the positive feedback indicated by two or three 'stars', and the one 'wish', indicating where development could be made. This can be completed as self-assessment or can be used to guide peer assessment. The teacher can then talk to the child about how they might work on the area they have identified in the wish category. This approach can be flexible and children can be allowed to give only one star, or no wish, or there may be situations where wishes are not appropriate, as its overuse could have a negative effect. Children can find it difficult to begin with, and focus on holistic areas of their work including the presentation rather than the learning objectives or success criteria agreed for the lesson; the teacher may need to remind them about the focus of their feedback for themselves or others. A key element here is that the success criteria are clear and accessible for all learners. Be aware that children can also focus on trying to please the teacher rather than making judgements against the criteria for themselves.

Another approach to self-assessment uses a star diagram, where the child is asked to rate themselves against the items indicated. In the case of Figure 13.2, it is some general

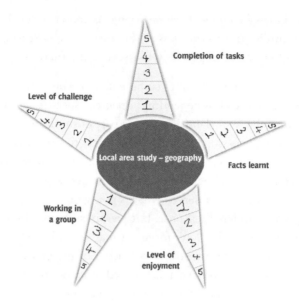

Figure 13.2 Star diagram

items in relation to a geography topic on the study of a local area. 1 represents a low score and 5 is high. The star can have additional arms so more items can be included. You can use the results from individuals to evaluate teaching approaches and plan for future approaches to learning.

Activity
Look at your last piece of written work from your course and try the 'two/three stars and wish' approach by first looking at the marking criteria and assess your own work.

Role of peer coaching

Linked to peer and self-assessment is the role of mentoring and coaching in the classroom. Mentoring and coaching are terms that are often used interchangeably for two people working together to change outcomes for one of the pair. Sometimes that can be a directive relationship, relying on the coach or mentor being a more knowledgeable person than the other.

Children can develop the skills of a coach, as Briggs and Van Nieuwerburgh (2010) have shown in their work with Year 5 and 6 children focusing on giving and receiving feedback. Figure 13.4 is an example of feedback given on the drawing of a giraffe, and how the child has responded to the feedback in another drawing.

Coaching continuum

←————————————————————————————————→

Directive, coach seen as
having expertise in
the area.
Instructional and could be
seen as tutoring, the coach
drives the actions.

Non-directive coach
does not have any
expertise in the area,
coachee takes
responsibility for action.

Figure 13.3 Coaching continuum

Figure 13.4 Children's drawing of a giraffe pre- and post-coaching

Although the research was carried out with the oldest children in Key Stage 2, in one school a Year 1 teacher had already been working in this way, encouraging her class to give and receive feedback.

Tests

You will probably remember spelling and times tables tests from your own school days. Tests can be very useful for teachers to check what pupils know, and for pupils to see how much they have learnt. Tests can be a source of stress for some pupils and as a teacher you will need to be aware of how different pupils cope with them. You will need to read the schools policy on assessment and identify any requirements for using tests in your teaching for monitoring progress.

With the changes in the National Curriculum and the assessment arrangements for tracking progress, a large number of commercial publishers advertise testing and tracking packages for schools to use to support them with the new arrangements. Some of these include electronic databases for compiling information about individual pupils, classes and schools. You will need to find out if the school you are working in is using any of these systems and if so how you will be required to input data from your teaching and assessment.

Tracking pupils' progress

As a result of the changes made to the National Curriculum and the associated assessments, pupils' progress has become a significant aspect of the assessment process. In arriving at judgements about progress, inspectors will usually consider whether and how well:

- pupils' work shows that, where possible, they have the knowledge, understanding and skills expected for their age as set out by the curriculum and assessment system;

- all pupils are set aspirational targets and that they are on track to meet or exceed these expected standards by the end of each key stage;

- assessment, including test results, targets, performance descriptors or expected standards are used to ensure that all pupils make the progress their teachers expect and that more able pupils do work that deepens their knowledge and understanding;

- progress in literacy and mathematics is assessed by drawing on evidence from other subjects in the curriculum, where this is sensible;

- pupils' strengths and misconceptions are identified and acted on by teachers during lessons, and more widely, to:

  - plan future lessons and teaching

  - remedy where pupils do not demonstrate knowledge or understanding of a key element of the curriculum;

- deepen the knowledge and understanding of the most able. (Ofsted, 2014)

Inspectors are not looking for the same system of tracking progress in every school. You will find that there are differences in the ways schools carry out this process, and you will need to ask specific questions about the systems any school you will work in is using.

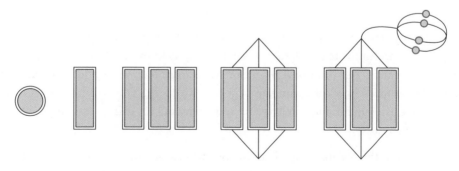

Figure 13.5 The SOLO taxonomy – structure of observed learning outcomes

In exploring tracking progress, teachers have been looking at existing approaches that don't use levels. One such approach is SOLO (Hook and Mills, 2011), which is a taxonomy providing a structure of observed learning outcomes (see Figure 13.5). It describes five stages of increasing complexity in a student's understanding of a subject.

Pre-structural level of understanding, where a task has been started but a pupil may need help as they do not understand;

- Uni-structural level of understanding, at a surface level where the pupil may have grasped one aspect of the task;

- Multi-structural, also at the surface level of understanding, where the pupil is grasping parts of the task but not the whole;

- Relational level, where the pupil links the aspects of the task and as a result develops a deeper and more coherent understanding of the task as a whole;

- Extended abstract level of understanding, which enables pupils to look at the task in a new way, creating a new understanding.

Although SOLO is not a new way of looking at learning and tracking progression, this work is being used in very different contexts from Bloom's taxonomy of the 1950s (Bloom, 1956).

High:	**synthesis** – hypothesising, showing originality by creating, inventing and composing
	evaluation – judging, rating and giving opinions
	analysis – categorising and comparing; distinguishing between fact and opinion or relevant and irrelevant information
Middle:	**application**/use – transferring knowledge from one situation to another similar one
Low:	**comprehension** – summarising and putting ideas or information into other words
	knowledge – remembering, reciting or listing facts.

Figure 13.6 Bloom's taxonomy

Some schools have been working with combining SOLO and Bloom's taxonomy to make judgements about pupil's progress in relation to the programmes of study:

- emerging
- developing
- secure
- exceeding.

You will see that these are used as the basis for the record-keeping example below.

Record keeping

All teachers keep records of children in their class; these can take a variety of forms, from notes scribbled on sticky notes while teaching, to in-class test results and assessments against NC programmes of study (POS). What is important about record keeping is that apart from being useful it links with tracking pupils' progress. You may like to ask yourself the following questions in relation to your own records.

- Can you identify groups of children for whom it would be helpful to work as a group with you on a specific topic they find difficult from your records?

- Does your record keeping help you to compile summary information about children's progress and attainment? If not, what other information would you need to collect?

- Would your records allow someone else to be able to pick up and plan for your class rather than trying to assess them all again?

You may have been asked to record information to indicate whether or not targeted learning objectives have been achieved in a specific lesson (see Figure 13.7). The three categories of judgement come from the reform of the National Curriculum group and the work of Professor Mary James, who suggests that only these are needed. Emerging means that pupils are not reaching the expected outcomes; expected means that they are reaching the expected outcomes; and exceeding means that pupils are working beyond expected achievement against the programmes of study in the NC. Pupils in the highest category are expected to deepen their understanding, moving towards mastery.

Name	Attendance register		Emerging	Expected	Exceeding
	Present ✓	Absent ✗			
	I	I			

Figure 13.7 Class record sheet

What kind of information does this give you, and is it helpful in identifying specific groups of children for guided group work, or for future planning or for summative assessment purposes?

What kinds of records would give you more comprehensive information in order to address these questions?

Activity

With a small group of trainees on your course, pool any examples of record keeping that you may have collected or been given and see if you can evaluate their effectiveness. Construct a list of the most useful information that you need to keep as a record in the class, and say why. Compare the ways in which schools are tracking progress and the categories they are using to judge progress against. If schools are using a commercial system they may break the categories down into more than the three parts mentioned above. Some, for example Learning Ladders, have editable templates and include the facility to download booklets for each pupil, to keep track of progress and attainment. Other popular systems include Target Tracker, which was developed by the Essex local authority. This breaks down the learning from the National Curriculum year expectations into six categories, and can store information at an individual, group, class and school level. Whether the school you are working in uses one of these systems or have developed their own, you will need to find out what is being used and how your judgements about progress and attainment can feed into the records.

Summative assessment points across early years and primary age range

Several significant changes are planned in this area that will have an impact on individual teachers and schools practice as well as the inspection process. A new floor standard for schools will be introduced from 2016. This expects 85 per cent of pupils to achieve a standard broadly equivalent to the pre-2014 'old NC Level 4b' or above by the end of Year 6 in all core subjects: reading, writing, grammar, punctuation and spelling, maths, science. Schools that don't achieve this standard will be judged on a progress measure; this is why the process used by schools to measure this progress will be very important. Progress will be assessed relative to the national average, which will change year on year. From 2022, schools' progress will be measured from a new baseline test administered in Reception from 2016 onwards. Schools must administer an approved baseline test in order to be judged on the progress measure from 2022 onwards, or choose a different measure (see below for details about the baseline).

The rationale of the changes to the measures for summative assessment and the move away from levels can be seen in Tim Oates' overview, available from https://www.youtube.com/watch?v=-q5vrBXFpm0&index=31&list=UU4NkS_w8o50U6jw2oksEMxQ.

Early Years Foundation Stage (EYFS) profile

The *Assessment and Reporting Arrangements* (DfE/Standards and Testing Agency, 2014) contain guidance on the early years foundation stage (EYFS) profile curriculum assessment and reporting arrangements. These are updated regularly, so ensure that you have the most up-to-date copy.

The EYFS profile is a way of summarising each child's development and learning attainment at the end of the EYFS. For most children, this is at the end of the Reception year (Year R) in school. Others may be assessed in settings such as nursery schools, private, voluntary and independent (PVI) settings and by Ofsted-registered childminders. It identifies children's learning needs for the next stage of school, helping Year 1 teachers to plan an effective and appropriate curriculum for each child.

Baseline assessment

To enable progress to be measured from the time that cohorts of children start school, a new Reception baseline was introduced in 2015. This short, teacher-administered, age-appropriate assessment is conducted in the first few weeks of a child starting school. From September 2015 schools can choose from a range of baselines to use. The Reception baseline will be the part of the measures used to assess progress for children who start school in September 2016 and beyond. From September 2016, the assessment burden will be reduced, as teachers will no longer be required to carry out and submit data on the EYFS profile. From 2016 schools will only be able to use their results from Reception baseline to Key Stage 2 to measure progress. In 2022 the government will then use whichever measure shows the most progress for each school: the Reception baseline to Key Stage 2 results or the Key Stage 1 to Key Stage 2 results. If schools choose not to use the Reception baseline, from 2023 schools will be held to account by their pupils' attainment at the end of Key Stage 2. You will need to check with your individual placement school about whether they have decided to use a baseline assessment tool. In 2015 the list of providers for the baseline were as follows:

- Centre for Evaluation and Monitoring, Durham University (CEM)
- Early Excellence
- GL Assessment
- Hodder Education
- National Foundation for Educational Research (NFER)
- Speech Link

End of Key Stage 1

Ensure that you have the most recent copy of the assessment arrangements for Key Stage 1, with the most up-to-date information for this age group. At the end of Key Stage 1 teachers summarise their judgements in relation to the National Curriculum expectations. These teacher assessments are informed by tests in English grammar, punctuation and spelling, English reading and mathematics

End of Key Stage 2

Ensure you have the most recent copy of the assessment arrangements for key stage two as this will give you the most up to date information for this age group. At the end of Key Stage 2 teachers summarise their judgements in relation to the National Curriculum expectations. These teacher assessments are informed by tests in English, reading, mathematics, English grammar, punctuation and spelling, and sampling tests for science.

The National Centre for Excellence in Teaching of Mathematics (NCETM) is working on the new tests at Key Stage 2 level in order to deepen the understanding, especially in mathematics, working towards a mastery of the subject. At the time of writing, the draft rating scale shown in Table 13.2 was as far as the thinking had progressed in relation to the tests.

Strand	Rating scale			
	1 (low)	2	3	4 (high)
Depth of understanding	Recall of facts or application of procedures	Use of facts and procedures to solve simple problems	Use of facts and procedures to solve more complex problems	Understand and use facts and procedures creatively to solve complex or unfamiliar problems

Table 13.2 NCETM rating scale for tests

Reporting results of tests to parents/carers

Schools must ensure that they explain pupils' progress and attainment to parents/carers at each stage. You will need to find out how the school or other setting you are working in is organising this for all parties: pupils, teachers and parents.

The following information needs to be reported to parents or those with parental responsibility in each year of pupils' education in the school.

- comments on general progress;
- results of any national curriculum tests taken during the year;
- attendance record;
- arrangements for discussing the report.

Inclusion issues in relation to national tests

A small number of children within this age group may need to be considered for a slightly different arrangement for their tests. Access arrangements are allowed for children who have a long-term illness or have an injury, such as a broken arm, for children who have limited fluency in English, and for children with special educational needs. The support given must not result in a change in the test questions, and the answers must be the child's own. When considering these arrangements schools may look at the following groups of children:

- those with a statement of special educational needs as described in special educational needs and disabilities (SEND);

- those for whom provision is being made as part of an Education and Health Plan (EHP) and whose learning difficulty or disability significantly affects their ability to access the tests;

- those who require alternative access arrangements because of a disability;

- those who are unable to sit and work for a sustained period because of a disability or because of behavioural, emotional or social difficulties;

- those with English as a second language and who have limited fluency in English.

P-scales

The use of P-scales is statutory for children with special educational needs who are working below the expectations of the National Curriculum. This is the only area of the curriculum where levels remain. In this context, special educational needs are defined in the *Special Educational and Disability Code of Practice* (DfE/DOH, 2014). Schools will need to use P-scales to record and report the achievements of those children in English, mathematics and science. The P-scales must not be used to assess children with English as an additional language (EAL) at any age, unless they have additional special educational needs. For further discussion about including all children, read Chapter 5.

Reporting religious education

Religious education is a statutory subject for all children registered at a maintained school, except for those in nursery classes, and unless they have been withdrawn from such classes by their parents or persons with parental responsibility under section 71 of the School Standards and Framework Act 1998. It is not a subject within the National Curriculum and there is no national programme of study. It is a general requirement that schools report children's progress in religious education to their parents or carers, but there is no required format for national reporting. *Religious Education: The non-statutory national framework* (DfE, 2004) provides guidance for schools and local authorities on assessing progress in religious education using two attainment targets which may be used for reporting progress.

Information that is exempt from disclosure

Schools must report a child's National Curriculum test scores to their parents or persons with parental responsibility. A head teacher can disclose the marks awarded to a child in the tests or allow their parents or carers to see, or have copies of, marked test scripts, but there is no requirement in education law to do so.

School level analysis of assessment data

Schools make appropriate use of pupil-tracking approaches; year, class and group curricular targets are set, linked to analysis of assessments. Teachers:

- use a range of summative assessments to judge attainment; identify children's progress; inform groupings of children;

- use statutory and commercially available tests to monitor and assess progress;

- use assessment to establish challenging targets for pupils.

Schools make use of data from the foundation stage, baseline tests and end of key stage tests for tracking progress. Other sources of information include tests, tasks, judgements made against NC expectations, and age standardised scores, for example for reading ages or other commercially available schemes.

Tracking can take place across a variety of time periods: across key stages, annually, termly or half yearly, half termly and day to day. With shorter-term periods, curricular targets, key objectives, progress books and any half-termly or termly tests are used as data for judgements made about progress. For day-to-day tracking teachers use marking, observations, annotations of work and plans, feedback, both oral and written, and any notes taken as part of lesson evaluations.

Attainment needs to be measured against age-related expectations and progress is measured against the child's starting point. By analysing data teachers can begin to address the following questions.

- How well are we doing? – *Analyse current performance of children.*

- How well should we be doing? – *Compare with national standards and similar schools.*

- What more can we achieve? – *Set clear and measurable targets.*

- What must we do to make it happen? – *Identify and implement improvement plans.*

- What went well?

- What can we do better? –*Take action – review success – start again.*

With the changes to assessments at the end of key stages, assessment no longer focuses on that key stage alone. There is more emphasis on ongoing assessments and a greater need for consistency of judgements.

Case Study

As a placement task, Sheila had to find out about the system used in school to track children's attainment and discuss how often teachers add data to this system and the frequency with which they review all the data and what they do as a result. The head teacher showed her a line graph of three children in her class and how they had all increased in attainment over their time at the school.

In addition to this, Sheila was required to track the attainment of three individuals in her class during the placement. She chose the same three children, but was staggered to find that their progress was less than smooth and that the topic being studied had a significant impact on their attainment.

Sheila's mentor explained how, over time, learning may appear smooth, but at any one point learning is a challenging process and is far from linear. They discussed why assessment was such a crucial part of teaching, reflecting on Sheila's revelation.

You can read more about the process of learning in Chapter 4.

School self-evaluation and target setting

Reporting and Analysis for Improvement through School Self-Evaluation (RAISEonline) provides interactive analysis of school and children's performance data. This system aims to enable schools to analyse performance data in greater depth as part of the self-evaluation process while providing a common set of analyses for schools, local authorities, inspectors and school improvement partners.

The system allows the generation of reports and analysis covering the attainment and progress of children in Key Stages 1 and 2, as well as for secondary, and these include the facility to explore hypotheses in relation to children's performance. Contextual information about the school is part of the key information and this in turn allows comparison with schools nationally and locally. The program allows for question level analysis to investigate children's performance in specific subjects. In addition there is a facility to set targets which supports schools in the process of monitoring, challenging and supporting children's performance. The final part of the system provides the ability to import and edit child-level data and create school-defined fields and teaching groups. This information is then used by schools to set targets as part of their Learning Improvement Plan (LIP) or Raising Achievement Plan (RAP); these replace the School Improvement Plan (SIP). See www.raiseonline.org.

Consultations with parents and reporting to parents

As a teacher you will be in a position to discuss children's learning, behaviour, attitudes and any other aspects of education with their parents/carers. This can be quite a daunting prospect for a new teacher. It is an activity you should try to observe first, then undertake as a mentored task while you are in school.

Learning Outcomes Review

Thinking about the school in which you are currently placed, or in which you most recently undertook a placement, respond to the questions which follow each of the intended learning outcomes, as a means of identifying your knowledge and understanding of the issues covered in the chapter.

- **Consider what assessment is and its relationship with learning and teaching:**

  - Look at your lesson plans to identify how you have used assessment to plan and teach specific curricular subjects. Have you used assessment in different ways for different subject areas? What might you improve for your next teaching placement?

- **Consider your role in monitoring and assessing children's progress in learning across the curriculum:**

  - Look at your lesson evaluations to identify how you have monitored children's progress over a sequence of lessons in specific curricular subjects. What strategies have you used for monitoring and recording progress? What have you done as a result of your monitoring – for example, selecting children for guided group work? What might you improve for your next teaching placement?

- **Explore how to share assessments with children:**

  - Look at your plans and specifically the success criteria. How have you shared these with the children?

- **Consider how to feedback to children on their work and/or responses:**

  - Consider examples of the written feedback you have given to children and review any notes you made in preparation for oral feedback sessions. What responses did you get from the children? Could you see any impact on their progress and/or attainment as a result of the feedback?

- **Consider the role of recording assessments:**

  - Look at the records you have kept. Can you evaluate its usefulness? What might you improve/change for future teaching placements?

- **Consider the statutory assessments:**

  - Consider the experience you have of any statutory assessment procedures and target any gaps for your next teaching placement. Have you read the current arrangements for primary schools?

- **Consider reporting to parents/carers and consultations:**

  - Review the experience you may have had of reporting to parents/carers. What else might be helpful experience? Have you attended parents' evenings?

Further Reading

Further issues associated with continuity and progression are addressed in Chapters 6 and 14 of this book.

Hook, P. and Mills, J. (2011) *SOLO Taxonomy: A guide for schools. A common language for learning*, Book 1. New Zealand: Essential Resources Educational Publishers.

Hook, P. and Mills, J. (2012) *SOLO Taxonomy: A guide for schools. Planning for differentiation*, Book 2. New Zealand: Essential Resources Educational Publishers.

Hook, P. and Cassé, B. (2013) *SOLO Taxonomy in the Early Years: Making connections for belonging, being and becoming*. New Zealand: Essential Resources Educational Publishers.

Lilly, J., Peacock, A., Shoveller, S. and Struthers, D. (2014) *Beyond Levels: Alternative assessment approaches developed by teaching schools*. Research Report, Wroxham transformative learning alliance and the South Farnham teaching school alliance. Nottingham: NCTL.

RAISEonline. Read about using RAISEonline in Hansen, A. and Vaukins, D. (2011) *Primary Mathematics Across the Curriculum.* Exeter: Learning Matters.

References

Black, P., Harrison, C., Lee, C., Marshall, B. and Wiliam, D. (2002) *Working inside the Black Box.* London: King's College.

Bloom, B. (ed.) (1956) *Taxonomy of Educational Objectives*, Vol. 1. Harlow: Longman.

Briggs, M. and Van Nieuwerburgh, C. (2010) The development of peer coaching skills in primary school children in years 5 and 6. Paper presented at the World Conference for Learning, Teaching and Administration, American University, Cairo, Egypt.

Brooks, V. (2009) Marking as judgement, *Research Papers in Education*, pp.1–18.

DfE (2004) *Religious Education: The non-statutory national framework.* London: QCA/DfE.

DfE (2011a) *Independent Review of Key Stage 2 Testing, Assessment and Accountability: Government Response.* London: DfE.

DfE (2011b) *Teachers' Standards.* Available from www.education.gov.uk/publications

DfE (2014) *Assessment Principles: school curriculum.* Available from https://www.gov.uk/government/publications/assessment-principles-school-curriculum

DfE/DoH (2014) *Special Educational Needs and Disability Code of Practice: 0 to 25 years.* Statutory guidance for organisations who work with and support children and young people with special educational needs and disabilities. London: DfE/DOH.

DfE/Standards and Testing Agency (2014) *Early Years Foundation Stage: Assessment and Reporting Arrangements (ARA).* London: DfE/STA.

Hook, P. and Mills, J. (2011) *SOLO Taxonomy: A guide for schools. A common language for learning*, Book 1. New Zealand: Essential Resources Educational Publishers.

Ofsted (2014) Inspecting Schools: note on the use of assessment information. Note for inspectors: use of assessment information during inspections in 2014/15. Available from https://www.gov.uk/government/publications/note-for-inspectors-use-of-assessment-information-during-inspections-in-20141

Sadler, D.R. (2005) Interpretations of criteria based assessment and grading in higher education. *Assessment and Evaluation in Higher Education* 30, pp.175–94.

Williams, P. (2008) *Independent Review of Mathematics Teaching in Early Years Settings and Primary Schools.* Nottingham: DCSF.

14. Planning

Mary Briggs

Learning Outcomes

By the end of the chapter you will have:

- become aware of the essential components of planning that are undertaken in schools including children's previous experiences, teacher's subject knowledge, vocabulary and resources;
- become aware of the levels of planning that are undertaken in schools;
- looked at the necessary elements of lesson planning in detail including evaluation;
- considered the planning requirements for additional adults;
- considered opportunistic planning and the issues surrounding different locations.

TEACHERS' STANDARDS

A teacher must:

1. Set high expectations which inspire, motivate and challenge pupils

- establish a safe and stimulating environment for pupils, rooted in mutual respect
- set goals that stretch and challenge pupils of all backgrounds, abilities and dispositions
- demonstrate consistently the positive attitudes, values and behaviour which are expected of pupils.

2. Promote good progress and outcomes by pupils

- be accountable for pupils' attainment, progress and outcomes
- plan teaching to build on pupils' capabilities and prior knowledge
- guide pupils to reflect on the progress they have made and their emerging needs
- demonstrate knowledge and understanding of how pupils learn and how this impacts on teaching
- encourage pupils to take a responsible and conscientious attitude to their own work and study.

3. Demonstrate good subject and curriculum knowledge

- have a secure knowledge of the relevant subject(s) and curriculum areas, foster and maintain pupils' interest in the subject, and address misunderstandings
- demonstrate a critical understanding of developments in the subject and curriculum areas, and promote the value of scholarship

- demonstrate an understanding of and take responsibility for promoting high standards of literacy, articulacy and the correct use of standard English, whatever the teacher's specialist subject
- if teaching early reading, demonstrate a clear understanding of systematic synthetic phonics
- if teaching early mathematics, demonstrate a clear understanding of appropriate teaching strategies.

4. Plan and teach well-structured lessons
- impart knowledge and develop understanding through effective use of lesson time
- promote a love of learning and children's intellectual curiosity
- set homework and plan other out-of-class activities to consolidate and extend the knowledge and understanding pupils have acquired
- reflect systematically on the effectiveness of lessons and approaches to teaching
- contribute to the design and provision of an engaging curriculum within the relevant subject area(s).

5. Adapt teaching to respond to the strengths and needs of all pupils
- know when and how to differentiate appropriately, using approaches which enable pupils to be taught effectively
- have a secure understanding of how a range of factors can inhibit pupils' ability to learn, and how best to overcome these
- demonstrate an awareness of the physical, social and intellectual development of children, and know how to adapt teaching to support pupils' education at different stages of development
- have a clear understanding of the needs of all pupils, including those with special educational needs; those of high ability; those with English as an additional language; those with disabilities; and be able to use and evaluate distinctive teaching approaches to engage and support them.

6. Make accurate and productive use of assessment
- know and understand how to assess the relevant subject and curriculum areas, including statutory assessment requirements
- make use of formative and summative assessment to secure pupils' progress
- use relevant data to monitor progress, set targets, and plan subsequent lessons
- give pupils regular feedback, both orally and through accurate marking, and encourage pupils to respond to the feedback.

8. Fulfil wider professional responsibilities
- deploy support staff effectively.

Introduction

In order to plan effective lessons and sequences of lessons for any subject in the curriculum there are a number of areas that need to be explored. When a trainee teacher observes experienced teachers teaching, it can appear that they can perform without any apparent planning and very little written down. This can be misleading as it can make you think that this is how you need to operate. The experienced teacher is only able to operate effectively in this way through building up their expertise by initially planning lessons in more detail as this helps with the thought processes needed to plan good lessons. It is tempting to want to cut this process short, as it is very time consuming and it may feel like an unnecessary workload during your training course. However, it is worth seeing this as part of the training process like any other and, although it appears that it is the written plans that take precedence, you will be going through a process that involves a number of other elements. Your teaching of a specific topic within the curriculum could be the only time that children are introduced to that area during the year, so it should be well planned, organised and taught. In time you will be able to plan good lessons without the weight of apparent paperwork but you will have still undertaken the cognitive activity of thinking through each lesson or session in detail and it will be no less rigorous as a result. This will include the necessary consideration of elements of contingency planning which may well initially look intuitive to the observer but are skills developed over time.

Essential components of planning

The areas listed below are the general starting points for all planning regardless of the amount of detail that is actually recorded. Your course will have guidance about the requirements and expectations for planning at each stage of your progress, which will also guide your thinking and your actions.

The School Curriculum and the National Curriculum

The School Curriculum in England (DfE, 2013) comprises all of the learning and other experiences that each school plans for its pupils. The National Curriculum forms one part of the school curriculum. Details of the plans should be available on a school's website by subject and academic year. The National Curriculum is the statutory document you are legally obliged to teach if you teaching are in a state-maintained school. For information about what schools are expected to identify on their websites, see http://www.legislation.gov.uk/uksi/2012/1124/made.

Once you know the curriculum areas and topics you will be planning to teach you need to look at the National Curriculum and the detail of the expectations of the outcomes for the age group you will be teaching.

Children's previous experiences

Securing pupils' progress that builds on their prior learning is a central curricular objective. Because progress is goal-related, the goals of learning must be explicit in order to guide planning and teaching, whether cross-curricular or focused on discrete subject content (Rose, 2009, para. 35).

Previous experience of the topic by the age group you will be teaching

This has two elements: the detail of the activities and tasks given to the children – the teaching that has been undertaken – and, more importantly, assessments of the pupils' learning and indication of any errors, misconceptions or areas that occurred during the previous lessons that need to be recapped. It is useful to know how long ago this area of the curriculum was last undertaken by the group or class, and also the focus of the lesson immediately prior to the lesson you will be planning. With this information you can think about making connections within the subject and across the curriculum. This can be content knowledge as well as skills developed in other lessons. Even when children appear to have had no previous experience of the topic to be taught, they will bring their own ideas about the area to the lesson. This can include any preconceptions they may have established when making sense of their world. For example, they may think that clouds cry when it rains. Part of the planning process is to allow space in your lesson to explore ideas that children may bring to school with them; only then can you begin to use these in your teaching and address misconceptions and errors. If you don't address these they become harder to shift and can create barriers for future learning in any subject.

Teachers' subject knowledge

In order to plan and teach effectively you will need to look at the progression within a specific topic and the links between the topic to be planned and other areas within the subject being taught or between curriculum areas. Once you know what you will be teaching and you have asked your class teacher and/or mentor about pupils' previous experiences, attainments and misconceptions, you are ready to explore your own subject knowledge. Your course will include sessions on subject and pedagogic knowledge. Look at your notes for the specific topic you are planning, to explore the details of the progression. Use these to understand where the lessons you will be planning and teaching fit into this progression. Try to identify any aspects that you may want to revisit in relation to your own understanding. Explain the key aspects to a colleague to try out your approaches and check your understanding. Be honest with yourself at this point as it is possible to make assumptions about your knowledge.

Vocabulary

Your understanding of the vocabulary needed during any unit/session/lesson is a crucial part of planning effective teaching. Think about how you will explain what each of the words means in the context that it is used within the curricular focus, particularly if they are everyday words that have a subject-specific meaning. Part of your planning will be to have the words available to introduce to the children on an interactive whiteboard, poster, display and/or cards.

Activity

Choose a subject you are less confident about teaching. Look at the appropriate School Curriculum and associated National Curriculum expectations, schemes of work and any long-term planning you have access to. Identify the progression of subject knowledge required for the learner and the teacher. Check your understanding of terms, processes, procedures and all other aspects of content.

Resources

What kind of resources will be needed to help you teach the topic? Ensure that you are familiar with the resources available in the school you will be working in. Do they use an interactive whiteboard (IWB) to present and manipulate ideas? How can you vary the resources that you plan to use to support different learning styles or different age groups of children?

Levels of planning in settings and schools

Levels of planning in settings and schools can be classified as long term, medium term and short term. As a trainee teacher, you will receive details of the medium- and long-term planning by your placement setting/school, but you are not likely to have access to staff discussions about this level of planning while you are on placement, particularly if it is of short duration. If you do have the opportunity it is good experience to be present at the discussions even if you will mainly be listening to the other teachers. It would also be worthwhile talking to teachers about how the plan was developed so that you can gain a sense of the process. Schools evaluate this level of planning through work trawl scrutiny and a review of children's progress in learning across the curriculum in preparation for the next year's teaching.

Long-term planning

This planning is usually the focus for the whole setting or school and is designed to ensure continuity and progression for children in a subject. In terms of coverage this level of planning should ensure that the requirements of the Early Years Foundation Stage and the National Curriculum are met for all children.

Medium-term planning

Medium-term planning focuses on greater detail than long-term planning and usually comprises half-term to termly plans. As a trainee you may find yourself being given the existing medium-term plan or scheme of work. It can be difficult to work from someone else's plans as you may not have been part of the discussion about the order of topics or the amount of time to be given for teaching those topics. It is worth making these plans your own by looking at the medium-term plan for the placement's duration and adding appropriate detail to support your work and to address the specific standards related to planning across the curriculum.

Mixed year group classes

It can be particularly important to gain an overview of what is to be taught when dealing with a mixed year group class. You will need to ensure that the subjects of the whole curriculum to be covered by the year groups coincide so that the same areas are being taught at the same time. This will make it easier to plan in the short term and for you to offer a coherent approach to all children. This level of planning is evaluated either by the whole school or by a member of staff who has responsibility for a subject area or teaching and learning and is usually the agenda for a whole staff meeting, year group or key stage, depending upon the size of the school and its organisational structure. On a longer placement, you may be asked to evaluate the planning for a sequence of lessons within a subject area or thematic approach, and here you will draw on individual lesson evaluations in order to make judgements about the effectiveness of learning and teaching across the sequence. You can also draw upon any feedback you have had from observations of your teaching of appropriate lessons as part of your evidence base.

Blocking subjects

You may find that some subjects are blocked on the timetable over a number of weeks; rather than having a weekly lesson in geography, for example, the school may have decided to block a humanities topic for a specific year group or across a key stage. When mapping out blocks over the term or year, the interrelatedness of the content and pitch of the material needs to be taken into account. Blocked topics can be pieced together in various ways to provide children with a coherent learning experience and the blocks can be adapted to suit the specific school context and the pupils' needs. This will be based upon previous teaching and assessment of pupils' learning. Some schools produce their own block plans for subjects like science, and they allocate blocks of time on the timetable for teaching these areas.

Other starting points

You can think about planning and the starting points for lessons in various ways. For example, a book could be used as the stimulus for planning across the curriculum, or a topic approach – neither of which may cover all areas of the curriculum. The reasons for this are explained in

Chapter 2. These cannot detail all the possible activities, but they offer you a starting point to think about your planning from differing perspectives.

Commercial schemes

Some areas of the curriculum may be taught using a commercial scheme which structures the teaching and learning and supports the teacher's planning. Materials can include pupil books, teacher books, large text books, posters, IWB resources and other items. Be sure that you use these only as a guide or loose framework so that you continue to focus first and foremost on the children's needs and prior experiences, as textbooks cannot be written for a specific class and the potential range of needs.

Research Focus

Despite the importance of planning as part of the teaching process there is little research specific to this area. Much of the research looks at the effectiveness of implementing a teaching strategy and how this is planned by the teacher. Beyer and Davis' (2009) research looked at pre-service teachers' use of 'educative curriculum materials' for science teaching in Canada. They argue that teachers need to cultivate the capacity to critique and adapt curriculum materials in productive ways and that for new teachers this is a challenging task. They found that the lesson-specific nature of the supports made it difficult for the pre-service teachers to recognise the principle underlying the ideas in the supports. Thus, most of them did not use the principle within the educative supports to analyse the lesson plan more broadly or analyse other lesson plans, resulting in missed opportunities to further improve the materials beyond the suggestions given in the support (p.699). This raises questions for how trainee teachers work with curricular materials and the support you may be given to enable you to work with materials more effectively. It also points to trainee teachers being aware that they need to unpack the principles within materials before use with a class.

Activity

When you are on placement, find out which subjects are taught using a commercial scheme. How does this impact on planning? Does this mean that the planning, teaching and learning for this subject is a separate area and that there is no integrated planning with this area of the curriculum? Look at the commercial scheme material available to you on placement for a specific subject.

- Read through the lesson plan and any guidance.
- Adapt the plans to take account of the least and most able children.
- Annotate a copy of the plans to meet your pupils' needs.

- What ideas could you take for activities from the material?
- How could you change the worksheet offered into a practically based activity?
- If you intend to use a prepared plan as part of your planning, consider how you will intervene to monitor progress during the lesson and inform and redirect learning when necessary.
- Discuss any use of scheme materials with your school-based tutor/class teacher/ mentor.
- How does this compare with the issues raised in the research focus?

Short-term planning

Short-term planning is the level you will have most autonomy over as a trainee teacher. The other chapters in this book encourage you to consider many issues related to planning for children, such as meeting individual needs, planning a motivating lesson, the need to plan for assessment opportunities and so on. This section considers the 'nuts and bolts' of lesson planning.

Daily or lesson planning and lesson formats

Most teachers use their weekly or block plans as the main short-term planning rather than working on individual lessons, although you may find yourself in a school where teachers plan daily lessons. As a trainee, though, you are likely to be required to plan individual lessons, especially when you are being observed. This will also allow you to gain evidence against a number of standards for QTS.

Below is a list of the typical content you will find required in a trainee teacher's lesson planning pro forma. While each course will vary as to its format and precise content, what is important is that your plans include all the key elements to ensure you have a clear effective plan that will support your teaching and progress in learning in the classroom.

The list is clearly intended for planning lessons according to the features of a three-part lesson. Some teachers always use this lesson format to structure their lessons; others will vary the format according to what is being taught. In the introduction at the beginning of the lesson you make the links to previous learning and connections between aspects of the subject. A review/plenary at the end of the lesson assists with assessment and gives children time to reflect upon their learning. The lesson can be stopped at any point for a mini review, which would allow you to monitor progress, pick up on any misconceptions and extend or redirect learning where needed.

In addition to noting the subject/theme, date, class, and number of children, you will need to consider:

Children's previous experience: Work to be built on from previous lessons, units, years.

The previous lesson: Make notes from evaluations and assessment, including children's errors and misconceptions that need to be addressed in this lesson.

National Curriculum references: Include statutory requirements.

Learning objectives: Should be specific to this lesson and measurable and may vary for different groups of children and say how you will share these with the class.

Possible errors and misconceptions or sources of difficulties: This should show your awareness of potential difficulties children might encounter.

Assessment: **What** precisely do you want the children to achieve in this lesson? **Who** is to be assessed: individuals, group, class? **How** will the assessment be made, e.g. observation during introduction, group work questioning; marking work?

Cross-curricular focus: Links with other subjects, themes.

Teachers' Standards: Trainee teacher's personal targets to be addressed during this lesson. Two or three maximum.

Resources: Materials, equipment, ICT, texts.

Safety issues: This could include what you say to the class about the use of potentially dangerous equipment e.g. scissors, compasses, or the need for children to wear appropriate clothing if working outside, or awareness of allergies if cooking.

Subject-specific language: Including introducing and using key vocabulary both by the children and the teacher.

Specific expectations for behaviour: Make clear to children; this could be a general focus on a show of hands or specific targets for individuals or groups.

Language and literacy objectives, including spoken language, reading and writing and vocabulary development: As appropriate to this subject/lesson.

Introductory activity: Focus on the teacher and the children. Include assessment. May be an oral/mental starter in a mathematics lesson. Include timings.

Introduction to the main activity: Focus on teacher input to start the lesson. What are the key concepts that you want the children to learn? What stimulus will you provide to focus the children's learning?

Main activity: Will include differentiated tasks, including Education, Health and Care plans (EHC) where appropriate. Include differentiate assessment. Consider mini plenaries where appropriate. What will your role be? What is the role of other in-class supporting adults? Timings?

Plenary: Key questions to ask/objectives to revisit/areas to discuss; consolidation activity; introduce homework where appropriate; note any errors/misconceptions to address.

Evaluating lessons

In addition to considering the above aspects, your lesson plan should provide space for an evaluation of the lesson. Annotate the plan, using a different colour. Add other working notes or changes directly to the plan. After the session, consider both the quality of the teaching and whether each of the children really progressed in their learning. Make any relevant notes that will help you plan the following sessions. This may include: comments on timing; the appropriateness of the resources; additional ideas to reinforce the learning; suggestions for alternative organisational strategies.

Did each child really learn what was intended? Remember, you can't judge learning just by completion of the work or activities set. Also remember to think about the children's understanding of vocabulary used in the lesson. Make reference to specific children (which may or may not need to go on their records). Make notes on how you might help the children progress in their learning; this can include areas for recap as well as what, where and when, with next steps.

In the case study below you will see these headings in practice, in a plan for a Key Stage 2 history lesson planned by a trainee teacher. As you read the plan, think about the extent to which the trainee is responding to each of the areas in her planning.

Case Study: Planning for a history lesson

Subject/Theme	History – Life in Tudor Times. The Tudor Monarchs
Date:	20th October
Class/year group	Class: 5B Number of Children: 28
Children's previous experience:	In Year 3: Explored past photos from 1900s as a source of evidence about changes in the local area. Throughout KS2 children have been encouraged to use exploring different sources of evidence in order to find out about a specific period of history as part of historical enquiry skills.
Notes from previous lesson	Last couple of lessons on Who were the Tudors? and Early Tudors Explored pupils' existing knowledge about the Tudors. Arranged dates of Tudor Monarchs in chronological order. Placed pictures of Tudor Kings and Queens on a large family tree S.N. and M.J. had difficulty sequencing large numbers in dates (pick up on this in numeracy as well).
NC references	A study of an aspect or theme in British history that extends pupils chronological knowledge beyond 1066.

→

Learning objectives	By the end of the lesson most children will:
	• Know the Tudor family were a family of kings and queens who reigned in fifteenth and sixteenth centuries.
	• Specifically know who Elizabeth I was and key facts about her reign.
	• Have discussed the evidence and bias about the character and images of the Tudor Monarchs as presented in contemporary portraits, e.g. Holbein's portrait of Elizabeth I.
	• Have made at least one inference based on the evidence contained in the Tudor portraits.
Possible errors and misconceptions or sources of difficulties	Children may have difficulty relating the centuries to the dates, e.g. sixteenth century and 1500s.

Assessment	**What?** Can the children identify some aspect of the portrait as evidence to make inferences about the life, status or character of the king or queen, e.g. the padded clothes make the queen look big, strong, powerful. Symbolism used in Elizabeth's portrait. **Who?** Orange group (T), TA to assess J, M, E, S, D and K. **How?** Observation/questioning during intro, focus group activities and plenary.
Cross-curricula	Art. Artists and portraits. Hans Holbein, Nicholas Hilliard.
Focus	Maths. Ordering larger numbers – dates. Group collaboration.
Resources	National Gallery posters, postcard – Tudor portraits, http://www.marileecody.com/eliz1-images.html
Safety issues	Manage transitions group by group. Discourage dashing from carpet. Bring back if necessary.
Subject-specific language	Primary source, evidence, inference, portrait, artist, costume, facial expression symbol, chronological order, family tree.
Specific expectations for behaviour	Work as a team. Allocate a person to record your ideas about the portraits. Share your ideas. Listen to others. Encourage everyone in group to contribute.
Language and literacy objectives: *including spoken language, reading and writing and vocabulary development*	Spoken language – expressing ideas to an audience. Paired and group discussion.

(Time: 10 mins)	Introductory activity/Mental Oral:
Teacher:	Children:
Manage groups to carpet.	Gather on carpet
Review previous lesson on Tudors	
IWB. Display large portrait of Richard III	

Discuss portraits	Partner talk. Review. What do you remember about the Tudors? Two things you learned about the Tudors.
Valuable, important source of evidence/ information about people and life in the past	
Why no photographers to take their pictures?	
• Q.A./Partner talk	
• Who do you think these people are?	
• What clues are there?	
• Give one or two examples, e.g. jewellery, background, facial expression	
• Why might they be made to look stern, wealthy, etc.	Children discuss other clues and what they might tell us about the Tudor Kings and Queens as they are presented in the portraits.

- **Assessment:** Can the children identify at least one aspect of the portrait as evidence to make an inferences about the life, status or character of the king or queen e.g. the padded clothes make the king look big, strong, powerful. The map in the background suggests they ruled over other lands.

(Time: 5 mins)	Introduction to the main activity
Teacher:	Children:
Display portraits of Henry's children in early life and as monarchs so that children can see how children were dressed and any changes once they become monarchs, Edward and Mary and Elizabeth.	In groups at tables.
	Each group of 'Time Detectives' discuss Henry's children as presented in the portraits.
Explain Task	Examine carefully. Describe what they can see.
Use famous portraits of Tudor Kings and Queens.	Identify what might it tell us? Elect a recorder.
Become Time Detectives. What can we discover about each monarch from the portraits?	Use large sheets to record the clues and what it might tell us about the character or life of each monarch.
Model example on flip sheet. e.g. Edward V	
Arrange groups (6x5)	
• Orange to Teacher	
• Support group with TA	

(Time: e.g. 30 mins)	Main activity:	
Group (TA)	Groups	Group (with Teacher)
Pomegranate, with J, M, E, S, D and K	**Swan,** Edward	(White Rose)
To work on carpet	**Hawk,** start with portrait of Mary Queen of Scots	To examine Rainbow portrait of Elizabeth
Use IWB Coronation portrait of Elizabeth		

Supervise recording or scribe for the children. Record clues and pupils' ideas. **Assess each child** as below.	**Red Rose,** Mary Each group to discuss and record clues/evidence and inferences about monarch.	Discuss some examples of symbolism, e.g. serpent, wisdom, dog loyalty etc.
Assessment: Can these children: identify at least one aspect of the portrait as evidence to make inferences about the life, status or character of the king or queen, e.g. the padded clothes make the king look big, strong, powerful? The map in the background suggests they ruled over other lands.	Can these children: identify at least two aspects of the portrait as evidence to make inferences about the life, status or character of the king or queen, e.g. the padded clothes make the king look big, strong and powerful? The map in the background suggests they ruled over other lands.	Can these children: identify at least three aspects of the portrait as evidence to make inferences about the life, status or character of the king or queen? *In addition* can they identify some of the symbols and what they might mean? E.g. crown, orb, serpent? Visit website for information. http://www.marileecody.com/eliz1-images.html

Differentiation/target setting including IEPs where appropriate:

AK – EHC plan (EAL support) encourage use of vocabulary for everyday items – king, queen, clothes, picture, portrait, costume

Encourage T, W, KM to use mother tongue where helpful.

Teacher's role during the main activity:

Develop Rose group's appreciation of symbolism and use internet search if available.

Use of in class support, including guidance to supporting adult(s):

See above.

(Time e.g. 15 mins)	Plenary:

Gather children on carpet

Key questions to ask/objectives to revisit/areas to discuss:

What has each group of Time Detectives learned about their child of Henry from their portrait?

What did they notice about the representation of them as children and then as monarch?

What makes Mary Queen of Scots the odd one out? Each group to display chart and briefly report Explore the idea of 'bias' in the pictures.

Do you think the portraits are accurate? Why might an artist's portrait be biased?

What would you do if you were an artist in the time of the Tudors?

Reinforce and praise original or independent inferences drawn from portraits.

$\longrightarrow$

Consolidation activity

Hot-seat an artist

Choose a volunteer to be Holbein or Hilliard.

Ask them to describe the monarch they painted.

Children ask questions about what they were really like!

Introduce homework where appropriate:

Find other pictures of the Tudor Family which might tell us something of their lives or characters.

Activity

Use the following lesson plan discussion sheet to evaluate the history lesson above. If possible, talk to other trainees/tutors/your mentor about your findings. What would you alter from the plans?

Lesson Plan Discussion Sheet   Title:

      Date:

Focus	Yes/no/ partly	Notes and suggestions
Are there clear and appropriate references to the EYFS, School Curriculum, NC, commercial schemes? Do they match age-related expectations? If not why not?		
Are the learning objectives and intended outcomes specific and clearly defined? Is it clear what knowledge, skills, understanding or attitudes the children will gain from the lesson? Are there sufficient opportunities for challenging children? Remember that children who find activities either too easy or too hard can become bored, frustrated and disruptive in the lesson. Does the plan indicate how children will know what the objectives for this lesson are?		
Does the plan identify potential errors, misconceptions and difficulties that the pupil's might have with the content or processes?		

(Continued)

(Continued)

Does the plan show that the trainee's knowledge and understanding are accurate?		
Will this be an interesting lesson, set in an appropriate context, relevant to the children's experiences? Remember that children who are bored can be disruptive in lessons.		
Does the lesson plan demonstrate that the trainee teacher is building on an evaluation, assessment and knowledge of the pupil's ability, achievements and needs?		
Does the lesson cater for children with a range of different abilities – SEN, G&T or those with EAL?		
Is there an opportunity to find out what the children already know at the start of the lesson?		
Are there planned opportunities for the children to contribute, talk, interact, communicate and engage in activity?		
Is it clear where and how the class will be organised for the activities, e.g. whole class, group, paired and individual work?		
Are health and safety issues considered?		
Are the activities explained in sufficient detail for another teacher to be able to lead the lesson if necessary?		
Is it clear what both the teacher and children will be doing at each stage of the lesson?		
Have any additional adults in the classroom been planned for?		
Does the lesson have an obvious structure, e.g. beginning, middle and plenary?		
Has the timing of each stage of the lesson been considered?		
Can the outcomes be realistically achieved in the allocated time?		
Have appropriate questions and the introduction of new vocabulary been planned for? Does the plan show how the new vocabulary will be shared with the children?		
Is it clear what resources, including ICT, will be used and how they are to be organised?		

Is it clear who and what is to be assessed and how this links to the learning objectives?		
Are the activities to be used as opportunities for formative or summative assessment?		
Is it clear what the purpose of the plenary for this lesson is?		
Are there appropriately planned mini plenaries to allow reinforcement of specific issues/address misconceptions/monitor progress with activities/ share feedback with the class group from pairs or small group work?		

One issue you may have considered is the standard ability groups within the plans for the main activity. What other ways are there for organising the learning during this phase of the lesson? You may consider individual work, pairs, small groups, but not necessarily by ability, splitting the class into two, and whole class working, depending on the content and focus of the lesson to be taught. You may also notice that one of the aims of the lesson was key facts about Elizabeth, yet the main focus was Henry VIII's children. What would you do about this? How might you extend this lesson to look at the changing power of monarchs during the Tudor reign?

Planning for other adults in the classroom

Many classes have other adults present who support the learning and teaching of individuals and groups. They can be supporting children with additional learning needs, English as an additional language, behavioural issues or as a learning mentor. They will need to know what is expected of them during the lesson and you may not have much time to discuss your plans ahead of time. A written plan to support them is helpful for both you and them as everyone is clear about expectations.

Subject/theme	
Date	
Group or set including number of children or individual you will be working with	
Children's previous experience Work to be built on from previous lessons, units, years.	

(Continued)

(Continued)

Notes from previous lesson Based on evaluations and assessment. (Include children's errors and misconceptions that need to addressed in this lesson.)	
Learning objectives	
Activities Here detail the activities to be undertaken with the group/individuals.	
Assessment by additional adult **What** the children to achieve are to achieve. **What will you be looking for?**	Notes from assessments made by additional adult.
Resources **Materials, equipment, ICT, texts**	
Safety issues It is your responsibility as the teacher to indicate if there are any safety issues that other adults working in the class should be aware of in relation to the specific tasks you are asking them to undertake with groups/individuals.	
Subject specific language Including key vocabulary.	
Any specific expectations for **behaviour** for group/ individuals	
Language and literacy objectives: including spoken language, reading and writing and vocabulary development.	

Activity

Plan for another adult in your placement class and then gain some feedback about the details of your instructions for future planning for other adults with whom you will work.

Alternatively, plan for the additional adult for the previous history lesson.

Research Focus

Panasuk and Todd (2005) describe a method of evaluating lessons: the Lesson Plan Evaluation Rubric (LPER). This is an instrument derived from the Four Stages of Lesson Planning (FSLP) strategy (see Figure 14.1) and some empirical results that provide insight into the elements of lesson planning with a specific focus on mathematics. They explore previous writers discussing planning, for example Clark and Dunn (1991), who said that planning is a psychological process of envisioning the future, and considering goals and ways of achieving them. The teacher makes decisions that affect their behaviour and their students. Schön (1983) described lesson planning as pre-active decision-making in that it takes place before instruction.

OBJECTIVES formulated in terms of students' observable behaviour HOMEWORK matches the objectives DEVELOPMENTAL ACTIVITIES reflect the objectives, advance development and learning MENTAL MATHEMATICS activates prior knowledge, prepares students for the acquisition of new concepts	ELEMENTS OF INSTRUCTION *Instructional environment* • Inquiry-based instruction • Expository/direct teaching • Labs and projects *Instructional approaches based on* • Problem solving • Multiple representations • Critical thinking • Communication • Connections *Class arrangements* • Individual • Group work • Pair work

Figure 14.1 Four stages of lesson planning (Panasuk and Todd, 2005, p.216)

Each element of the plan was scored for each teacher's plan and the results identified four factors that influenced the effectiveness of the lesson plans.

1. *Worked out problems* – this is about working out the answers to questions that the teachers would ask the children and, by examining the questions that the children would complete during the lesson, the teachers had a better picture of scope of the concepts that were going to be taught.

2. *By-products of the Four Stage Lesson Plan (FSLP)* – this was related to the organisational structure of the lesson, not always the same but planned carefully.

3. *Lesson coherence* – this is related to the links between the different elements of the lesson to maximise the learning for the pupils.

4. *Representations* – these were the mathematical representations used by the teachers to support the pupils learning.

Activity

Look at one of your lessons using this framework and discuss it with other trainee teachers on your course and or teachers in school. What can you learn from this research about planning and its importance?

Opportunistic planning

The following extract, taken from the Rose Review of the primary curriculum, sums up the use of opportunities that arise in the classroom which teachers can take advantage of in their teaching.

> **3.58** *As well as planning work, primary teachers are invariably skilful opportunists, always ready to capitalise on the unexpected to build from children's interests. For example, when a 5-year-old announced, 'My new baby brother was born last night,' what followed was a lively class discussion covering several aspects of personal development: thinking about the care of babies, how to hold them, why they are weighed frequently, and why milk is better than water for feeding them. This was followed by an invitation to mum and baby brother to visit the class to celebrate the baby's birth and learn more about how to care for him.*
>
> *(Rose, 2009, p.75)*

Activity

Think about a time when you:

a) Allowed an unplanned event to impact on your teaching. How did this affect the children's learning? Or:

b) Chose not to follow up an unplanned event and therefore kept following your planned lesson. How did this impact on the children's learning?

Location and planning

So far we have considered planning within a classroom, but you will sometimes need to plan for other locations. Planning resources for outdoor work is important; you need to consider weather conditions, and how you protect the recording of work that children may complete as part of their activities. For outside lessons you can plan larger-scale tasks, or use the children themselves as a main resource.

Activity

Walk around the school in which you are on placement. Note the outdoor areas, including playgrounds, fields, and nature environments. Find out how they are currently used as a location for learning and teaching. Plan, in consultation with your school-based tutor/mentor/class teacher, to use one of these locations as part of your plans and evaluate the lesson(s).

Learning Outcomes Review

Thinking about the school in which you are currently placed, or in which you most recently undertook a placement, respond to the questions which follow each of the intended learning outcomes, as a means of identifying your knowledge and understanding of the issues covered in the chapter.

- **Become aware of the different levels of planning that are undertaken in schools:**

    - What were the long-term plans for the class you were teaching?
    - How were the plans organised? Were they organised in subjects or were they cross-curricular?

- **Consider the required elements of planning, children's previous experiences, subject knowledge, vocabulary, resources:**

    - Identify examples of planning during your placement that show how you have taken account of:

        o pupil's previous experiences;
        o your own subject knowledge required before teaching;
        o the necessary vocabulary for lessons;
        o appropriate resources including the use of ICT to support learning.

- **Become aware of the documentation you need to be familiar with before planning any area of the curriculum:**

    - Show examples of how you have linked your planning to the appropriate statutory and guidance materials for the curriculum and how this has influenced the decision you have taken in planning learning and teaching activities. This is more than quoting the references in your planning.

- **Look at the elements of lesson planning in detail:**

    - Identify an example of lesson planning during your placement where the lesson was successful in promoting learning and one where the lesson was less successful. Try to identify what the differences were in your planning that supported the more successful lesson. Why? What changes will you make to the process of planning as a result in the future?

- **Consider the planning required for additional adults:**

    - Identify an example of planning for another adult during your placement where the activity was successful in promoting learning and one where the activity was less successful. Try to identify what the differences were in your planning that supported the more successful activity for both the children and the other adult. Why? What changes will you make to the process of planning for additional adults as a result in the future?

- Consider how to evaluate planning, teaching and learning and how to use this information to feed into future planning:

  - Identify examples of lesson evaluations during your placement which show how you have altered elements in the next lesson as a result of your review. Discuss these with another trainee teacher on the course and compare methods of review. Between you can you draw up a list of questions to assist you both in reviewing future lessons?

  Further issues associated with continuity and progression are addressed in Chapter 13 on assessment.

Further Reading

Medwell, J. (2006) Approaching long term and medium term planning. In Arthur, J., Grainger, T. and Wray, D. (eds) *Learning to Teach in the Primary School.* London: Routledge, pp.81–9.

Medwell, J. (2006) Approaching short term planning. In Arthur, J., Grainger, T. and Wray, D. (eds) *Learning to Teach in the Primary School.* London: Routledge, pp.90–101.

Superfine, A. C. (2008) Planning for mathematics instruction: a model of experienced teachers' planning processes in the context of a reform mathematics curriculum. *The Mathematics Educator* 18(2) pp.11–22.

Threlfall, J. (2005) The formative use of assessment information in planning: the notion of contingency planning. *British Journal of Educational Studies* 53(1) pp.54–65.

References

Ausubel. D.P. (1968) *Educational Psychology: A cognitive view.* New York: Holt, Rinehart and Winston.

Beyer, C.J. and Davis, E.A. (2009) Using educative curriculum materials to support preservice elementary teachers' curricular planning: a comparison between two different forms of support. *The Ontario Institute for Studies in Education of the University of Toronto Curriculum Inquiry* 39(5) pp.679–703.

Clark, C.M. and Dunn, S. (1991) Second-generation research on teachers' planning, intentions, and routines. In Wanen, H.C. and Walberg, H.J. (eds) *Effective Teaching: Current research.* Berkeley, CA: McCatehum Publishing, pp.183–200.

DfE (2011) *Teachers' Standards.* Available from www.education.gov.uk/publications

DfE (2013) *The National Curriculum in England: Key Stages 1 and 2 framework document.* Available from www.gov.uk/dfe/nationalcurriculum

Panasuk, R. M. and Todd, J. (2005) Effectiveness of lesson planning: factor analysis. *Journal of Instructional Psychology* 32(3) pp. 215–32.

Rose, J. (2009) *Independent Review of the Primary Curriculum: Interim Report.* Nottingham: DCSF Publications.

Schön, D. (1983) *The Reflective Practitioner.* New York: Basic Books.

15. Managing behaviour for learning
Kate Adams

Learning Outcomes

By the end of this chapter you should be able to:

- reflect on your own behaviour as a learner;
- understand the importance of identifying why some children behave inappropriately;
- understand that teaching, learning and behaviour are linked;
- know some strategies for achieving effective behaviour in the classroom;
- recognise links between theory and practice in managing behaviour for learning.

TEACHERS' STANDARDS

A teacher must:

1. Set high expectations which inspire, motivate and challenge pupils
- establish a safe and stimulating environment for pupils, rooted in mutual respect
- set goals that stretch and challenge pupils of all backgrounds, abilities and dispositions
- demonstrate consistently the positive attitudes, values and behaviour which are expected of pupils.

2. Promote good progress and outcomes by pupils
- be accountable for pupils' attainment, progress and outcomes
- demonstrate knowledge and understanding of how pupils learn and how this impacts on teaching
- encourage pupils to take a responsible and conscientious attitude to their own work and study.

5. Adapt teaching to respond to the strengths and needs of all pupils
- have a secure understanding of how a range of factors can inhibit pupils' ability to learn, and how best to overcome these
- demonstrate an awareness of the physical, social and intellectual development of children, and know how to adapt teaching to support pupils' education at different stages of development.

7. Manage behaviour effectively to ensure a good and safe learning environment
- have clear rules and routines for behaviour in classrooms, and take responsibility for promoting good and courteous behaviour both in classrooms and around the school, in accordance with the school's behaviour policy

---

- have high expectations of behaviour, and establish a framework for discipline with a range of strategies, using praise, sanctions and rewards consistently and fairly
- manage classes effectively, using approaches which are appropriate to pupils' needs in order to involve and motivate them
- maintain good relationships with pupils, exercise appropriate authority, and act decisively when necessary.

Defining 'good' and 'bad' behaviour

Imagine a school in which every child in every class was on task, put their pencil down as soon as the teacher asked, walked down the corridors without being tempted to run, lined up in silence, always spoke politely to staff and fellow children and hung on every word of the teacher ... even on a Friday afternoon when the rain had been pouring since 9 a.m. confining children to the dreaded indoor playtimes. Perhaps you have been fortunate enough to have experienced such a school, in which case you will be the envy of your fellow students, but for many of you this is probably a scenario you could only dream of.

The behaviour of children is a key concern for all trainees and many experienced teachers alike (ATL, 2006). After all, it only takes one child in a class who displays inappropriate behaviour to unsettle the calm ambience of the classroom and disrupt the learning of other children. For you, as the adult responsible for the lesson, it is essential that children's 'good' behaviour is maximised and their 'bad' behaviour is minimised, either through prevention or by a quick response which ends it quietly wherever possible without a drama.

Life in school is, however, rarely as simple as one would like, particularly because the classroom is a complex setting involving group interactions with social actors who bring with them a wide range of experiences and assumptions which may or may not concur with those of their peers. There are, as the final report of Sir Alan Steer's government-commissioned review of behaviour in schools made clear, no simple answers to the issue of poor behaviour. However, there is the potential for all schools to 'raise standards if they are consistent in implementing good practice in learning, teaching and behaviour management' (DCSF, 2009, p.3). This chapter takes you through some of the key issues inherent in managing behaviour for learning. It encourages you to engage in reflective thinking to clarify your own ideas about what constitutes appropriate classroom behaviour and to explore the reasons why some children do not engage in the type of behaviour you anticipate. Practical advice is offered to help you nurture children's behaviour for learning, while recognising the complexities of the task and understanding the links between theory and practice.

At the centre of this chapter is you, the aspiring teacher, so before we explore children's behaviour in more detail, it is necessary to engage in self-reflection. Self-reflective practice is a key element in the role of a teacher and a requirement of qualified teacher status. It can bring many advantages, not only in improving your own practice but also in developing yourself – bringing insights into your ideas, motivations and behaviour. But to achieve this also demands an honesty which can be difficult for some people. It is particularly challenging when addressing the issue of children's behaviour because we need to reflect on our own actions within learning settings; we need to be honest about our own behaviour when we are students.

Activity

Thinking of yourself as a learner in a classroom setting (a university seminar/an evening class/as a school child/college student), answer the following questions with as much honesty as you can. Have you ever:

- engaged in a whispered conversation while the tutor was talking?
- written notes to a friend while the tutor was talking?
- gone off task during an exercise or activity, discussing something completely different?
- failed to have done the prerequisite reading?
- sent a text message to a friend during the session?
- while working on an online task, checked your personal email?

You may well be the model student and have answered 'no' to all of these, in which case you are to be commended. If you have, you are unlikely to be a serial offender, perhaps only occasionally having indulged in such behaviour, as indeed I confess I have. Whatever your response, you will no doubt recognise these traits in some of your peers. Some students argue that sending a text message during a session is inconsequential because it does not disrupt anyone else's learning; that discussing last night's party is not a problem because the other group members wanted to know what happened, and besides, the task prescribed by the tutor was not that engaging anyway. Fellow students and tutors may well take a different stance, expecting all to take responsibility for their own learning and engage at all levels and demonstrate respect and politeness in the learning environment.

The perceived 'rights' and 'wrongs' of adult students' behaviour could be debated endlessly, but at the heart of the issue is this: how do you feel when the children in your classroom behave in similar ways? When you are the teacher, the relatively harmless act of children passing notes to friends or whispering to each other while you are talking has the potential to make a strong impact on you, especially if several children are engaging in such behaviour rather than just one or two. One minor incident is not an issue, as you can end it swiftly and silently, with an appropriate stare to convey your disapproval, but if several pockets of mildly disruptive behaviour erupt, the impact on you can be quite disconcerting. You can feel powerless and frustrated, demotivated by the fact that you have spent so long preparing the lesson only to find that few children are interested and few are learning. If you are being formally or informally observed the stress and pressure can be quite overwhelming. In order to avoid being in such a situation there are simple steps you can take to prevent and minimise disruptive behaviour and resolve many issues quietly before they create problems. This chapter will outline some of those steps but it is equally important to consider them alongside the complexities of behaviour in classroom settings, whether it be the behaviour of adult students or young children. One of the most fundamental issues to consider is what is meant by the terms 'good' and 'bad' behaviour, or appropriate and inappropriate behaviour.

Activity

Alongside a friend, independently make lists of what you consider to be 'good' and 'bad' behaviour for primary school children during a lesson. Also include a middle column for behaviour you do not desire, but would not find offensive, such as a child writing a message to a friend. Now compare them with your friend's list. Are there areas of difference?

While you and your friend will have undoubtedly placed some incidents in the same column, such as a child hitting another in the unwanted behaviour section and working quietly and conscientiously in the 'good' column, you may find that there are areas of disagreement, particularly in the middle column, as this case study illustrates.

Case Study: What do you mean, that was *bad* behaviour?

Carrie, a student teacher, had completed a practical science lesson on magnetism and was receiving feedback from Mr Laughlin, her school mentor.

'So, Carrie, how do you think that went?' he asked.

'I know what you're going to say,' she responded. 'It was awful, especially the noise. The children were so excitable as soon as they got hold of the magnets. At one point I couldn't hear myself think but I did use the hand signals to get their attention, though they were too involved with the materials to notice that I was trying a non-verbal technique.'

'So you think that the noise levels were too high?'

→

'Oh, yes! It was deafening.' But Mr Laughlin disagreed. Their ongoing conversation highlighted the fact that on a personal level they both had differing tolerance of noise levels. Certainly, he explained, too high a level can be dangerous if you need to attract the attention of the class immediately for safety issues. Noise can also make it difficult for some members of the class to concentrate. However, what Carrie needed to focus on is what the children were talking about. If they were excitedly discussing the lesson then that was a positive sign; if they were discussing last night's television viewing then that would be another matter.

In addition to the issue of noise levels, other aspects of behaviour are particularly prone to being classified as grey areas, being acceptable to one teacher but not to another. These types are the most commonly found in schools and are referred to as 'low level' disruptive behaviours.

Research Focus

Government reports such as the Elton Report (DES, 1989) and more recently those from Ofsted (2005a, 2005b) consistently note that low-level disruptive behaviours are the most commonly reported type of misbehaviour in schools. These are inoffensive behaviours, which Rogers (1998) notes include talking while the teacher is talking, leaving one's seat, calling out or not having equipment. Hayes (2003) adds tapping an object on a table, leaning back on a chair, giggling instead of concentrating and making silly comments at inappropriate times. The most effective means of reducing low-level disruptive behaviours is through good-quality teaching and learning (Ofsted, 2005a; DCSF, 2009). Serious incidents, including violent acts, remain rare according to the most recent government reports (see DCSF, 2009). While newspaper reports often portray the opposite, presenting a picture of schools in a crisis situation with regard to unruly behaviour, Haydn (2007) argues that these are unhelpful given that research shows that serious incidents remain in a small minority.

Why children behave in the ways they do

Given that there are various ways of labelling classroom behaviours, it is important for you to be clear in your mind what you deem appropriate. However, this understanding needs to be viewed within the context of your school's behaviour policy and ethos. You also need to be flexible in your definitions. A practical lesson is, for example, likely to result in much higher noise levels than a creative writing lesson, so you cannot use a blanket approach to defining an acceptable level of the volume of children's talk.

Alongside your flexibility with regards to definitions, you will need to consider why children behave inappropriately, as these reasons can vary from one child to another. Every child is different. They come from different backgrounds and have different life experiences and they will not necessarily respond to you, or any other member of staff, in the same way. The more you are able to understand the reasons for a child's inappropriate behaviour, the more easily you will be able to minimise or manage it.

Activity

When next on placement, at the end of your first day, write down the names of the children you have learnt. Clearly, you will not be able to recall all 30 immediately, so it is useful to reflect on why you have remembered the names that you have. It is quite common to have remembered those who had been eager to welcome you and offer help (showing positive behaviour) and those who misbehaved, but very few of the remaining group.

You will have walked away from any classroom with some warning bells in your head, to be mindful of certain children who have the potential to show disruptive behaviour. This is what sociologists call labelling; it is a natural human response but it is potentially damaging for the child who, if labelled as a troublemaker, may well fulfil this prophecy by acting according to adults and other children's expectations of them. Instead it is important to explore the 'why' of the child's behaviour in order to identify the root of their actions.

Case Study: Identifying reasons for behaviour

Shannon was nearing the end of her final block placement and was particularly worried about losing control of her class, taking a relatively strict approach to behaviour management to compensate. She followed the principles of consistently enforcing the school's behaviour policy with little flexibility. One day Robbie, a normally quiet, conscientious and compliant six year old, began to show disruptive behaviour, throwing rubbers and pencils across the room and refusing to stop. Shannon was taken aback by his unusual behaviour and continued to implement her zero tolerance approach, which only caused Robbie to be more defiant. Feeling overwhelmed by her loss of control of the situation, Shannon spoke to her mentor, who then went to see Robbie's mother at the end of the day, to be told that his father had left home the previous night. Clearly, Robbie's behaviour was a reaction to this devastating event in his personal life. Shannon then realised that she should not have been so inflexible with Robbie and vowed to take time to explore the reasons why children misbehaved in the future.

The reasons for children's appropriate and inappropriate behaviour are extremely wide. Tables 15.1 and 15.2 note some of the most common reasons underlying children's behaviour but are by no means exhaustive lists.

Appropriate behaviour in class	Possible causes
On-task behaviours	Engaging lesson
	High levels of motivation
	Good self-esteem
	Strong school and class ethos
	Children have clear expectations

Table 15.1 Possible causes for appropriate behaviour

Inappropriate behaviour in class	Possible causes
Off-task behaviours	Uninspiring lesson
	Low levels of motivation
	Low self-esteem
	Weak school and class ethos
	Children have no clear expectations
	Special educational needs (not necessarily diagnosed)
	Health issues
	Emotional problems
	Disruptive home life
	Being bullied

Table 15.2 Possible causes for inappropriate behaviour

You will see that the first five causes listed in Table 15.2 – uninspiring lesson, low levels of motivation, low self-esteem, a weak school and class ethos and no clear expectations – are effectively the opposite of the first five potential causes of appropriate behaviour. This is good news because they are elements on which you can have a significant influence, as we will see in the next section. The other possible causes of inappropriate behaviour are not necessarily as daunting as they might first seem, because you can still take a role in supporting the child, whether directly or by contacting the relevant people including parents or other agencies. The most important element to recognise is the need to understand why a child behaves as they do. Many children with disruptive behaviours cannot or will not articulate why they display them, so it is important to work in partnership with parents/carers, other staff and other agencies as appropriate in order to begin to explain their behaviour.

Finally, in reflecting on the 'whys' of behaviour it is valuable to consider your own actions in learning settings. At the outset of this chapter you identified situations when you or your peers went off task while you were a student/child. Revisit that list and now consider why you did so. It may be that you/they discussed last night's film during a practical task because you believed that the task was boring or irrelevant. Or perhaps you had finished the task early? Did you send text messages to your friend during the lecture because you were bored with the lecture content or were you worried about a situation at home and could not concentrate? Whatever the reasons, they will have implications for your role as the teacher when your children go off task, so always be mindful of them.

Your role in supporting children's behaviour for learning

Thus far, the chapter has shown how important it is for you to acknowledge your definitions of appropriate and inappropriate behaviour, the need for flexibility in applying those definitions and the importance of understanding why children in your class behave as they do. These are underlying fundamental concepts which are essential to your role, but there is also a wide range of practical actions you can take to maximise positive behaviour for learning. This section outlines some of those actions that will soon become second nature to you, but are fundamental to your role as a teacher.

It is essential to note that behaviour management is not an 'add-on' to your teaching role; it is not something which is done on top of your lesson planning. Rather, there is no separation between good behaviour and good teaching and learning/planning (DES, 1989; Cohen et al., 2006; Adams, 2009). Ofsted (2005a, p.15) further endorses the link between teaching, learning and behaviour, commenting that in their own inspections, 'effective teaching and learning is a key to encouraging good behaviour and engaging with those children who have the most difficult behaviour'.

Lesson planning

The previous chapter was dedicated to discussing planning. However, it is worth revisiting because it is a complex notion and one that is crucial to consider in relation to behaviour for learning. From day one of your training, you will be taught to plan lessons in significant detail. Your plans are unlikely to make any explicit reference to behaviour, yet their content will be inextricably linked to the children's behaviour. How?

One of the key features of a lesson in which children are engaged and on task is that children are sure of what they need to do. Clear aims and objectives are therefore important, because if children are unsure of what is expected of them they are more likely to engage in behaviours off task. Naturally, those clear aims and objectives need to be conveyed to the children effectively, which needs to be combined with a stimulating and clear delivery of the lesson itself. It needs to incorporate a range of teaching strategies to cater for different learning styles and keep children purposefully occupied. Further, it needs to be delivered at an appropriate pace (Pollard et al., 2008); too fast and the children will not be able to consolidate learning, and too slow and many will lose interest, again creating unnecessary opportunities for off-task behaviour. Overall, Moyles (2001) observes that much unacceptable behaviour can occur when children are unsure of what to do, or are bored with work which is unvaried, so your planning has a crucial role to play.

Personalised learning is also important to your practice. This involves the tailoring of teaching and learning to individuals' needs, providing clear progression routes for children based on assessment for learning and, where relevant, incorporating interventions such as one-to-one support (see Chapter 5 for a detailed discussion).

The physical classroom environment

In addition to your planning, you can also take other practical steps to prevent much inappropriate behaviour, via the preparation of the physical classroom environment. An experienced teacher will have given considerable thought to the layout of the room – something that is not necessarily discernible to the untrained eye, yet is relatively obvious once you understand the thinking behind it.

The physical layout of the room has a major positive influence on children's behaviour if set out carefully. Seating plans are crucial for ensuring that appropriate combinations of children are grouped together (DfES, 2006) and it is common for these to be altered over the course of a term as children's relationships with each other change. You have a variety of issues to consider here, such as:

- Will seating friends together enhance their work ethic or allow them to engage in excessive idle conversation?

- Should children with disruptive behaviour be seated with children who are conscientious learners so that the latter can set good examples, or will the disruptive behaviour distract them from their own learning?

- What should you do if the relationship between two children on a table turns sour?

- Does seating children in ability or mixed ability groups enhance their behaviour for learning more effectively?

There are no clear-cut answers to such questions and the answers can change according to the different personalities involved – what works for one group of children may not work for another.

Research Focus

Haydn (2007) collected the views of over 100 teachers, 300 trainees and 700 pupils to identify factors that aid teachers to manage learning effectively. A prominent issue in discussions related to whether or not moving children to different places within the classroom was effective, but he found no clear consensus of opinion, even within the same school. Likewise, the use of seating plans gave rise to different views, although some respondents noted that it was difficult for trainees to change established seating plans as this often gave rise to resentment among children. Wannarka and Ruhl (2008), reviewing the literature on the effects of seating arrangements on behaviour, found no consensus in the literature on seating arrangements and their effects on behaviour and academic attainment. However, some contradictory findings may have arisen due to different methodologies, and Wannarka and Ruhl argue that the nature of the task should influence the seating plans, a view also supported by Muijs and Reynolds (2001). For example, seating children in groups may be ideal for discussion-based tasks while seating in rows may benefit independent work. That said, children were given a voice in Haydn's (2007) research; 45.5 per cent stated that teachers who allowed them to choose where they sat in class were having a positive influence on their learning by doing so.

In addition to seating, making resources accessible for children not only minimises opportunities for time wasting but also encourages independence and responsibility. Consider where you keep pencil sharpeners, spare pencils and rubbers; children will need these regularly throughout the day and if they are placed in a tub on the other side of the room, you are providing children with the opportunity to 'waste' considerable learning time by wandering around 'looking for the pencil sharpener'. You can appoint different children to hand out resources such as books or practical equipment. This approach gives children responsibility but also ensures that you avoid groups hovering around one area of the room at the same time, potentially giving rise to unwanted low-level disruptive behaviour.

In all aspects of the physical layout of the room, routines are of critical importance. Clear procedures for entering and leaving the classroom or what to do when a child cannot find a pencil sharpener are essential. When children are unsure of what to do, you have unwittingly provided an opportunity for losing learning time at best, or engaging in disruptive behaviour at worst. Clear expectations are vital with regards to all aspects of behaviour management.

The social environment

A second feature of the classroom environment is the social. It has long been recognised that some schools have a strong positive ethos – a warm, caring atmosphere, dominated by respect and strong values. In such schools, children's behaviour tends to be very positive.

While you will be able to develop your own classroom atmosphere this will need to fit into the wider school ethos. Ravet (2007) emphasises the importance of a whole school approach to developing and sustaining it; it is not about presenting words in a policy that have little influence on practice, but it relates to a school where rights, responsibilities, open communication and collaboration are embedded in all areas of the school. It is the responsibility of all staff, not just teachers, to ensure that such values are lived.

Creating a positive ethos permeates all activities and all areas of the curriculum. Historically, key drivers have been the spiritual, moral, social and cultural development (SMSC); personal, social, health and citizenship education (PSHCE); the social and emotional aspects of learning (SEAL) and the Every Child Matters agenda (ECM). Aspects of these various elements combine to enable children to develop a strong sense of identity, self-efficacy, self-esteem and self-confidence; they learn to understand their role as being part of a wider community within the classroom, school, neighbourhood community and as a global citizen; they encounter moral issues and learn to manage their feelings and recognise and respond appropriately to others' feelings. For a more detailed discussion of the impact of issues such as identity and self-confidence on behaviour, see Adams (2009). Read also Chapter 5 in this book.

Strategies for managing children's behaviour

Combined with these practical steps undertaken in planning and preparing the classroom environment, you will also employ a range of strategies for managing children's behaviour.

Make the most of your opportunities to see other teachers in action while you are training as it is easy to become locked into your own relatively small repertoire of techniques which will not necessarily have long staying power with a class, and may not be effective at all with another group of children. All strategies need to be clearly explained to the children so that they are aware of your expectations of them. For example, you can employ some of the following for gaining the attention of a class as noise levels rise, but be advised that they may well become ineffective after a certain length of time, and in some cases may never make an impact at all, thereby highlighting the need for a wider range to draw upon.

- Count down from five to one, by which time all children should be silent and listening.
- Ring a bell to indicate that noise levels are becoming too high.
- Raise your hands in the air, indicating that all children should do the same and refrain from talking as they do so.
- Hand out stickers to children who are working quietly.
- Place marbles in a jar as noise levels become higher, using a marker to show that when the marbles reach that point, then noise levels are too high.

Activity

Wider issues, some of which are noted in the table below, are also helpful to ensure that you are fully prepared. Before your next teaching session, use this checklist to evaluate your preparation.

Preparation	Check this box if prepared
Ensure that I have a 'teacher presence'.	
I am aware of the school's behaviour management policy.	
I am aware of my role in managing behaviour while the teacher is teaching.	
I am aware of individual children's special educational and emotional needs which may impact on their behaviour.	
Resources for my lesson are easily accessible.	
My lesson plan has clear learning objectives and a range of teaching strategies and I am confident that I know how to communication them effectively to the children.	
I have considered the seating plan for my lesson.	
I have planned for any transitions such as moving children to their tables, back to the carpet, or into another part of the school.	
I have a range of non-verbal strategies to complement the use of my voice.	

Behavioural theories

While it is tempting to simply collect a list of tips and practical strategies, theory is important in fully understanding the reasons for poor behaviour and how to manage/prevent it. Theory does not stand alone. It has strong links with practice and in fact underpins many of the routine actions that teachers undertake in the classroom. Take, for example, the use of rewards and sanctions in the school. Each institution will have its own policy and practice, with good reason. As the Steer Report (DfES, 2005, p.22) states: 'Consistent experience of good teaching promotes good behaviour. But schools also need to have positive strategies for managing behaviour that help children understand their school's expectations. These strategies must be underpinned by a clear range of rewards and sanctions.' You will have seen a range of these on placements. Rewards commonly include stickers, verbal praise, certificates, team points, while sanctions may include withdrawal of privileges, a system of warnings, being sent to the head teacher and parents being informed. Behind such apparently simple strategies are, however, theoretical frameworks, a selection of which is discussed here.

LEEDS TRINITY UNIVERSITY

Behavioural approaches have a long history in education, offering principles for describing behaviour and theorising that learned behaviours can be altered using conditioning. Psychologist B.F. Skinner developed the theory of operant conditioning, which involves voluntary responses to situations whereby a person acts on their environment to achieve a desired outcome. For example, a child who wishes to receive praise from the teacher will work conscientiously in order to receive praise. They will make an association between the situation of working hard and the teacher's response of praise, which is called a positive reinforcer or a reward. Receiving praise may then encourage students to work conscientiously in the future. Conversely a punisher, or negative reinforcer, weakens the association. Long (2005) gives the example of making children collect litter from the school grounds and then allowing them to stop when their behaviour improves. One of the limitations of behaviourism is that it does not consider children's thoughts and feelings.

Assertive discipline is an approach developed by Canter and Canter (1992) which involves presenting clear boundaries to behaviour and the use of non-verbal methods. A key feature is to consciously seek and recognise children's good behaviour. For example, if a child is sitting quietly, the teacher should consistently praise the child for doing so, explaining what they are being praised for. Rules are often displayed and are regularly reinforced, with a child facing a sanction if they break one, such as their name being written on the board. As Long (2005) notes, assertive discipline is a commercial venture, but you will regularly see elements of it in classrooms which are common practice. For example, class rules are often created with children and displayed. Indeed, Steer's final report (DCSF, 2009, p.62) states that 'all parties need to be aware of the expectations of the schools and the rules that apply. Good behaviour management requires excellent communication and intelligent, sensitive and consistent application of the rules.' Similarly, praise is undoubtedly important and Steer's report states that all schools have the responsibility to praise children where appropriate. However, as Muijs and Reynolds (2001) advise, it needs to be sincere and realistic otherwise it becomes tokenistic.

A student-centred approach has long been advocated in education, which is particularly relevant to children's behaviour and focuses on the emotional life of the child. Psychologist Carl Rogers (1983) argued that it is vital for teachers to empathise with children to maximise their learning and personal growth. According to this theory, children who feel that their teacher does not judge them are more likely to share their thoughts and feelings, in turn contributing to a strong class ethos, and positively influencing their behaviour. The concept of empathy has been central to the notion of emotionally literate schools. Weare (2004) argues that strategies establishing clear expectations and administering sanctions are not sufficient for addressing behaviour alone, and that the theory of emotional literacy is essential to understanding children's behaviour. She suggests that teachers need to understand the emotional origins and outcomes of inappropriate behaviour. The notion of emotional literacy has become increasingly mainstream in UK schools in recent years, with an emphasis on encouraging children to explore and share their feelings through activities in PSHCE and SEAL, for example. Yet the concept has been strongly critiqued by Ecclestone and Hayes (2009) who argue that a rise in what they term 'therapeutic education' is actually damaging the aspirations and resilience of learners, instead turning them into self-preoccupied individuals.

More recently, the 'behaviour4learning' approach has emerged following a study for the Evidence for Policy and Practice Information and Co-ordinating Centre (EPPI-Centre) at the Institute of Education, London (Powell and Todd, 2004). This was a systematic review of studies which explored the theoretical links to learning behaviour in school contexts. Ellis and Todd (2009) expand upon the framework which has relationships at the heart of children's behaviour: their relationships with themselves, with others and with the curriculum. Each of the three types of relationships has a bearing on children's learning and behaviour but given that relationships are fluid by nature, quick-fix strategies are not readily available. Rather, teachers are encouraged to prepare for positive relationships, and encourage children to also work positively towards them. It is not a theory that is intended to replace behaviour management techniques, but rather is intended to complement them and aims to reduce the common misunderstanding that behaviour management is separate from teaching and learning (Adams, 2009; Ellis and Todd, 2009).

Activity

All theories can be critiqued, so consider the strengths and limitations of these theories. Some notes have been made for you – can you add to them?

Theoretical argument	Strengths	Limitations
Breach of a class rule can lead to a sanction whilst obeying rules brings rewards.	Children are given clear expectations.	It does not teach children to obey rules because it is the right thing to do.
Praise should be offered regularly.		
Empathy is central to the teacher–child relationship.		
It is important to understand the emotional origin of a child's inappropriate behaviour.		
Quality relationships with self, others and curriculum can enhance positive behaviour for learning.		

Where do I go from here?

Managing children's behaviour is a never-ending learning curve because every class and every group of children is different, and some children's behaviour can be different from day to day. Even the most experienced of teachers face disruptive behaviour, albeit from a very small minority of children. Yet that is not a reason to be disheartened. Instead, you should embrace the variety of human nature and recognise that all children are different and will therefore react differently to the same classroom environment. You have many tools at your disposal to prevent inappropriate behaviour from the outset via effective planning and practical organisation, and by your ability to understand why some children display disruptive behaviour. Through self-reflection and the understanding and application of theory, you have the ability to build a repertoire of techniques, and learn from your own experience and that of others. That ideal, 'dream' class will never behave perfectly every day of every school year, so do not impose unattainable targets on yourself but make it your goal to ensure that the learning environment maximises positive behaviour to the best of your ability.

Learning Outcomes Review

Thinking about your own behaviours as a student teacher, respond to the questions which follow each of the intended learning outcomes, as a means of identifying your knowledge and understanding of the issues covered in the chapter.

- **Reflect on your own behaviour as a learner:**

    - When I am a learner, do I behave in the ways that I expect from children?
    - What causes you to behave in particular ways when you are learning?

- **Understanding the importance of identifying why some children behave inappropriately:**

    - What types of behaviour do I not expect from children? Are there times when I can make an exception?

- **Understand that teaching, learning and behaviour are linked:**

    - How effective are my lesson plans for preventing inappropriate behaviours?
    - What do I need to do to improve my behaviour management to maximise children's opportunities for learning?

- **Know some strategies for achieving effective behaviour in the classroom:**

    - How effective are my lesson plans for preventing inappropriate behaviours?
    - How can I create a positive ethos in my classroom?
    - How willing am I to learn new strategies and keep in mind the theories behind some of them?

- **Recognise links between theory and practice in managing behaviour for learning:**
  - How well do I understand the links between theory and practice?
  - What do I need to do to improve my behaviour management to maximise children's opportunities for learning?

Further Reading

Behaviour4Learning website, available from http://webarchive.nationalarchives. gov.uk/20101021152907/http:/www.behaviour4learning.ac.uk/ViewArticle2. aspx?ContentId=13206. In addition to covering the theoretical components of the B4L approach, the website also contains research, policy and practice.

Cohen, L., Manion, L. and Morrison, K. (2006) *A Guide to Teaching Practice.* Abingdon: Routledge. Chapter 15 provides a relatively concise but thorough overview of approaches to behaviour management, which is grounded in theory.

Rogers, B. (2011) *Classroom Behaviour: A practical guide to effective teaching, behaviour management and colleague support.* London: Paul Chapman. An accessible text that provides a wide range of practical strategies, which are also supported with theory.

References

Adams, K. (2009) *Behaviour for Learning in the Primary School.* Exeter: Learning Matters.

ATL (Association of Teachers and Lecturers) (2006) *Poor Behaviour is an Ongoing Problem, ATL Survey Finds.* Available from www.atl.org.uk

Canter, L. and Canter, M. (1992) *Assertive Discipline.* Santa Monica: Lee Canter Associates.

Cohen, L., Manion, L. and Morrison, K. (2006) *A Guide to Teaching Practice.* Abingdon: Routledge.

DCSF (2009) *Learning Behaviour, Lessons Learned. A review of behaviour standards and practices in our schools.* Nottingham: DCSF.

DES (1989) *The Elton Report: Discipline in Schools.* London: HMSO.

DfE (2011) *Teachers' Standards.* Available from www.education.gov.uk/publications

DfES (2005) *Learning Behaviour: The Report of the Practitioners' Group on School Behaviour and Discipline.* London: DfES.

DfES (2006) *Learning Behaviour, Principles and Practice – What Works in Schools.* Nottingham: DfES.

Ecclestone, K. and Hayes, D. (2009) *The Dangerous Rise in Therapeutic Education.* Abingdon: Routledge.

Ellis, S. and Todd, J. (2009) *Behaviour for Learning: Positive approaches to behaviour management.* Abingdon: Routledge.

Garner, P. (2005) Behaviour for learning: a positive approach to managing classroom behaviour. In Capel, S., Leask, M. and Turner, T. (eds) *Learning to Teach in the Secondary School: A companion to school experience.* Abingdon: Routledge.

Haydn, T. (2007) *Managing Pupil Behaviour: Key issues in teaching and learning.* Abingdon: Routledge.

Hayes, D. (2003) *A Student Teacher's Guide to Primary School Placement: Learning to survive and prosper.* London: Routledge.

Long, M. (2005) *The Psychology of Education.* London: RoutledgeFalmer.

Moyles, J. (2001) *Organising for Learning in the Primary Classroom: A balanced approach to classroom management.* Buckingham: Open University Press.

Muijs, D. and Reynolds, D. (2001) *Effective Teaching: Evidence and practice.* London: Paul Chapman Publishing.

Ofsted (2005a) *Managing Challenging Behaviour.* London: Ofsted. Available from www.ofsted.gov.uk/Ofsted-home/Publications-and-research/Care/Childcare/Managingchallenging-behaviour/(language)/eng-GB accessed 04/08/10.

Ofsted (2005b) *The Annual Report of Her Majesty's Chief Inspector of Schools 2003/2004.* London: Ofsted.

Pollard, A., Collins, J., Simco, N., Swaffield, S., Warin, J., Warwick, P. and Maddock, M. (2008) *Reflective Teaching: Evidence-informed professional practice.* London: Continuum.

Powell, S. and Todd, J. (2004) *A Systematic Review of How Theories Explain Learning Behaviour in School Contexts.* London: EPPI-Centre, Social Science Research Unit.

Ravet, J. (2007) *Are We Listening? Making sense of classroom behaviour with children and parents.* Stoke-on-Trent: Trentham.

Rogers, B. (1998) *You Know the Fair Rule.* Harlow: Pearson Education.

Rogers, C. (1983) *Freedom to Learn for the 80's.* Columbus: Charles E. Merrill.

Wannarka, R. and Ruhl, K. (2008) Seating arrangements that promote positive academic and behavioural outcomes: a review of empirical research. *Support for Learning* 23(2) pp.89–93.

Weare, K. (2004) *Developing the Emotionally Literate School.* London: Paul Chapman.

16. Managing the learning environment
Jonathan Leeming

Learning Outcomes

By the end of this chapter you will:

- appreciate that the physical layout of the classroom has a huge impact on teaching and learning;
- have developed a rationale as to how you will arrange the seating in your own classroom;
- have the necessary knowledge to make informed decisions about how to organise the equipment in your own classroom;
- have a clear rationale about how you will plan and set up the display in your classroom;
- have clear ideas about classroom routines and how they can facilitate the smooth running of a classroom.

TEACHERS' STANDARDS
A teacher must:

1. **Set high expectations which inspire, motivate and challenge pupils**
- establish a safe and stimulating environment for pupils, rooted in mutual respect
- demonstrate consistently the positive attitudes, values and behaviour which are expected of pupils.

2. **Promote good progress and outcomes by pupils**
- demonstrate knowledge and understanding of how pupils learn and how this impacts on teaching
- encourage pupils to take a responsible and conscientious attitude to their own work and study.

4. **Plan and teach well structured lessons**
- impart knowledge and develop understanding through effective use of lesson time.

5. **Adapt teaching to respond to the strengths and needs of all pupils**
- have a secure understanding of how a range of factors can inhibit pupils' ability to learn and how best to overcome these.

7. **Manage behaviour effectively to ensure a good and safe learning environment**
- have clear rules and routines for behaviour in classrooms, and take responsibility for promoting good and courteous behaviour both in classrooms and around the school, in accordance with the school's behaviour policy

- have high expectations of behaviour, and establish a framework for discipline with a range of strategies, using praise, sanctions and rewards consistently and fairly
- manage classes effectively, using approaches which are appropriate to pupils' needs in order to involve and motivate them
- maintain good relationships with pupils, exercise appropriate authority and act decisively when necessary.

Introduction

The primary classroom is a busy and complex environment. Consider for a moment the vast range of activities that take place there: drama, arts and crafts, science experiments, writing, music activities, games … the list is endless. When setting up my classroom at the start of a school year I always bear in mind that the children in my classes and I may well spend more time in this room than in any other room during our waking hours. This inspires me to create a comfortable and cheerful environment. Much more important than the aesthetics, however, is the fact that classroom arrangement significantly impacts on student behaviour; there is evidence to suggest that it impacts on achievement as well (Pace and Price, 2005). It is, therefore, crucially important that we maximise the potential of the rooms that we inherit so that they present a motivating and purposeful setting for learning.

Until 20 years ago, much of the rationale involved in the layout of a classroom was based on teacher testimonials of 'what works for me'. More recently, however, research has produced some principles that can guide us to make informed decisions. In this chapter we shall consider research evidence as we discuss the physical layout of the classroom (already briefly mentioned in Chapter 15). The aim is that you will have a clear idea and rationale about how to set up your own classroom. We will discuss seating arrangements, organisation of resources, displays and routines.

As I write this chapter my school is expanding from two to three forms and I am in the fortunate position of having some say on the furniture and layout of the newly constructed classrooms. Despite having over 15 years of classroom experience, I have found much of the research evidence in this chapter both informative and useful in guiding my decisions. I trust that you will find the same!

Seating arrangements

Standard practice in England is for teachers to seat children in table groups with usually four to six children in each group (Figure 16.1). I am sure that this is true of your experience. In fact this configuration is so normal that rarely does anyone ask about its rationale or question its appropriateness. Hastings and Chantrey Wood (2002), however, suggest that although such an

Figure 16.1 Typical seating arrangement in England

arrangement is suitable for small group teaching and collaborative group work, it is not ideal for individual, whole class or paired work. They point to several research studies that show that children's attention to their work increases when they are seated in pairs or in arrangements where no one is seated opposite them. This increase in attention is particularly pronounced for the most distracted pupils who reportedly double their time on task. Hastings and Chantrey Wood (2002) recommend a flexible approach to classroom organisation where the seating arrangement is modified to match the learning task. Therefore, during group and collaborative work children may sit in groups, yet during individual work children may be seated in rows.

This flexible approach has certainly paid dividends in my own experience. A few years ago I had a class of 32 Year 6 pupils, several of whom presented significant behavioural needs. As a result, I decided to switch from the established practice of seating children in groups. Instead, I sat them in rows of four to minimise potential disruption (Figure 16.2).

When I wanted children to work in groups of four, they turned round and faced the pair behind them. It worked very successfully and since then I have favoured this approach in upper KS2. Now that I teach a Year 2 class, however, such an arrangement does not allow enough room for carpet space nor does it complement the increased use of group work. As a result, I have adopted the configuration of a horseshoe and two grouped tables (Figure 16.3). This allows me flexibility to work with groups and presents less distraction for children who are working individually. When the whole class are working in groups I move three tables so that there are five groups.

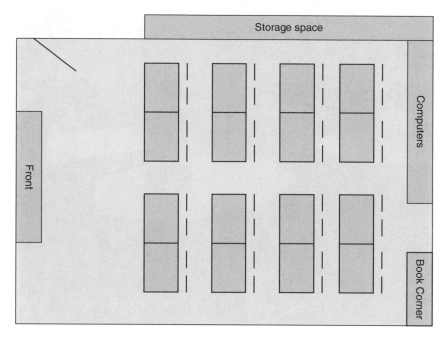

Figure 16.2 My classroom layout in Year 6

*Figure 16.3 Horseshoe and group table layout in my Year 2 classroom
(front of the class is to the right of the picture)*

As well as pupil concentration, there are other important considerations to take into account when arranging seating.

- Can children see the board?

- Can children easily access necessary resources?

- Are high-traffic areas free of congestion?

- Can the teacher easily monitor the room?

- Is there sufficient space for children to sit on the carpet?

Activity

Research shows that seating arrangements should match lesson purpose (Evertson et al., 2003). Think about a lesson that you have taught or will teach soon. How could you have arranged, or will arrange, the seating to maximise learning and minimise potential distraction? Try it out if you have the opportunity!

Plan a default classroom seating arrangement for your current class, or a class with which you are familiar, which maximises time on task and minimises potential distraction.

Positioning of pupils

Once the arrangement of desks has been decided, it is necessary to consider where individuals will sit. It is important to be aware that the interaction and involvement of pupils depends to some extent on where they are seated in the classroom.

Research Focus: Action zone

Generally research indicates that there seems to be differences in student involvement dependent on position, with an 'action zone' of increased involvement across the front and down the middle of a room that is set up in rows (Figure 16.4) (Good and Brophy, 1980). Interestingly, Moore and Glynn (1984) found evidence that the differences of pupil involvement can be attributed to the questioning and attentiveness of the teacher rather than the students' behaviour.

$\longrightarrow$

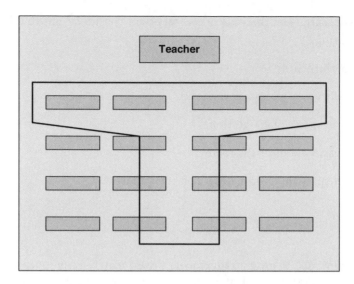

Figure 16.4 Action zone radiates from the teacher

This 'action zone' will obviously vary depending on the seating configuration but it is useful to be aware of it. It is recommended that children who are the most likely to become distracted should be placed in forward and central locations of the action zone. This will decrease the likelihood that these students will be off task while also improving their degree of interaction with the teacher. It is also the responsibility of the teacher to be cognisant of the students located farther away from the action zone by circulating around the classroom to keep them involved.

As well as considering the position of pupils in terms of pupil–teacher interaction we must also take into account pupil–pupil interaction. As with the seating configuration, the rationale for the positioning of pupils will be to maximise learning. In fact, a seating plan is one of the best pre-emptive measures a teacher can use to reduce potential disruption. As discussed in Chapter 15, there are many issues to consider. Should talkative pupils be seated next to quiet pupils? Should a dominant child be seated next to a passive child? Are disruptive children seated at the front? What about children with special needs? There are no definitive answers to the myriad questions; they will depend on the individual students involved and you as teacher.

Working in Key Stage 1, I have found it useful to have a seating plan for children on the carpet as well as in their seats. With the increasing use of 'talk partners' in lessons, it is crucial that children work well with those who sit next to them.

Case Study: Seating children with ADHD

Lucas seems to move around more than all the other pupils and he never pays attention in class. He is always staring into space or kicking the chair in front of him. Lucas has attention deficit hyperactive disorder (ADHD) and because of this his teacher, Sarah, has adapted her seating plan to accommodate his needs. She knows that usually children with ADHD learn better when placed in close proximity to the teacher in the front area of the classroom (Doberman, 2011). She also knows that children with ADHD often work better when seated alone, but as she doesn't want Lucas to feel excluded and she wants to develop his social skills, she decides to surround him with well-behaved, attentive classmates as desk neighbours (Carbone, 2001). Finally, she decides to sit Lucas away from windows or the doorway as there is less distraction. These decisions do not constitute a panacea, but Lucas is now generally more attentive and less distracted.

Research Focus: Attainment grouping

Standard practice in primary classrooms in England is to seat children in attainment groups for mathematics and English lessons. In fact, in mathematics classrooms England utilises attainment (sometimes referred to as ability grouping) more than anywhere else in the world (Boalar, 2009). The rationale behind this is that children have different learning needs and therefore work can be pitched at the appropriate level for the different learners within the cohort. In her influential book, *The Elephant in the Classroom: Helping children learn and love maths* (2009), Boaler argues that this practice is extremely damaging for some pupils, especially those deemed to be 'low ability'. She suggests that it gives them the message that they cannot 'do maths'. She points to research evidence that shows that many children are given work that is too easy because they are judged to be low ability.

Case Study: Girls and maths

Michael is a trainee in a small school. He has a discussion with the class teacher about Sofia, a Year 5 pupil who, like many girls her age, lacks confidence in mathematics and is making less progress than many of the boys in her class (DfES, 2007). Together they decide to sit her in a girl-only group with her peers who also lack confidence, as advocated by the local County Council Mathematics Team. They notice that she now feels less threatened and enjoys the increasing opportunity for collaborative tasks within the group.

> ## Activity
>
> Create a seating plan for your current class considering which children are placed in the action zone as well as those with special educational needs and disabilities (SEND).
>
> If you had an ADHD student like Lucas, or any other learning disabled student in your classroom, how would that influence your classroom design?

Organisation of resources

The smooth running of the classroom is the primary concern when considering how resources will be organised. Well thought out storage minimises disruption and leads to more time spent learning (Gump, 1987; Loughlin and Suina, 1982). The priority is for children to have easy access to the equipment that they need without too much equipment, as this may cause a distraction. The way that resources are organised, just like the seating, will to some extent vary depending on the age group of the children. For example, in my school children do not commonly use handwriting pens until KS2 so these do not need to be readily available. The organisation of resources will also vary depending on the furniture and the specific resources available.

Many teachers choose to organise stationery in pots that are placed in the centre of the table (Figure 16.5). These pots can be purchased from educational providers, or cutlery pots can

Figure 16.5 Stationery organiser

be used. There is no correct way of organising these pots but they can very quickly become cluttered so choose carefully what will be stored here. I have just reorganised mine in my Year 2 class and removed scissors and glue sticks as these are not used every day and can be given out quickly when needed. Mine now have pencils, rubbers, whiteboard markers, whiteboards and wipers only.

A good idea gleaned from a TES Forum (https://community.tes.co.uk/tes_primary/ f/36/t/599619.aspx) was removing pencil sharpeners from table pots so that children do not waste valuable lesson time sharpening pencils. I have sharpened pencils available and a pot near the bin where blunt pencils can be placed. Children who arrive in class early after breakfast club sharpen the pencils in the five minutes before school starts.

In my school, desks in Key Stage 2 have trays so each child is responsible for his or her own equipment. This makes organising stationery easy but it is essential to ensure that trays are regularly tidied otherwise they become cluttered and then children cannot find resources!

Labelling resources around the classroom enables children to access them quickly and it can also help them to acquire language. Ensure that cupboard spaces where books are stored are clearly labelled; children then know where to retrieve and place books at the start and end of a lesson. I spend some time on the first day of the year showing the children where everything is stored. It is amazing how a small amount of time invested in the layout and labelling of resources can save much time later on.

Research Focus: Mathematics equipment

It is widely accepted that apparatus can help children to understand complex mathematical ideas (Drews and Hansen, 2007) and every primary classroom will have a variety of resources available including manipulatives, images, ICT-based resources, games, textbooks and every-day materials. Turner and McCullouch (2004, p.65) suggest that allowing children the choice of resources (either from a wide range or a selection chosen by their teacher) 'enhances the ability of children to apply their knowledge to new situations', yet this alone is not enough. Drews (2007) reminds us that the effective use of resources is only achieved when the teacher understands both how a particular representation helps to develop mental imagery and how to use the resource to support pupils' understanding of mathematical concepts.

There are implications here in terms of storage and usage, and I would like to present some practical advice. First, allowing young children the opportunity to 'play', or interact, with resources before using them for a specific mathematical task helps to remove novelty value and increases their focus on the task. This is particularly the case when pupils are presented with equipment for the first time.

Second, resources must be readily available for children. Often resources are stored away in cupboards and only one resource is used in a single lesson. Some teachers are now storing equipment in open view (like on a windowsill) so that children can use it as and when it is needed.

Classroom display

How a teacher approaches display is largely dictated by the philosophy of senior leaders and the culture and policy of the school. Prevailing practice seems to follow a belief that display forms an important part of inspiring children's learning and so it is often expected that classrooms have the 'wow' factor. Classrooms are, therefore, often full of decoration. A class studying rivers, for example, may have blue material representing a river stapled to the ceiling, a waterfall made out of strips of crepe paper in a corner of the room, and windows decorated with water droplets. I have even been in classrooms where as you opened the door an Egyptian mummy would sit up in a coffin to greet you! Some, however, focus more on the classroom as a working environment, and feel that such decoration causes too much distraction.

Currently as part of a Dinosaur topic with a Year 2 class I have created a 3D dinosaur village on a windowsill in my classroom. Although it has generated much excitement in the topic, it has also caused great distraction with children playing with the dinosaurs at every opportunity. Reflecting on this with colleagues, we considered that perhaps the 'wow' displays can be used temporarily for introducing a topic and arousing curiosity and then changed after a few days to remove the distraction. Perhaps the 'wow' displays are more effective in corridors where we want to attract the attention of pupils and adults.

There are three main aspects of display: celebrating children's work, providing information to consolidate and extend learning, and arousing curiosity.

Arousing curiosity and providing information

Whether subjects are taught 'holistically' or discretely, teachers want to provide information about the topics of study in order to arouse interest and provide additional information. These displays tend to include a word bank, posters and interactive questions. Some schools use QR codes to make displays more interactive.

Working walls

Working walls are display areas that are designed to help children with their current learning (Figure 16.6). They are principally used for English and mathematics and often include key vocabulary, images and examples.

Figure 16.6 Year 1 working wall

Displaying children's work

Showcasing children's work is a key aspect of display because it celebrates their achievements, promotes self-esteem, offers an audience and encourages them to value their own work and the work of others. It also informs all who visit the school of the work students are engaged in. Different schools have different expectations of how children's work is presented, whether it is mounted and what colours are used. Whichever way we mount children's work, it should be presented in a way that makes them proud. It is important that all children are given the opportunity to show their work.

Research Focus: Effects of display on pupils' attention

A recent study (Fisher et al., 2014) investigated whether displays can affect children's ability to maintain focused attention during instruction and to learn lesson content. Kindergarten children were placed in a laboratory classroom for six introductory science lessons, and the visual

→

environment in the classroom was experimentally manipulated. The outcome was that children were more distracted by the visual environment, spent more time off task, and demonstrated smaller learning gains when the walls were highly decorated than when the decorations were removed. Researchers drew attention to the paradoxical relationship between student age and typical classroom design where younger learners are often placed in learning environments that are rich with potential sources of distraction.

This research supports the premise of Communication Friendly Spaces™ (http://www.elizabethjarmantraining.co.uk/), an initiative aimed at improving speaking and listening skills in the Early Years Foundation Stage, which suggest that many children are overstimulated by the current cluttered environment found in most settings. The bright colours, displays and noise give the children a kind of sensory overload. A general neutral background environment is seen as an aid to learning.

Activity

What is your philosophy of display? Do you follow the idea that bright interactive display inspires children, or do you think that it distracts children's learning? How will this affect the way that you plan the display in your classroom?

Plan a display for the next topic that you will teach that will arouse pupil interest.

Plan a working wall for mathematics.

Classroom routines

Taking the register, pupils entering and leaving the classroom, hands up for asking or answering a question … anything that we ask pupils to do repeatedly is a routine. Research, as well as common sense, shows that effective classroom routines can positively affect students' academic performance as well as their behaviour (Vallecorsa et al., 2000). When daily routines are entrenched, teachers are free to devote more time to instruction and to the unforeseen events that occur during the day. They allow for the smooth running of the classroom.

Routines will vary depending on a range of factors including the age of the students being taught and the goals of the teacher. They can be divided into different categories: administrative, instructional and interactive (Colvin and Lazar, 1995; Savage, 1998). The administrative routines include packing books away and doing the register. The instructional include routines for setting out work, and the interactive include what to do when working in a group. We can see here that there is some degree of overlap between rules and routines.

Principles of executing routines successfully

It is not so much the particular routine that you choose that is important as the way that you execute it, and there are some good principles that can help to ensure that routines are effective.

First, and this is often overlooked, is that the routine must be taught explicitly and in many cases modelled and practised. How do pupils work in a group? When a child needs the toilet, do they get out of their place and tap the teacher, do they raise their hands, or are they allowed to leave the room without permission? Should pupils underline their title and write a date? How do we expect pupils to sit? The first week of school is the best time to set these expectations and teach routines.

Second, routines need to be reinforced. Consistency is absolutely crucial. In some cases rewards can be used for those who follow the routines and sanctions for those who do not. For example, I have the routine that when I want to call my Year 2 class to attention, I clap a short rhythm and the children clap the rhythm back and then fold their arms (so that they are not tempted to continue with the task!). If I do not follow up on those who fail to comply then gradually other children will not clap and the routine will fail. In this case I clap the rhythm again and remind the children of the need for compliance. Sanctions for not following routines will depend on many different factors including the teacher, the routine and the age of pupils. A sanction for not setting out work correctly for my Year 6 pupils was to copy the work out again during breaktime. It often only took the application of one sanction for this routine to become automatic!

Finally, it is important to review routines and revise those that do not appear to work. If the teacher observes that many students do not successfully engage in the desired behaviour, perhaps it is a signal that a different routine is required. This happened recently at my school where we have successfully changed the end of breaktime routine. We used to blow a whistle twice. The first blow would signal for children to stand still and be quiet; the second for them to line up silently in their classes. The children were good at being quiet on the first whistle, but started to talk again as they walked to their lines. It was hard to police and seemed to frustrate both children and adults. Now the first whistle signals that breaktime will be over in two minutes and that children need to finish games, put the playground equipment away and line up. Only when the second whistle is blown are children expected to be silent. This allows for a smoother transition from breaktime to lessons.

Case Study: No hands up!

James, a trainee in a Year 5 classroom, began his placement asking children questions and expecting them to raise their hands to respond with the right answer. He noticed that it was invariably the same children with their hands up and he was concerned that those who didn't raise their hands were perhaps feeling that they were less able and were losing motivation (Clarke, 2005). As a result, he changed to a 'no hands up' routine. He used talk partners and gave children thinking time. When he wanted a response he chose *anyone*. This he found helped to raise the level of focus and increased participation in the classroom.

Concluding thoughts

When people visit the classroom of an experienced teacher, they often get the impression that teaching is easy. Managing the classroom environment effectively, however, is not something that merely occurs on its own, or happens because a teacher has been teaching for years. It needs to be intentionally planned and carefully thought through. It can require great effort and be time-consuming, yet the outcome of a well-managed classroom is an environment that promotes success, which makes it well worth it!

Learning Outcomes Review

Thinking about the school in which you are currently placed or in which you most recently undertook a placement, respond to the questions which follow each of the intended learning outcomes, as a means of identifying your knowledge and understanding of the issues covered in this chapter.

- **Appreciate that the physical layout of the classroom crucially impacts on teaching and learning:**

  - Think about your own school days and the different classrooms that you learned in. Which classrooms were best managed and why?

- **Have developed a rationale as to how you will arrange the seating in your own classroom:**

  - What is your default table arrangement? For which kind of learning (collaborative, group, individual) is it best suited?
  - How could you efficiently reorganise the classroom to make the seating appropriate for different kinds of tasks?
  - Is your seating plan allowing all children to learn effectively?

- **Have the necessary knowledge to make informed decisions about how to organise the equipment in your own classroom:**

  - Will you use table pots to store stationery?
  - What equipment will need to be immediately accessible to children?
  - How will you organise pencil sharpening?

- **Have a clear rationale about how you will plan and set up the display in your classroom:**
  - What is the school policy/culture of display and how does this fit in with your philosophy?
  - Is it possible for your classroom to have the 'wow' factor and not cause children to be distracted?

- **Have clear ideas about classroom routines and how they can facilitate the smooth running of a classroom:**
  - How will you organise the distribution and collection of books?
  - What routines will you explicitly teach to your class?
  - How will you follow up on children who are not sticking to your routines?

Further Reading

For further reading about seating arrangements including case studies see: Hastings, N. and Chantrey Wood, K. (2002) *Reorganizing Primary Classroom Learning*. Buckingham: Open University Press.

For further reading about routines and embedding positive behaviours see: Savage, T.V. and Savage, M.K. (2010) *Successful Classroom Management and Discipline: Teaching self-control and responsibility*. Los Angeles: Sage.

For some interesting ideas about setting up the classroom, display and routines see: Chang, M.L. (2004) *Classroom Management in Photographs*. New York: Scholastic.

References

Boalar, J. (2009) *The Elephant in the Classroom: Helping children learn and love maths*. London: Souvenir Press.

Carbone, E. (2001) Arranging the classroom with an eye (and ear) to students with ADHD. *Teaching Exceptional Students* 34(2) pp.72–81.

Clarke, S. (2005) *Formative Assessment in Action: Weaving the elements together*. London: Hodder Murray.

Colvin, G. and Lazar, M. (1995) Establishing classroom routines. In Deffenbaugh, A., Sugai, G. and Tindal, G. (eds) *The Oregon Conference Monograph 1995*, Vol. 7. Eugene, OR: University of Oregon, pp. 209–12.

DfES (2007) *Keeping Up – Pupils who fall behind in KS2*. Nottingham: Crown Copyright.

Doberman, F. (2011) Classroom Management of Attention Deficit/Hyperactivity Disorder. Available from www.karnercare.com/classroom-management-of-child/ accessed 16/06/15.

Drews, D. (2007) Do resources really matter in primary mathematics teaching and learning? In Drews, D. and Hansen, A. (eds) *Using Resources to Support Mathematical Thinking: Primary and Early Years*. London: Learning Matters.

Drews, D. and Hansen, A. (eds) (2007) *Using Resources to Support Mathematical Thinking: Primary and Early Years*. London: Learning Matters.

Evertson, C.M., Emmer, E.T. and Worsham, M.E. (2003) *Classroom Management for Elementary Teachers* (6th edition). Boston, MA: Allyn and Bacon.

Fisher, A., Godwin, K. and Seltman, H. (2014) Visual environment, attention allocation, and learning in young children: when too much of a good thing may be bad. *Psychological Science* 25(7) pp.1362–70.

Good, T.L. and Brophy, J.E. (1980) *Educational Psychology: A realistic approach*. New York: Holt, Reinhart and Winston.

Gump, P.V. (1987) School and classroom environments. In Stockol, D. and Altman, I. (eds) *Handbook of Environmental Psychology*, Vol. 1. Oxford: Wiley.

Hastings, N. and Chantrey Wood, K. (2002) *Reorganizing Primary Classroom Learning*. Buckingham: Open University Press.

Loughlin, C.E. and Suina, J.H. (1982) *The Learning Environment: An instructional strategy*. New York: Teachers College Press.

Moore, D.W. and Glynn, T. (1984) Variations in question rate as a function of position in the classroom. *Educational Psychology* 4(3) pp.233–48.

Pace, D. and Price, M. (2005) Instructional techniques to facilitate inclusive education. In D. Schwartz (ed.) *Including Children with Special Needs*. Westport, CT: Greenwood Press, pp. 115–31.

Savage, T. (1998) *Teaching Self-control Through Management and Discipline*. Boston, MA: Allyn and Bacon.

Turner, S. and McCullouch, J. (2004) *Making Connections in Primary Mathematics*. London: David Fulton.

Vallecorsa, A. L., deBettencourt, L. U. and Zigmond, N. (2000) *Students with Mild Disabilities in General Education Settings: A guide for special educators*. Upper Saddle River, NJ: Merrill Prentice-Hall.

Index